D0874178

Changing Consumer Cultures
of Modern Egypt

Social, Economic and Political Studies of the Middle East and Asia (S.E.P.S.M.E.A.)

(Founding editor: C.A.O. van Nieuwenhuijze)

VOLUME 101

Changing Consumer Cultures of Modern Egypt

Cairo's Urban Reshaping

by

Mona Abaza

BRILL

LEIDEN • BOSTON
2006

This book is printed on acid-free paper.

Library of Congress Cataloging-in-Publication Data

ISSN 1385-3376
ISBN 90 04 15277 6

PRINTED IN THE NETHERLANDS

For W.M.L., who reoriented me in Berlin

CONTENTS

ACKNOWLEDGEMENTS

There are many people who helped shape this book. The late Cynthia Nelson, my mentor and dear friend for many years who mothered me after my mother's disapperance provided support during the difficult year of 2004. Cynthia's recent departure in March 2006 is deeply felt on all levels. I miss her energy, her spirit, her intellectualism and her generousity. These qualities constituted a fundamental pillar in consoling me when I was down. She always encouraged me to write and rethink matters. Marlis Weisenborn and Merhi Foda were a great delight to get me out of my work and incite me to relax. Our escapades out of Cairo were wonderful. Furthermore, Mehri Foda helped intensively in organising meetings with various members of the Foda family. Mark Linz has been extremely supportive during difficult times. This book would not have seen the light without his sharp way of wrapping issues in a remarkable aesthetic style. Sharon Siddique, in Singapore, a lifelong friend enriched me with the comparative perspective. Sharon has always been generous with her ideas, time and emotional support. Susan Watts' sensitive and intelligent editing elevated the text. She helped me to reshuffle the whole work and challenged the chaotic way I tend to put down my flow of ideas.

Ahmad Hamid gave an inspiring lecture in my class at the American University in Cairo (AUC) on consumer culture in Egypt in 2003. It sparked many ideas, but mostly, he introduced me to Bauhaus in Egypt. Joel Beinin commented on the project proposal; we had intensive discussions, which certainly reshuffled my work. Jennifer Robertson and Celeste Brusati's sharp comments and critiques of an earlier version of the text were illuminating. I wish to thank Ahmed Youssef and Ahmed al-Sherbini for being part of the research team, which conducted interviews in Cairo's shopping malls. The project was financed by the AUC. Mustafa Abdel Rahman was of great help in some of the interviews.

I have obtained several grants from AUC to conduct interviews in shopping malls. The Social Science Research Council, New York, funded my research to undertake a comparative study of Beirut and

Cairo. I was part of a team that won an award in the project of "Reconceptualizing Public Spheres in the Middle East and North Africa". Seteney Shami's support was extremely valuable. Her capacity at stirring topics and opening doors is remarkable. I would like to thank Franck Mermier for his help and hospitality in Beirut; and thanks to the whole group: Melhem Chaoul, Nelida Fuccaro, Anh Nga Longva, Franck Mermier, Sharon Nagy and Khaled Ziadeh for the intellectual exchanges, writings and lively discussions we had during the series of conferences at which we met. The Social Science Research grant enabled me to explore the life of department stores, and the shopping Malls of Beirut. The Rockefeller Foundation invited me for a month at the wonderful villa Serbelloni in Bellagio. The magical atmosphere allowed me to complete the final revisions of this work under the spell of the most inspiring landscape of Lake Como.

I wish to thank my fellow sociology students from the class we took together: Contemporary Sociological Theory 310, during the spring semester 2004. We enjoyed reading the writings of the Frankfurt school and applying consumer culture to Egyptian weddings. Special thanks to my student Rasha al-Gamal. The seminars I conducted on "consumer culture in Egypt" during 2000, 2001 and 2004 at AUC were very instructive and I have learned a great deal from my students. Anna Vinea, my assistant at AUC undertook the superb task of researching in the Arabic magazines of the 1960's. Her assistance was invaluable in preparing the glossary and the bibliography. She was always a patient and thorough scholar. Finally, I would like to thank the anonymous reader for the intelligent and critical comments that helped me to re-write the text.

Sections of this book have been presented in a symposium at the American University in Cairo in 2004 on Consumer Culture in Egypt and a paper titled: "On Fashion Life Style and Consumer Culture" was presented at The International Institute for the Study of Islam in the Modern World (ISIM), Amsterdam, 15–16 April, 2005 *Muslim Fashions-Fashionable Muslims*.

Parts have been published in various journals and newspapers: "Shopping Malls, Consumer Culture and the Reshaping of Public Space in Egypt" in *Theory, Culture and Society*, 18 (August 2001): 97–122; "Advertising History" *al-Ahram Weekly* (1–7 July, 2004): 24;

"Brave New Mall," also *al-Ahram Weekly* 16–22 September 2004, Issue No. 708 (http://weekly.ahram.org.eg/2004/708/feature.htm). A forthcoming article on Nasr city's shopping malls will soon appear in an edited volume by Diane Singerman and Paul Ammar; published by the American University Press in Cairo.

GLOSSARY

ʿabayya	type of long and large cloak usually considered a modest and Islamic form of dress.
affandiyya	initially a title in the Ottoman Empire, later used to generally refer to white-collar workers.
aʿyan	large land owner.
ʿamal	evil spells.
ʿashwaʾiyyat	slums, unplanned construction, scattered areas, squatters.
ʿasr	afternoon, the Muslim afternoon prayer performed between noon and sunset.
badron	underground floor where servants lived in upper middle and upper classes houses.
baladi	literally country or local as opposed to foreign, more broadly refers to traditional urban practices and people, it also means popular.
batata	sweet potato.
bawab	doorkeeper.
biʾa	literally "environment", a negative term used by middle and upper classes to refer to the bad taste of lower classes, in the last years it started to replace *baladi*, but used in a pejorative way.
bitaqat al-tamwin	ration card.
(al)-bitaqa al-thakiyya	"intelligent" ration card.
daftar al-tawfir	savings account opened at a post office.
dikkah	oriental large sofa.
fajr	dawn, also refers to the prayers carried out at this time of the day.
(al)fan al-habit	literally decadent culture, it might include popular music and singers, theatre shows
fatiha	the opening chapter of the *Qurʾan*.
fatwa	non-biding legal opinion usually delivered by a *mufti* (jurisconsult)
feddan	*One Feddan equals 4200.83 sqm.*
fetir mushaltit	special pastry done by peasants.

fitar	breakfast, it also refers to the first meal served after the sunset during Ramadan that marks the end of the fast.
fitir	type of pastry with diverse fillings.
funduq	hotel.
ful	a popular dish made of beans. *Ful* is known to be the basic diet of the poor in Egypt.
galabiyya (*jalabiyya* in high Arabic)	loose, flowing gown usually associated with the urban popular classes and the peasants.
gamʿiyya (*jamʿiyya*)	state cooperative that sells subsidized goods; also rotating credit association which many women participate in it.
ghafir	supervisor of workers on large estates (*ʿizba*)
hagg (*hajj*)	title given to a person who made the pilgrimage to Mecca, also used as a respectful term of address for old people.
hakawati	storyteller who usually used to perform in coffee-houses.
halawa	mixture of water, lemon juice and sugar used as depilatory.
halwa	type of sweet usually made of pressed sesame seeds.
hammam	public bath.
haram	religiously prohibited.
hara	small alley, also used by extension to refer to a popular quarter or neighbourhood.
hassad	evil eye, envy.
higab (*hijab*)	veil.
ibn/bint al-balad	literally son/daughter of the country, large designation for Egyptians, narrow designation of a person that comes from popular quarters.
ʿid	generally feast, in Islam it refers to the two major feasts—*ʿid al-fitr* that follows the fasting month of Ramadan and *ʿid al-adha* that commemorates the sacrifice of Abraham.
infitah	the open door policy of economic liberalization promoted by Anwar al-Sadat starting with 1974, which implied privatization and more opportunities for foreign investors.

intifadat al-haramiyya	literally the outbreak of thieves, term used by Sadat to refer to the 1977 food riots that followed the lift of the subventions to bread, oil and other basic goods.
'isha	the Muslim evening prayer.
ishta	cream.
'izba	large estate owned by landowners.
jinn (*ginn*, colloquial Arabic)	non-human being that can be either bad or good.
karar	large room used for storing large quantities of food and other household items.
kelim	Oriental carpet.
khawaga	used by Egyptians to define foreigners living in Egypt, it included the Levantines, Greeks, and Italians of Egypt, contains some irony.
khutuba	engagement.
kushari	a popular Egyptian dish, it consists of a mix of rice, noodles, lentils, fried onions and tomato sauce.
L.E.	Egyptian Pounds
madrasa	school, before it referred to the traditional schools where the *Qur'an* was taught.
marmiton (marmatun in Arabic)	cook in the elite usage of French.
mashrabiyya	type of wood work in which small pieces of wood are interlocked in order to form elaborate patterns.
mastabah	Ottoman furniture.
mawa'ed al-rahman	public banquets for the needy organized during Ramadan month
mezza	appetizers.
milaya laff	type of large and long veil that can be wrap up around the body, also used for showing or covering the face according to the circumstances, usually wore by women form popular urban quarters.
misyar	"ambulant" marriage imported from Saudi Arabia according to which the man has no economic obligations towards his wife.

mowazaffin	government employees.
muhaggaba (muhajjaba, high Arabic)	a woman who wears a veil covering the hair and the neck.
munaqqaba	a woman who wears a type of veil that covers the entire face as well as gloves.
namliyya	kitchen cupboard used for storing food (such as rice, oil) used especially in the 1960's.
naksa	setback, term used to refer to the Arab defeat by Israel in 1967.
niqab	type of veil that covers the entire face leaving only some space for the eyes.
ʿud	musical instrument.
qahwa	coffeehouse.
quftan	long-sleeved outer garment, opened in front and wore with a belt.
riwish	refers to a fashionable youngster. This word has been newly introduced in the Arabic language.
roba vecchia	Italian expression, literally, "old stuff", shouted by ambulant salesmen.
sabil	public fountains.
shaʿbi	popular.
shariqat al-taʾmin	insurance company.
shisha	water pipe.
sitt	literally woman, also used to refer to the famous singer Umm Kalthoum.
suffragi	domestic servant (valet) whose duty was to receive guests and serve at the table.
suq	market.
suq al-kanto	popular market situated in Bulaq where second hand clothes are sold.
(al) suq al-hurra	free market.
taʿmiyya	also called falafel, dish made of mashed chickpeas and spices fried in a patty.
tabliyya	low table used by peasants.
taqsit	installments.
tally	tinsel needlework.
tarahil	seasonal, migrant workers.

tarbush	also called fez, type of red head cover with a long black tassel, very popular during the Ottoman Empire and in Egypt until the 1952 revolution.
tin shoki	prickly pears.
thanawiyya 'amma	general secondary school certificate or baccalaureate.
tiqil	literally heavy, implies becoming unavailable or unapproachable in order to make oneself desired.
tuggar al-shanta	literally coffer traders or suitcase merchants, ambulant merchant women who sold smuggled imported goods (especially clothes) by coming to homes during the '60's.
'ulama	collective noun, jurists and theologians of Islam.
'umra	also called the small pilgrimage, refers to the pilgrimage to Mecca that can be performed during any month of the year.
'urfi	literally customary, especially used to refer to unregistered marriage.
warsha	small shop in the informal sector.
wikala	sometimes called caravanserai, medieval merchants hostel with rooms for sleeping in the upper floor, the round-floor had rooms used for storage.
zaffa	marriage procession.
zuhr	noon, also refers to the prayers from this moment of the day.

INTRODUCTION

The idea for this book grew out of my interest in consumer culture, as a result of my two years in Singapore (1990–92) and later one year in Malaysia in Kuala Lumpur (1995), when I undertook research on contemporary Islamic discourse and the networks Malaysian intellectuals developed with Middle Eastern centres of learning. One particular memory of my stay was the long hours I spent walking in Asian shopping malls. To escape the terrible heat and horrible traffic jams, it was natural to make appointments to meet in such places. These were easy meetings points in the city, especially during heavy rains and everybody seemed to agree that the malls were pleasant and cool spaces.

Singapore has also often been designated as a huge shopping-mall island. My two years in Singapore were extremely fruitful and rich in human and intellectual encounters. I came into contact with the sociological works of Chua Beng Huat, Anandah Rajah and Habib ul-Haq Khondker from the Department of Sociology at the National University of Singapore, which brilliantly reflected upon the local-global dynamics and the "glocalization" effect on consumer culture in Southeast Asia. The works of Chua Beng Huat on McDonald's in Singapore and the hybridization of cuisines, which I refer to later in addition to his reflections on Singaporean youth *vis-à-vis* consumption, were illuminating and inspired me to draw parallels with the Middle East. Singapore, with its multiethnic structure – the majority of which were Chinese, followed by Malays and Indians – became for me a fascinating place where the tourist industry has successfully promoted shopping among other activities. But it also promoted an image of an ethnic diversity whereby traditions: cuisines, attires and furniture are constantly reinvented, resulting in an ever-growing hybridization of tastes. Besides that, it was very hard for me to avoid becoming an avid shopper. Little by little, I developed the hobby of studying markets and I imagined myself becoming a potentially "intelligent" shopper. At a later phase, I became obsessed with computers, cameras and shopping in general, thanks to the extremely appealing Singaporean computer and software markets. In the early nineties, the specialized shopping centres such as the Funan Centre in Singapore offered much more sophisticated services than European markets. My memory was that the salesmen and women dedicated their time generously to the customers. It is in Jakarta and Singapore that I have encountered the most capable software "freaks" and of course an unimaginable variety of pirated programs. However, I realized how easy and pleasurable it was to slip into an uncritical and indulgent consumerist lifestyle. Later, Sharon Siddique in Singapore initiated me to the famed gigantic Mustafa Centre where we spent a long time shopping and observing extended Indian families endeavouring in purchasing jewellery and consumer durables for the young brides. Flâneuring, an expert and a witness of the tremendous transformation of the quarter, was enlightening and inspiring for drawing analogies between Singapore and Egypt.[1]

I returned to Cairo in 1998 after a long absence to observe developments very similar to those I had seen in Kuala Lumpur before the Asian crisis. The flow of cash had increased among certain classes, and along with it conspicuous consumption. Competent and professionally made shopping guides which included information on accessories, electronics, beauty, fashion, jewellery, entertainment and books, became available in the market.[2] Advertising companies flourished and they seemed to be doing very well in the region of the Middle East in contrast to other parts of the world.[3] According to the latest CAMPAS study of Egyptian consumption patterns in 2001, the standard of living in both rural and urban areas was on the rise. Egyptian families spend yearly 127,3 billion LE.[4] These are spent on the following items (in L.E. billion): food and drink – 56.1, housing 18.7, clothing 12.8, transportation 7.2, education 6, private lessons 2.1, sports, entertainment and cultural activities 5.6, health, 5.3, cigarettes 4, furniture and household items 3.1, cafes and hotels 2.6 other 3.8.

---

[1] See the brilliant anthropological study on the quarter by Sharon Siddique and Nirmala Purushotam, *Singapore's Little India*, Institute of Southeast Asian Studies, Singapore. ISEAS, 1982.

[2] *The Ultimate Guide to Shopping in Cairo*, Shopping Supplement, issue 2, 2004.

[3] The Middle East showed a 22 percent growth in agency performance in 2001, to a total of $454.3 million in gross income. Source *Egypt Almanac, The Encyclopedia of Modern Egypt*, Egypto-file Ltd. LLC Wilmington 2003, p. 240.

[4] *Egypt Almanac, The Encyclopedia of Modern Egypt*, Egypto-file Ltd. LLC Washington 2003, p. 109. This number however, does not say much about the class disparities in consumption.

Today Cairenes can order local fast food to be home delivered, through www.otlob.com and other websites. The service of home delivery is extremely efficient and fast. Websites have an available facility, which offer a wide variety of information about where to shop according to the range of prices desired. With increasing consumer appetites, shopping malls – such as the World Trade Centre (WTC) and the newly opened (2001) Arkadia Mall next to the WTC – had proliferated in various areas of Cairo. I was fascinated by how youngsters, both poor and rich, had conquered these spaces of consumption and how these are turning into specifically gendered spaces at specific times of the day. New forms of leisure socialization are in the making among middle class Cairenes. I was equally caught by the fact that the urban texture of Cairo has been facing a rapid transformation, falling prey to wild neo-liberal tycoons whose major projects were directed towards land speculation, and the construction of gated and resort communities. I quickly became interested in the capitalists behind such constructions and tried to find out if there was a pattern in investment.

If we take into account phenomena such as the spread of McDonald's, ATMs, mobile phones, condominiums, email usage, and gated communities, then Egypt has indeed entered the age of globalization. But to jump from that premise to the conclusion that these types of phenomena are leading to a homogenization in lifestyle is too simplistic. For example, the McDonald's frequenting public in Cairo is certainly different from that in Singapore and in India. The volume edited by James Watson, *Golden Arches East: McDonald's in East Asia,*[5] was a discovery for me because in the introduction it conveyed exactly the same sentiments I felt when I was living in Malaysia. Watson states that the idea of undertaking research on such a topic came from the fact that when one does field work, one lives, eats and behaves in a manner similar to the people one studies. By looking at the everyday life of middle-class people in East Asia, he came to the conclusion that they increasingly frequent McDonald's and shopping malls.[6] Furthermore, the book provided a comparative study of McDonald's in various Asian countries: Tokyo's McDonald's opened (1971), Hong Kong (1975), Taipei (1984), Seoul (1988), and Beijing

---

[5] Stanford University Press, Stanford, California, 1997.
[6] (Preface viii).

(1992). The study was fascinating in revealing the different local variations and how the fast food industry has affected certain habits such as for the Japanese eating with their fingers for the first time, while for Taiwanese youth, French fries became popular and were integrated into their daily diet.[7] The most significant consumers in Asia turned out to be children who discovered pizza, chicken and French fries. In Egypt, fast food is socially handled as an outing for the well to do middle classes, which can afford it. It is possible to draw similarities with Beijing and Seoul where McDonald's restaurants have turned into arenas of conspicuous consumption that cater to yuppies.[8]

Although I could see that one can trace growing homogeneity across cultures and regions, much as theorists of globalization are talking about organizational ecumenism in the making,[9] they are also faced with particularisms, "invention of traditions" and the "folklorization of culture".[10] To quote Waters: "The absolute globalization of culture would involve the creation of a common but hyper differentiated field of value, taste, and style opportunities, accessible by each individual without constraint for purposes either of self-expression or consumption".[11]

The recently constructed district of Madinat Nasr (Nasr City), dominated by the emerging middle classes, who accumulated wealth through migrant work in the oil-producing countries such as Saudi Arabia over the past thirty years, has seen five giant shopping malls built recently, in an architectural style that emulates that of Singaporean and Malaysian malls.[12] The largest of these is City Stars, next is the Geneina Mall, consisting of 12,000 square meters. Large numbers of malls were erected during the 1990's, such as the Horeyya Mall in Heliopolis, the Maʿadi Grand Mall in Maʿadi district, the two malls of Hilton Tahrir and Ramses, the Yamamah Centre in Zamalek

---

[7] James Watson, "Introduction: Transnationalism, Localization, and Fast Foods in East Asia" in: *Golden Arches East, McDonalds's in East Asia*, Stanford University Press, Standford, California, 1997, p. 6.

[8] Ibid. Introduction, p. 9.

[9] Meaning that Fordism as a model of work organization has been exported worldwide, as Malcolm Waters argued. Fordism was not only mimicked because of its success in production but also because it created 'instrumental workers'. Malcolm Waters, *Globalization*, London and New York Routledge, 1995, p. 80.

[10] A term I borrow from Sami Zubaida *Islam, The People and The State*, London and New York, Routledge, 1989.

[11] Ibid., p. 126.

[12] Such as the al-ʿAqad, Geneina, al-Serag, Tiba and Wonderland Malls.

Fig. 1. Stars Centre, Nasr City. January 2006.

Fig. 2. Stars Centre, Nasr City. Entrance, January 2006.

Fig. 3. Yamama Centre Pegasus, January 2006, a dying mall.

district, the First Mall in Giza district. These malls symbolize the growing merge between foreign capital, expertise and Egyptian capitalists. The Yamamah Centre in Zamalek was created by Saudi funding, more precisely by Prince Bandar, very much like the Ma'adi City Centre, a large shopping complex which includes Carrefour, which was created by the Majid Al-Futtaim group of the Arab Emirates who runs a series of malls in Dubai, Abu Dhabi and Oman. The Ma'adi Grand Mall was constructed by the Bitter Lakes for Habitation and Development Company. It was meant to be the largest centre in the Middle East. The Chief architect is Ahmed 'Azmy, whose brother is Nabil 'Azmy, a previous Deputy Chairman of Osman Ahmed 'Osman, Suez Canal Bank and CEO of Suez Insurance. The Project's top eight investors represent 90 percent of the capital and they all belong to the 'Azmy family.[13] City Stars

---

[13] Samir Ra'afat, "Ma'adi Grand Mall", *Cairo Times*, February 19, 1998. http://www.egy.com/landmarks/98-2-19.

Mall has been mentioned earlier, nevertheless, not all malls are the result of joint venture projects; some are purely local capitalists.

Inter-Personal and Inter-Textual Negotiations

I started to undertake research on the shopping malls of Cairo in 1999, first, through participant observation, hanging around in several malls at various times of the day to get the feel of them. Later, I conducted interviews with several managers of malls. I taught a class on consumer culture at the American University in Cairo (AUC) and together with the students we conducted several studies in various malls based on participant observation and interviews with some managers, shopkeepers and the public. During the year 2002–03, I conducted a more structured research project in eighteen shopping malls, with the support of funding from AUC, on which managers, workers, salesmen and the public were interviewed. With a team of three researchers, we conducted semi-structured interviews, which were tape-recorded. We encountered a number of problems. In the first place, not all managers were willing to be interviewed by my research assistants, who are sociologists trained at Cairo University, partly due to the fear of commercial and security leakages. In several cases, I had previously interviewed the same managers and found that being a female professor at AUC (perhaps also my privileged class background) facilitated the task. However, I now faced suspicion regarding my research. All the recordings of the public and shop keepers took place in the mall, against a background of constant noise such as music, television, and *Qur'an* reading, which certainly affected the quality of the recordings. I revisited several of these malls again in 2005 to find that quite a few "passed away" very quickly and new ones emerged. The velocity of change is indeed frightening. In some cases, it was extremely useful to refresh the information after the collapse of the mall.

However, I gradually realized that one couldn't tackle the social life of malls without addressing the broad issue of consumer culture in Egypt. I extended my interest to various related topics such as fashion, where the reinvention of "ethnic" and "Islamic chic" looks are today catering to wider classes and have become new social markers. Lifestyles, "salons" and living rooms have also undergone transformation. I also looked at changing tastes, coffee houses and the changing or imported cuisines. I became interested in the social handling of commodities, to use Arjun Appadurai's words in "the particular type of social potential of commodities"[14] and their "socialized" determinacy. I attempted to follow the intricate relationship of culture to commodities as the contributors of Appadurai's volume had demonstrated in their empirical case studies. To refer to Douglas and Isherwood's analysis of the usage of goods, it is the "social meaning" and the way goods maintain relations that triggered my interest:

> For Douglas and Isherwood, the essential function of consumption is not to fulfil needs in any prosaically useful way, such as food for eating, but rather its capacity to make sense (1979:62): it is not so much that food is good for eating, but that it is good for thinking.[15]

At a latter stage, I realized that to understand the social transformations, I had to look back and explore the period of the sixties and early seventies. I have attempted there to weave my personal recollections with historical data, magazines and newspapers documentation, to reconstruct a narrative of what consumer culture might have been for a Cairene middle, upper-middle class family and how a drastic change with the "open door policy" took place in the seventies and eighties. This was consolidated with interviews with middle-upper class acquaintances and relatives.

The introduction of Western lifestyles and consumer goods in Egypt dates back to before colonial times. Today the discussion focuses on the key word "globalization" and its pervasive effects of the "homogenization" and "Americanization" of the globe, and more precisely, on the articulation of the "right of difference" in the local context. Earlier debates, and in particular in colonial literature, stressed rather the "cosmopolitanism" of the local elites. Thus, much has been written about the colonial cosmopolitan architecture of downtown Cairo, the cosmopolitan lifestyles and the usage of foreign languages such as French, English, Italian, and Greek in Egyptian daily life, as well as the import of taste, furniture and goods. Cosmopolitan lifestyles produced different notions of leisure time such as horse riding, racing, polo and cricket. It also produced novel

---

[14] Arjun Appadurai, (editor) "Introduction: Commodities and the Politics of Value" in: *The Social Life of Things, Commodities in Cultural Perspective*, Cambridge University Press, 1986, p. 6.

[15] Peter Corrigan, *The Sociology of Consumption, An Introduction*. London Sage, 1997, p. 18.

Fig. 4. Nile Towers, Bulaq, view from Zamalek.

public spaces such as clubs, bars and hotels and department stores employing foreign employees (Greek, Jews and Italians). Foreign schools such as the Victoria College, the American College, the Lycée, the Franciscans, the Greek, Italian and Armenian schools and French catholic elite upbringing in the colony, were another testimony of cosmopolitanism.[16] After all, Egypt was already a tourist attraction for the English and French at the beginning of the nineteenth century. The French became known as the best guides to the Islamic part of Cairo. As mentioned by the historian al-Jabarti, the French even accompanied high Ottoman officials and Englishmen. Moreover, much trafficking in antiquities was already taking place then.[17] This means that interaction with the European culture dates back to two centuries. My impression however, is that this shift from "cosmopolitan culture" which was rather restricted to colonialism,

---

[16] For an overview of the history of foreign schools in Egypt, in particular English and French schools and their impact on the formation of the new and modern Egyptian woman and how this image was closely related to an new consumer culture, see the work of Mona L. Russell, *Creating The New Egyptian Woman. Consumerism, Education, and National Identity 1863–1922*. Palgrave Macmillan, 2004, pp. 107–125.

[17] Mohamed Scharabi, *Kairo Stadt und Architektur im Zeitalter des Europäischen Kolonialismus*, Verlag Ernst Wasmuth Tübingen, 1989, p. 35.

"elites" and the ruling classes of the periphery to "globalization", involves a complex dynamism when it pertains to local articulations.

As George Ritzer[18] argued, it is evident that the McDonaldization of the world is criticized because it is seen as part of the larger pattern of globalization involving a growing deregulation of markets and the dismantling of the social welfare system. For the anti-globalization movement, the wild, neo-liberal, free market economy has destroyed a long tradition of two centuries of working class struggle for acquiring an efficient welfare system, and the weakening of the trade unions. Zygmunt Bauman develops the fascinating thesis on the emergence of a fluid, ungraspable modernity with ephemeral volatile, elements. He speaks of a liquid modernity, in which a new form of capitalism is promoting an easily "disposable" work force. The magic of the system lies in flexible part-time jobs where retirement plans and pension systems would be ancient history. Likewise, disposable love relations can explain the growing pattern of serial monogamy and the proliferation of singles living in the modern metropolis, in addition to cheap Chinese disposable gadgets and garments, as well as disposable workers. In short, a whole disposable consumer lifestyle seems to be what humanity is heading towards. Ritzer developed the idea of the prevalence of the mediocrity of insecure McJobs, and the McDonaldization of academics and American sociology. Both authors thus speak of unstable and short-lived, restricted day-to-day survival, as if the forthcoming generations can no longer afford to be visionary. Surely, globalization has sharpened class difference, but the populist effect of mass culture and the semblance of "democratization" of desires and tastes through consumer culture requires further reflection in a Third World country such as Egypt.

Bauman's *Liquid Modernity* differentiates between lives organized around production from one that evolves around consumption. The first is normatively regulated, while life organized around consumption has to be without norms. He argues ". . . it is guided by seduction, ever rising desires and volatile wishes – no longer by normal regulation. . . . The idea of luxury makes little sense, as the point is to make today's luxuries into tomorrow's necessities, and to reduce the distance between 'today' and tomorrow to the minimum – to

---

[18] George Ritzer, *The McDonaldization Thesis*, Sage Publications, London, New York, 1998.

'take the waiting out of wanting'".[19] Society being organized around consumption instead of production creates a whole new understanding of individuality, and a different awareness of one's body. It sets new norms for pleasure. I am afraid that consumption has taken a dominant position in our part of the world. Perhaps even in a more prevalent manner than in industrialized countries.

Nancy Young Reynolds' thesis on consumption between 1910 and 1960 suggests how significant consumption played a role in nationalist articulations with the issue of the boycott of foreign goods and the dumping of local products.[20] Boycott of foreign products was strongly articulated among many bourgeois nationalists at the beginning of the last century. The rising nationalist bourgeoisie clearly suffered from the paradox of mimicking the colonizer whereas it could never really be on equal terms with the master. It was no one else other than Huda Sha'rawi who created the Wafdist Women's Central Committee, the (WWCC) consisiting of both Muslim and Coptic women, which in 1922 launched the boycott of British goods. These upper class women later advocated a larger economic embargo to include merchandise, banks, functionaries and doctors among other professions.[21] Reynolds' work on the other hand, focused on the history of department stores in Cairo, which she studied from the angle of the evolution of Egyptian cosmopolitanism in commerce and consumption. The department stores symbolized the Levantine and Europeanized way of marketing, and thus were the symbol of modernity. There is no doubt that consumption, and the social significance of goods, continues to become pervasive in our part of the world. Whether it is today designated as Islamic consumption, or simply consumption, it is omnipresent in everyday life and very powerful. It has changed eating, drinking habits and dress.

Consumption has affected our notions of beauty and self-perception. It plays a decisive role in distinction and value judgment on what is good and bad taste, distinguish what is classy from the *baladi* and *bi'a*. The term *bi'a* literally means environment. Cairenes have started

[19] Zygmunt Bauman, *Liquid Modernity*, Polity Press, 2000, p. 76.
[20] Nancy Young Reynolds, *Commodity Communities: Interweavings of Market Cultures, Consumption Practices, and Social Power in Egypt, 1907–1961*, Ph.D. submitted at the Department of History, Stanford University. 2003.
[21] This point is well elaborated in: Mona L. Russell, *Creating The New Egyptian Woman. Consumerism, Education, and National Identity 1863–1922*. Palgrave Macmillan, 2004, pp. 89–91.

Fig. 5. Popular market of Bulaq, located behind the World Trade Centre.

using it during the last few years to replace the word *baladi*. Thus one juxtaposes *bi'a* and chic malls, or *bi'a* and chic people. While *baladi* literally means from the "country" or "local" as opposed to foreign, more broadly it could encompass traditional urban as opposed to the modern urbanites. For many years *baladi* was used by so-called middle or upper classes to show contempt for the "vulgar" taste of inferior classes. Today *bi'a* is meant to define the bad taste of lower classes, a taste that is even more despicable than *baladi*, thus popular. Those described as *bi'a* are also imagined as smelly. It is also possible to link the term *bi'a* with a growing disgust of the culture of *'ashwa'iyyat (slums)*. *Bi'a* is used in a pejorative way and thus implies a much worse connotation than *baladi*. This brings me to the significance of the classical study of Sawsan El-Messri's *Ibn al-Balad*. The literal translation of *ibn al-Balad* means the "son of the country", but it certainly has other connotations. The term *ibn al-Balad* appears as such during the eighteenth century when the foreign Mamluk rulers used it. El-Messri states that it suggests ". . . such a person who is usually dressed in *gallabiyaa* (flowing gown), or who comes from a *baladi* (popular quarter), or someone who cannot be hoodwinked, or one who is never punctual, or one who is knowledgeable about folk traditions".[22] *Ibn al-Balad* is also a designation for Egyptians, for not all Egyptians are *ibn Balad*, if they have foreign ancestors. El-Messiri's anthropological study also explored the popular stereotypes related to that image. The image of *ibn al-Balad* entails positive connotations such as sharp instincts, a good knowledge of everyday life, and a sense of humour. If on the one hand *ibn* or *bint al-Balad* (daughter) has positive connotations for being courageous and reliable and was part and parcel of a distinct urban Egyptian identity, *bi'a* on the other hand, is mainly negative and clearly class biased. From this example, is it possible to draw the conclusion that class stigmatization and stereotyping has in recent years sharpened. This leads me to raise the question of how the new consumer attitudes would enhance such biases against the growing silent masses of slums.

Jean Baudrillard's analysis of consumption as collective, institutional behaviour, and his critique of affluent society aptly apply to the Egyptian case. Baudrillard's critique of consumer culture maintained that it ultimately leads to a growth that produces both wealth and poverty (at a parallel pace).[23] He furthermore argued that waste is functional and it is what provides short-term elusive satisfaction.[24] The inherent logic of consumption implies unequal abundance because, definitively, "some have rightful access to the miracle, while others end up with the by-products of the miracle".[25] Most important, it is the unlimited character of consumption; the infinite and unlimited activated desires and its uncontrolled aspects, inherently contradictory to the notion of satisfaction,[26] which are worth pondering upon. In a society where about 65 percent of the population is under thirty,[27] the public visibility of youth and youth culture have become obvious. It is as if youth is left with only two options: either violence which they come across in their daily lives exemplified in suicide bombs (in Palestine), wars and routine harassments, or dream of participating in the myth of consumption in a rather virtual manner.

---

[22] Sawsan El-Messiri, *Ibn Al-Balad: A Concept of Egyptian Identity*, Leiden, E.J. Brill 1978, p. 1.

[23] George Ritzer, Introduction to Jean Baudrillard, *The Consumer Society, Myths and Structures*. Sage Publications,1998. Reprint 2002, p. 2.

[24] Ibid., p. 5.

[25] Jean Baudrillard, p. 60.

[26] Jean Baudrillard, pp. 61–62.

[27] According to the Central Agency for Public Mobilization and Statistics 1996 census, youth aged 0 to 19 represent 49 percent of the population and 20 to 29, 16 percent.

The prospects are becoming increasingly restricted. Other than migrating, galvanizing desires without fulfilment will definitively lead to an unhappy end. It is clear that social life in malls invites a new reflection about "socializing" and gendering space in Cairo.

The Organization of the Book

In Chapter One, I discuss some theoretical issues in urban sociology. The utopia of islands of city-shopping malls dates back to earlier times. It attempts to raise the question of how these new spaces of consumption have widened the divide in Cairo. It challenges the following premises: can we still think of Cairo in dichotomous terms: i.e. the split city, Islamic-versus the modern, grid downtown, the Bazaar versus the department store? Or is it all rather scattered slums side by side with well off residential areas? I relate the "gentrification" of some old quarters with the creation of spaces of consumerism and hotels, a phenomenon which parallels the frightening growth of slums defined as unplanned, informal settlements, 'ahswa'iyyat.

Chapter Two raises the following question: why is it that consumer studies are facing a lacunae in the Middle East in spite of the flowering of consumer studies world wide? Is it because it is still considered as a new field in which no serious sociological work has been undertaken in that direction? The second part will tackle the issue of the public sphere developed by the German philosopher Juergen Habermas and differentiate between it and the emergence of "public spaces" such as coffee houses and department stores. These public spaces, which are the pre-requisite for the flourishing of the public sphere saw the light in the Middle East a century ago, but would the conjunction between the two, i.e. the public sphere and the public space be articulated in the same way across cultures? Second, I will raise some questions on the way the notion of the public sphere – which is being promoted by the religious oriented protagonists – has been mainly appropriated and interpreted by some social scientists in the Middle Eastern context. A brief overview mentions the significant role the grands magasins or department stores played in early Egyptian consumer culture.

Chapter Three looks back at the Nasser's consumer culture of the 1960's and tries to weave personal with documented historical data on the period. I will focus on the role of promoting national consumer durables, the impact of Bauhaus architecture and furniture as part and parcel of the project of the modernizing of the lifestyle of the nation. It seems to me that, with regards to consumer culture, much remained the same until after nationalization was imposed in 1962. For many, the fear of "scarcity", the long lines to obtain ration cards food and the dearth of luxury goods started to be felt seriously during the sixties. In this chapter, I argue that the transformation from the sixties' "state capitalism" to the "open door policy" did not constitute a break. And if it did constitute one, it took place with the collaboration of the pre-existing social agents. Thus, the "open door policy" was rather a logical continuation but with certainly clear mutations. A fusion between the surviving old feudal "decadent" classes with the rising "petite bourgeoisie" culture was already developing during the time of Nasser. It is possible to argue that the 1967 political defeat has fundamentally shaken the values, dreams and visions of all segments of the society. The collective dream of nation building was more than ever put into question, to wither away and be replaced with "individualistic" solutions such as migration, "internal migration into religion" and conspicuous consumption. By drawing attention to the notion of the "memory of scarcity", this chapter attempts to analyze the transformations that took place in the seventies and the shifts from a "socialist economy" to the "open door policy". Chapter Four could be read as a counter chapter to the previous one. One the one hand, I speak of the memory of scarcity, but on the other hand, I bring up examples of "affluence" and point to the "survival skills" of the old classes and how these adapted very well to the new regime's ideology. Opportunism and continuity of old wines in new bottles? Yet change through "newcomers" is what Egyptian society experienced in the transitional phase of the open door policy, to allow a free hand to the neo-liberalist tycoon culture of the nineties.

Chapter Five provides an overview of the new forms of consumer culture, such as the emergence of coffeehouses, the flowering of the art market and the transformation in the food industry. In this chapter, I also discuss the differing notions of beauty with the commercialization of the body, the popularization of gyms and plastic surgery. Fashion, both ethnic and Islamic is here discussed as a form of identity construction as part and parcel of authenticating one's roots with the advent of globalization. It is also expressed in the "ethnic look" i.e., jewellery, and oriental, Islamic or Ottoman furniture,

Fig. 6. Technology Mall. Nasr City. Mall-cum-flats. January 2006.

that could be seen as "recycled" artifacts, which are rediscovered
locally after the recognition of the Western gaze. Put differently these
items have been transformed into what Appadurai designates as
"tourist art".[28]

Chapter Six discusses the social life of Cairo's shopping malls in
relation to urban reshaping. It provides ethnographic information on
the malls in two main areas in Bulaq along the Nile, and in Nasr
City with the emphasis on the role of the army in going private in
malls. It is evident that the malls are an American invention, but in
our part of the world, they have detoured via a "Saudification" or
"Saudi Arabization" of tastes and lifestyles. It is no coincidence that
these have mushroomed in Nasr City, the new grid, satellite city on

---

[28] Arjun Appadurai by citing Graburn (1976) says about tourist art: ". . . in which
objects produced for aesthetic, ceremonial, or sumptuary use in small, face-to-face
communities are transformed culturally, economically, and socially by the tastes,
markets and ideologies of larger economies". Arjun Appadurai (ed.), *The Social Life
of Things: Commodities in Cultural Perspective*, Cambridge University Press, 1986, p. 26.

Fig. 7. Wonderland Mall. January 2006.

the fringes of the desert, which has the largest concentration of returnees from Saudi Arabia and the Gulf countries.

The book was completed before I came across the recent publication of Chua Beng Huat's, *Life Is Not Complete without Shopping, Consumption Culture in Singapore*.[29] It was a delight to find out that Chua Beng Huat had dealt with similar topics in this book such as fashion, ethnic clothes and bodies in shopping centres. This was a natural follow-up of his previous work, which certainly impacted my labyrinthine research.

Finally, I would like to state that my problem – and perhaps this is what rescued me – is that I am a firm believer in *bricolage*. This is how I conceived this work, a work in process, consisting of bits and pieces, a never-ending mosaic. A work exploding in all directions, suffering evidently from a lacking centre, a true post-modern condition for the fragmented outlook it conveys. While conducting research, I became fascinated with pastiche and montage, concepts

---

[29] Published by the National University of Singapore, 2003.

Fig. 8. Stars Centre, Nasr City. Escalators.

that are today popular among anthropologists. In *Takarazuka, Sexual Politics and Popular Culture in Modern Japan,* Jennifer Roberston focused on the ambiguous position of all female Opera cross-dressed stars, the Takarazuka who perform in one of the largest theatres in Japan. By analyzing the *Takarazuka Revue* Robertson has intelligently used the concept of the "montage-like effect" to highlight the significance cross-dressing and cross ethnicking as strategies of transgression. Her work is an attempt to weave gender sexuality, ethnicity and nationalism with the ambiguity of androgyny. "Pastiches of exotic otherness" is a concept, which Robertson develops to analyze the *Revuescope,* and to understand the way Japanese view themselves *vis-à-vis* the European other. One of the productions blended together various styles such as Art Deco interiors, tropical birds and Josephine Baker.[30] Inspired by Robertson's montage, *bricolage* helped me in ending up with collages of various topics which all merged towards consumerism.

---

[30] Jennifer Roberston,*Takarazuka, Sexual Politics and Popular Culture in Modern Japan.* University of California Press, Berkeley, 1998, p. 135.

Last but not least, forgery in the field of art has always been an inescapable influential parallel market. Fraud, forgery and pastiche, are in fact international phenomena with a long standing tradition. Today in Egypt, forging paintings by montage and pastiche seems to have become a form of "underground art" that needs further attention. Unknown paintings of late famous painters remade through a montage and collage from previous works are rediscovered every day and circulated for the demand of the new rich. Pastiche and montage, I have to confess, have been appealing tools in the construction of this book.

CHAPTER ONE

CONSUMER CULTURE IN DIVIDED CAIRO

If we try to imagine what the cities of the Middle East will look like in twenty or thirty years, we might predict that most of them will consist of creeping slums and rampant poverty, co-existing with international hotels, large spaces designed for consumption and leisure time for those who can afford it. Disney-fied satellite cities in the desert will provide suburban annexes for the well to do. Modern communication systems and technologies, at least in the formal sector of the economy, will be as efficient as those in any Western country.

Fig. 9. Nubian Villas El-Gouna. Courtesy of El Gouna Real Estate www.elgouna.com.

This world will not be totally sealed off from the world beside it. Within the city large-scale population mobility will be inevitable, as domestic workers, drivers, security staff, technicians, salesmen and women, waiters and other employees spend their life commuting between the two worlds. At a certain point, those living in the high-class areas will begin to feel threatened, and their spaces will have to be walled-off to be protected from the potential would-be violent poor. At least this is how I imagine the evolution of the city of Cairo.

Of course, things may turn out differently. But it is all too easy to imagine the evolution of cities such as Cairo in these terms. For walled-off, protected areas, gated communities, condominiums, private beach resorts, leisure islands of peace, snow cities in the desert and amusement parks, monitored by private security forces and most advanced technology against the outside "barbarians", are no longer just futuristic fantasies. They exist already, and many of them have recently become the subject of sociological investigation. For example,

the Egyptian Mediterranean north coast has been transformed into
a thousand kilometres long stretch of ugly cemented blocks of condominiums one after another. Cairo's slums are bound to expand
as Egypt copes with one million new citizens every year with a total
population already exceeding 70 million, an increase of 8 percent
since 1986.[1] Official sources are even more disturbing. They predict
that by year 2017 Egypt's population will reach 97 million.[2] Cairo,
the largest city in the Middle East and Africa today has an estimate
of between 16 and 20 million residents and commuters who move
into and within this densely settled area. Cairo could be described
as a fascinating site for constant negotiations about space. Negotiations
which reveal the genie and art of survival, but which could turn into
bloody feuds through the simplest everyday acts in crammed buses,
in pouring water from the window due to the lack of a sewage system, in walking long distance to buy water in slums, in sharing taxis
communally, in having the right to open a window in ones' flat, or
in the struggle of the courageous pedestrian against barbarian car
drivers. Tensions reach the peak during the fasting month of Ramadan
when drivers metamorphose into nasty pedestrian-witch-hunters and
the slightest wrong movement can turn into a bloody fight. Many
think that an explosion is bound to come, the question is only when.
Certain slums are witnessing drastic elimination through land speculation. Currently the slums are hidden by walls from the tourist
gaze. Not to forget the national obsession about the danger of tarnishing the country's image.

The city of Cairo has in recent years experienced the extended
and continuing growth of slums. In 1998, it was estimated that 43
percent of the built-up area of greater Cairo was informal. Also, in
the same year 57 percent of the population of greater Cairo lived
in informal areas.[3] David Sims predicts that, if the trend continues,
by 2020, 66 percent of the population of greater Cairo will be living

---

[1] *Egypt-Population*. http://countrystudies.us/egypt/55.htm.

[2] Hazem Mohammed, in the page of "Issues and Features" *al-Hayat*, Monday,
28 September 2004, p. 19.

[3] I draw this information from David Sims, personal communication, 5 May
2005, Zamalek. See also David Sims "Informal Residential Development in Greater
Cairo: Summary figures", *unpublished report*. See also David Sims "Residential Informality
in Greater Cairo: Typologies, Representative Areas, Quantification, valuation and
Causal Factors", for Egyptian Center for Economic Studies and Institute for Liberty
and Democracy, Cairo, 20 June 2000.

in informal areas. This will represent 55 percent of the residential area.[4] Social scientists specialized on Egypt, such as Asef Bayat and Timothy Mitchell, provide a pessimistic view of the growing rural and urban poverty and the unbearable urban density, which has exacerbated in the last decade to increasingly affect the deplorable living conditions of the silent majority.[5] Clearly, their findings are contradicting the previous CAMPAS statistics. Egypt witnessed in the 1990's the consolidation of the ideology of neo-liberalism after it accepted the conditions set by the IMF program. The economy experienced at that time a 5 percent growth.[6] This growth was however short lived. Egypt's exports and imports collapsed from 88 percent in 1985 to 47 percent in 1996–97. Its exports also began to rely on the burgeoning petroleum sector, but these were affected by the collapse of the world prices.[7] Mitchell's analysis of the previous decade's economic performance predicted a gloomy future. The figures reveal a sharp decline in real per capita consumption, a drop in real wages and an increase of the numbers of Egyptians living below poverty line.[8] The flotation of the Egyptian pound in January 2003 caused a generalized trauma. During the first weeks of the flotation of the pound, all prices of basic goods soared. Some estimates were as high as 40 percent inflation. The economic depression has led to job cuts for thousands in various sectors of the economy. Depression not only hit the working class, but also the managerial level and the banking sector.

Segregated Cities

Side by side with daily violent atrocities in Palestine, and the construction of the racist segregating wall, and the horrific war in Iraq, Arabic newspapers announce from time to time the opening of a fantastic 1001-nights new mega-mall or a supermarket in an eastern

---

[4] Ibid.

[5] See Asef Bayat "Cairo's Poor: Dilemmas of Survival and Solidarity" *Middle East Report*, 1997, Winter, pp. 2–8. Timothy Mitchell, "Dreamland: The Neoliberalism of Your Desires," *Middle East Report*, Spring 1999, 28–33.

[6] Timothy Mitchell, *Rule of Experts: Egypt, Techno-Politics, Modernity*, Berkeley, University of California Press. 2002, p. 272.

[7] Mitchell, ibid., p. 275.

[8] Ibid., p. 286.

Fig. 10. Nile Towers, Bulaq, view from Zamalek.

city. Hundreds of ads for a luxurious lifestyle in dream-like villas in Dubai[9] and the promotion of an image of an "Arab Riviera", *al-riviera al-'arabiyya*,[10] consisting of an island of luxury, bombard the Arab newspapers and satellite channels. *Al-Hayat* newspaper recently advertised a picture of the Spanish singer Julio Igliesias sitting amongst European looking friends, singing with his guitar in the garden of a villa. Underneath the ad, it was written Julio Igliesias lives (*ya'ish*) in *The Villa* complex of Dubai.[11]

It is as if "modernization" had become synonymous with never ending luxurious consumption, which often seems to be promoted in the media by sexy, hip-hop, infantile-paedophile singing stars. As if the road to "democracy" – a definitively loaded word which is becoming an alibi for hegemony, intervention and war – is being reconstructed to mean the "freedom to consume". "Consume but

[9] See *al-Hayat* Monday 7 February 2005. Advertisement: The Villa. infor@dubai-properties.ae.

[10] *Al-Hayat*, Monday 7, 2005, Advertisement: The Pearl www.thearlqatar.com.

[11] *Al-Hayat*, Tuesday, 31 May 2005, Issue No. 15400, p. 3.

shut up" could be promoted to encourage the adoption of an amnesiac state, vis-à-vis the flagrant class and inequality issues. But in countries like Egypt, which is clearly designated as the Third World, consumption is celebrated, while consumers' associations and consumers' rights are loathed. It was five years before scandals about high officials in the Ministry of Agriculture importing carcinogenic pesticides became public and the damage was long done.[12] The more one reads about urban planning in the Middle East, the more one goes over the projects that are currently lined up for us, the more one realizes that in the minds of our financial tycoons and multinational corporations, the concept of "development" means one thing and one thing only: the expansion of consumerism through the building of new shopping areas, annexed to international hotels and tourist resorts. What about the productive sector, you may ask? But no one in charge of these projects seems to be the least bit bothered by this question. It goes hand in hand with the image of Egypt being a recipient of aid, a "nation of beggars" seeking the assistance of international aid because it cannot keep its internal affairs in order. Every year, Egypt receives $2 billion in US in civil and military aid,[13] and it has so far received US $40 million for subsidizing the Egyptian army.[14] The US being the largest bilateral trade partner with Egypt means that the country has been involved in the largest cooperation with the USAID economic program in the world.[15] The whole country has been transformed into a mere aid recipient-consumer. We can only suppose that the entire working population will eventually have to become one huge undifferentiated mass, catering to the service sector. It is as if the crucial issue of the violation of human rights and the prevailing martial law could be forgotten by soporific consumption. The golden age of Egyptian liberal tycoons is paired with the regime's worse record of human rights, especially after the Taba Hilton bombing in October 2005 that led to the detaining of around

---

[12] This was the former deputy minister of agriculture Youssef Abdel Rahman who has been finally sentenced (2005) after having proven that he was involved in importing Carcinogenic pesticides between 1996–2004. See *Egypt Today*, Newsreel February 2005, p. 25.

[13] Sarah al-Deeb, "Aid to Government Opponents Rankles Egypt", Associated Press, 17 May, 2005. http//democracy.Egypt@aucegypt.edu.

[14] *Daily Risk Report, Enough, Enough,* April 05, 2005. www.crossborderreports.com

[15] Ambassador C. David Welch, "Mutual Support and Responsibility: The Course Ahead for the US-Egyptian Partnership, Council on Foreign Affairs", Cairo, Egypt, June 24, 2002. http://usembassy.egnet.net/ambassador/sp062402.htm.

2,400 persons under inhuman conditions and torture. Egyptian security forces have been identified by Human Rights Watch as com-
mitting mass human rights abuses.[16] For the first time in Egypt's
history, women who demonstrated against the 2005 May presiden-
tial referendum for amendments and foreign female reporters were
violently sexually harassed. In a country that prides itself on its
Islamic values and public morality, for the first time in a public
space, women were entirely stripped of their clothes from hooligans
paid by the party's regime. Dalal al-Bithri in *al-Hayat*[17] commented
ironically on the event by pointing to the double standards of the
regime's official discourse backed by the Bush administration about
the empty slogans of "women's empowerment", decision-making and
political representation. The consequence is that due to historical
antecedents, patriarchy has enhanced the image that women are only
accepted in public spaces when their chauffeurs drive them in shel-
tered, air-conditioned, enclosed cars. In other words, they are only
accepted when they themselves become consumer objects. Otherwise,
women clearly deserve to be raped if they protest in the street. Al-
Bithri wonders why is it then that such an appalling event could not
possibly have occurred in the political atmosphere of the sixties and
seventies?

The logic behind "walling off", be it the condominiums, gated
communities, islands of luxury, or shopping malls, became a model
for the projects erected by the emerging Egyptian capitalists. In our
part of the world, consumption definitively takes a crucial political
turn with the boycott of American and Israeli products. In the past
few years, Coca Cola and McDonald's, Marlboro and several American
food chains have been targeted and these certainly affected the market

---

[16] There has been much discussion recently in the press about the mounting
regime violence against political opponents. Moreover, the government's internal
security has been blamed for the injustices in jailing thousands of innocent people,
detaining them without trial and torturing them after the terrorist attacks in Taba
in 2004. See Gihan Shahine, "Terror as Vengeance", *al-Ahram Weekly*, 5–11 May,
2005, p. 4. About the appalling conditions of the jails and torture, see the most
recent Human Right Watch Report by Joe Stork, "Egypt Mass Arrests, Torture
Follow Taba Bombing. Human Rights Watch", http://hrw.org/English/docs/2005/02/
22/egypt10196.htm.

[17] Dalal-al-Bithri, "li-awwal marra fi tarikh al-Mahroussa" (For the First Time in
al-Mahrusa's History [Egypt]), *al-Hayat*, Sunday, 5 June 2005, issuee no. 15405,
p. 18.

opportunities of alternative local fast food chains and local beverages such as Zam Zam and Mecca Cola. Today the Egyptian anti-globalization movement (AGEG) has become one of the staunch boycott campaigners in support of the *intifada* in Palestine. Boycott campaigns seem to also be gaining momentum in Saudi Arabia, Bahrain, and Lebanon.[18] In addition, there are the worldwide anti-war activists, who added their voices to those calling for boycotts in Jakarta, Senegal, South Africa, Bangladesh, Malaysia, Japan, and all over Europe.[19] Whether these boycotts could lead to significant policy changes, needs still further research. However, Asef Bayat argues that after the American invasion of Iraq, millions of Arabs and Muslims have joined the boycott of products such as McDonald's, KFC, Starbucks, Nike, and Coca Cola. Furthermore, the success of local beverage products resulted in Coca-Cola losing 20 to 40 percent of its market share.[20] Another report identified a significant decrease in US imports to Arab countries in 2003 compared to the previous year. The following countries are: Qatar imported 28 percent less from the US compared to last year, Tunisia 28 percent less, Lebanon 24 percent less, Saudi Arabia 23 percent less, Egypt 18 percent less and Kuwait 3 percent less than the previous year. While the countries, which are importing much more than in the previous year are Bahrain, 1.04 as much, Jordan, 1.18 times more UAE, 1.5 times more Yemen 1.72 times more, Morocco 2.25 times more.[21] However boycotting foreign goods, as we know, is not a new policy. It was a major characteristic of nationalist movements in various colonized countries exemplified in Ghandi's boycott of British products and among the upper class members of the Wafdist nationalist Party in Egypt after the exile of the nationalist leaders in 1921. As Nancy Young Reynolds has written "Boycotts would become an important tactic in the nationalist movement, one that brought larger and larger numbers of people into the opposition, and the 1922–1924 boycott

---

[18] Sonia-Meyerson-Knox from Left turn Magazine, Echoes of Seattle: From Manama to Casablanca. http://www.lefturn.org/Articles/Viewer.asp?id=353&type=M.

[19] For the wider network of the boycott campaigns see http://www.motherearth.org/usboycott/global_en.php.

[20] Asef Bayat, "The 'Street' and the Politics of Dissent in the Arab World" in *Middle East Report*, Spring, 2003,http://www.merip.org/mer/mer226/226_bayat.html.

[21] "Year-end economic figures on the boycott" 2003–01–03, http:/www.boycottisraeligoods.org/modules 11584.php.

would retain a central part in popular memory about the revolution of 1919".[22]

City-Malls

By reading the cities as texts in which their topographies reveal the social stratification of urban life, previous studies have pointed to the reading of the mall as a city.[23] Nancy Backes pointed out that the mall, more than the city "with its recombinant properties, its reduction to basic forms not unlike those of abstract art offers a more democratic hope and possibility, despite its connection to private enterprise".[24] Already at the turn of the 20th century, urban futurists such as H.G. Wells, who predicted the diffusion of great cities as a series of villages connected by high speed transformation, have imagined the utopian city as a huge shopping mall. For H.G. Wells, the post-urban city

> will be essentially a bazaar, a great gallery of shops and places of concourse and rendezvous, a pedestrian place, its pathways reinforced by lifts and moving platforms, and shielded from the weather, and altogether very spacious, brilliant, and entertaining agglomeration.[25]

As Robert Fishman interpreted H.G. Wells, the city-shopping mall will end up pushing away the productive activities to the fringes and decentralizing the urban areas.[26] A similar idea of the ideal-consumer-city is to be found in the Utopian socialist Fourier whose phalansteries – which were meant to be new communities structures that consisted of producers and merchants – were inspired by the image of the bazaars and the Parisian arcades.[27] The theme of the utopian city is in fact not new, but more and more urban sociologists bring up the issue that for many futurists the 2000-year utopian city is

---

[22] Nancy Young Reynolds, 2003, p. 3.
[23] Nancy Backes, "Reading the Shopping Mall City" *Journal of Popular Culture*, Vol. 31 no.3, Winter 1997, pp. 1–17.
[24] Ibid. p. 1.
[25] Cited from Robert Fishman, "Beyond Suburbia: The Rise of the Technoburb", in: *The City Reader*, ed. Richard T. LeGates and Fredric Stout, London, New York, Routledge, 1996, p. 79.
[26] Ibid.
[27] Bill Lancaster, *The Department Stores, A Social History*, Leicester University Press, London and New York, 1995, p. 9.

Disneyland, the "degenerate utopia".[28] Disneyland is the "tomor-rowland", where science and technology will be overwhelming together with the "consumer paradise".[29] On the other hand, the counter image of utopia is the decadence of Babylon. Urban sociologists as well as novelists like Charles Dickens perceived the nineteenth century industrial "city as a problem"; a "monster" filled with crime, vice, slums, poverty, greed and miasmas. In short, the city as a mega-lopolis turned to be per se apocalyptic and evil; the only escape is then to return back to the pure and clean countryside.[30]

The question then remains: will the whole Middle East turn into dualistic torn apart landscapes (zones) of conflict, slums, on the one hand, and huge utopian shopping-city-malls on the other hand? Will the Middle Eastern futuristic metropolis turn into a huge consumer Moloch-Babylon of consumer culture? Another prediction: as long as the Gulf countries produce oil, they will continue to multiply huge shopping malls and sanitized areas where people will eternally indulge in leisure and drop before they could attack all shops. Dubai, Beirut and Cairo aspire to become associated at best with international shopping and tourism. At worst, these will be associated with current international terrorism and its local brand, which is bred in slums. But these capitals can still extract significant revenues from a clientele based in other oil producing countries.

Recently, Dubai announced the creation of the world's tallest tower in the world. It will be taller than Petronas Towers in Kuala Lumpur (452 meters) and the Chicago Sears Tower (442 meters). I find it interesting that national pride is closely associated with the Babylonian obsession of defeating height records. It is true that skyscrapers have been the symbol of "modern" architecture, which explains why Dubai aspires to be designated as "modern". My impression is that Dubai, similar to several Gulf countries, has in the background the successful Southeast Asian model. The island of Singapore, which consists, only of a few hundred square kilometres, has been often described as a big shopping mall, or a hotel. Former Prime Minister of Malaysia Mahathir Mohammad has previously boasted that he erected the

---

[28] Elizabeth Wilson, *The Sphinx in the City, Urban Life, the Control of Disorder, and the Women*, University of California Press, 1991, p. 14.

[29] Ibid.

[30] The idea of the city as a problem is brilliantly developed by Alexander Welsh, *The City of Dickens*, Harvard University Press, Cambridge Massachusetts and London, England, 1986. See in particular Chapter 1, the City of Satire.

longest shopping mall in Asia and the two tallest towers in the world.
All these empires of consumption are the modern temples glorifying
its indigenous leaders, as if development is equated with consumerism
and a "shop until you drop" mentality.

Back to Cairo

In today's Cairo, shopping malls are mushrooming, but malls multiplied equally in Sharm al-Sheikh and Luxor. In hot summers, these
are filled to capacity. A huge mall opened in the Cairo suburb of
Nasr City in 2005. The commercial development company Golden
Pyramid Plaza, controlled by the Sharbatly and Shobokshi Saudi
Arabian families purchased 115,000 square meters of land at the
junction of Nasr City and Heliopolis to open City Stars.[31] This centre, which evidently stands in competition with the many centres in
the Gulf, will save wealthy shoppers from flying to Dubai for shopping.[32] The press defines the new project as a city within a city.[33]
It is advertised as follows:

> The project's blueprints envision a complex housing three five stars
> hotels, 70,000 square meters of office space and 266 luxury apart-
> ments, all centred around a 550 shop mall. It's a retail centre larger
> than any in the Middle East or Europe – slightly bigger, in fact, than
> the gargantuan mall of America in Minnesota. Citystars' backers have
> so far sunk some 750 million $ (L.E. 4.27 billion) into the ground in
> Nasr City and are looking forward to a partial opening in November.[34]

Even before the official opening of the City Stars Mall, thousands
of people have started to flock there every evening simply to roam
around. Marvelling at the grandeur of this empire of consumption,
they wander aimlessly. The cafeterias, fast food restaurants and food
stalls are packed. The gigantic children's games section is already
fully operating with a frightening success. Another huge section of
the mall has been designed as a simulation of the Khan al-Khalili
Bazaar displaying the identical jewellers, handicrafts and items that

---

[31] Donna Mitchell, "Cairo's Wealthy Won't Need To Leave the City to Shop"
Shopping Centres Today, International Council for Shopping Centres May, 2002, http://
www.icsc.org/srch/sct/sct0502/page160html.
[32] Ibid.
[33] Nadia Mostafa, 'Retail goes Wild', *Business Today*, June 2003, p. 61.
[34] Ibid.

are sold in the old popular bazaar.[35] Only, it is cleaner, newer and cooler than the centuries old, dusty bazaar. Definitively, for the middle-upper class, uptight Egyptians and in-transit Gulf and foreign customers (the mall is located some twenty minutes from the airport), it will be faster and more comfortable to shop in the mall rather than in the Khan. The complex, which includes the adjacent Intercontinental hotel, is an amazing remake of kitsch facades guarded by huge statues of Pharaohs giving the illusion that one is entering a Pharaoh's temple. The mall is certainly inspired by a pharaonic temple. Except that one is immediately reminded that this temple of consumption has tight security measures, such as checking all the trunks of the cars when parking in the vast underground parking lots.

Among business circles, many gossiped that constructing shopping malls is the other side of the money laundering coin. Malls and mega projects have been used to obtain huge bank loans, which were smuggled out of the country. It resulted into a series of scandals and arrests of businessmen. This might explain why in spite of the short lifespan of malls, these will continue to multiply. But how would such a gargantuan project survive with the frightening current recession?[36] Certainly no one can answer that question.

How to Emulate the Asian Tigers?

In the late 1990's Egypt underwent a process of structural adjustment guided by international financial organizations, which led to further privatization and liberalization of the economy. This coincided with the birth of a new business class and tycoons, who are restructuring Egypt's economy. Is the Middle East heading towards an Asian model of development and would it be consummated by a similar financial crisis? In the Egyptian discourse on development, admiration of the Asian model seems to be central. Egyptian intellectuals

---

[35] Personal observations, visit to the City Stars Centre, 4 February, 2005.

[36] According to John Sfakianakis, a specialist on the business elites in the Middle East, many Saudi millionaires have encountered after 9/11 a tighter control on their business activities in the US and Europe. These businessmen had to redirect their investments to the Arab countries such as Egypt where they have evidently more freedom of action. Personal Communication with John Sfakianakis. Cairo, 20 March 2005.

ask whether the Middle East can follow a model of development like that of the Asian tigers. The Egyptian Marxist political scientist Mohammed El-Sayyed Said is quite pessimistic; commenting upon the 1999 change of the cabinet he stated:

> We want to imitate the Asian model, but we lack the traditional Asian virtues of self-discipline, strict precision and rigid austerity. We frequently boast our heritage and authenticity, but eagerness to learn, the desire to build and the appreciation of collective work are beginning to decay.[37]

Whether Egypt will emulate the Asian tigers is beside the point. What is of interest is precisely the analogy and the constant comparisons with the so-called Asian renaissance discussed by both leftists and Islamist intellectuals. "Why we will never be like them" is an idea that dominates debates in Egypt. Neither Sadat not Mubarak managed to transform the Nasserist statist and populist legacy of the state. Just as, so far both the indigenous and foreign capital failed to participate in industrial development.[38]

Some economists have argued that Third World countries undergoing structural adjustment suffer from an increase of impoverishment.[39] Recent reports between 1981 and 1991 are rather alarming, as the triumph of neo-liberalism takes place at the expense of the poor. Since the structural adjustment program implemented by the IMF in Egypt,[40] that rural poverty doubled and urban poverty increased more than 1.5 times between 1981 and 1991. Real wages in the public sector have dropped by 8 percent, and household expenditure surveys reveal a significant decline in real per capita consumption between 1990–1 and 1995–6. Mitchell remarks that a sign of increasing poverty is the reappearance of soup kitchens in Cairo. He adds "the proportion of people below the poverty line increased in this period from about 40 percent (urban and rural) to 45 percent in urban areas and over 50 percent in the countryside".[41] Bayat

---

[37] Mohammed El Sayed Said, "Coming up with the Right Formula," *al-Ahram Weekly* 14 October 1999.

[38] Moheb Zaki, *Egyptian Business Elite*, p. 80.

[39] Nader Fergany, "The Growth of Poverty in Egypt", Cairo: *Al-Meshkah Research Centre*, January 1998.

[40] Asef Bayat, "Cairo's Poor Dilemmas of Survival and Solidarity", *Middle East Report*, Winter 1997: 2–8, p. 3.

[41] Timothy Mitchell, "Dreamland: The Neoliberalism of Your Desires", *Middle East Report*, Spring 1999, p. 32.

states that more than half of Cairo and adjacent Giza were classified as poor and ultra poor. The most visible outcome of structural adjustment has been land speculation, which led to the enrichment of property owners while increasing social inequalities and poverty. Statistics reveal that in 1991, 35 percent of Cairenes lived below the poverty line.[42]

Beirut

In the same way, it seems that Beirut's reconstruction is closely linked with fast-growing fancy, post-modern, commercial centres. The reconstruction of the "centre ville" of Beirut under the auspices of the *Solidere* group, of the late al-Hariri, led to a boom in commercial activities. This attracted the growing interest of franchised companies such as Casper and Gambini, Bang and Olufsen, and Versage. The price of real estate in the centre of town rocketed to reach $9,000 per square meter. A mega project to rebuild the old markets of Tawile and Ayyas was proposed, as a hyper space consisting of 100,000 square meters which will be divided as follows: 12,000 square meters for a department store, 5,000 square meters for a jewellery market and a media complex with an 18,000 square meters for 8 cinemas, a super market of 7,000 square meters and a mall measuring 30,000 square meters which would potentially contain 200 shops. The French Galeries Lafayette has signed a contract to have a branch in Beirut through the group ADMIC, which already has the franchise for the French BHV and Monoprix supermarkets.[43] Shopping malls are also burgeoning in the luxurious rue de Verdun[44] to include the following malls: Plaza 1, Plaza 2, Dunes, Verdun 730 and Verdun 732. The Plaza malls 1 and 2, which were among the first to be constructed in Verdun (in 1992) by the Kamel Jaber

---

[42] Eric Denys, "Urban Planning and Growth in Cairo", *Middle East Report*, Winter 1996, pp. 7–12, p. 8.

[43] Guillaume Boudisseau, "Espace commercial. Les temples du shopping", *Le Commerce du Levant*, April 2002, (pp. 60–63), p. 61.

[44] For a comprehensive study of the commercial significance of both Verdun and Hamra streets in Beirut, see the extensive Ph.D. thesis of Guillaume Boudisseau, *Espaces commerciaux, centralités et logiques d'acteurs a Beyrouth: le cas de Hamra et de Verdun. Thèse présentée pour l'obtention du Doctorat de l'Université Francois-Rabelais de Tours*, octobre 2001.

Fig. 11. ABC BEIRUT.

Company have incorporated a total of seventy-four suites or apartments suites which cater to the Gulf visitors (who are called the *Khalijiin*) during the most high seasons. The items sold in the Plaza One shops are glittery, highly expensive clothes and jewellery, which are specifically made for the taste of the Gulf public. Although the two malls might look today as a bit "dépassé"[45] because they have turned into ghost spaces – with the exception of their coffeeshops which are well frequented, and its studios or suites which are fully booked all year round.[46] Verdun Street has been known for being among the most thirty-three most expensive streets in the world to reach a rent of US $800 per square meter with 120 franchises listed.[47]

The Christian quarter of Ashrafieh in Beirut witnessed the opening of another fancy shopping centre the ABC, a company, which

---

[45] Compared to Dunes and Verdun 730 and 732 which are new malls with fancy coffee shops like Starbucks and organic food coffee shops and they are all located in the same area.

[46] Personal communication with the general manager Darwish Hashoush, Plaza 1 Verdun, Beirut, 18 January 2005.

[47] Boudisseau 2002, p. 61.

has operated in Lebanon since 1936.[48] ABC today includes seven branches, and boasts that it could receive over 3 million shoppers.[49] The architect Dolly Debs – Braidi, who did a brilliant job of constructing the mall on a very steep slope, has designed the ABC Ashrafieh Mall. Her idea was to create a space that is an extension of the street. She had to take into consideration the high population density of the quarter, so that it looked naturally integrated into the quarter's life.[50] Debs managed to create different spacious terraces and levels, so that each level could have exits to the street. The mall, which its glass domes and arcades and its three large halls connected by different passages, Cineplex and games hall provides a futuristic post-modern atmosphere. With its 37,000 m² it is considered as the largest so far in the city.[51] Here again, the mall became the beloved place for youngsters and during holidays the manager stated that he has to increase the security guards from thirty-three persons (three shifts) to forty-nine, in order to contain possible sexual harassment and public disorder since up to 35 thousand people could visit the mall each day.[52] The 1500 parking places are full most of the time.

A City Mall just opened on the Dora highway in Beirut covers 200,000 m² of which 75,000 m² are for commercial purposes. It will include a hypermarket, a shopping mall, a Cineplex for nine cinemas, a parking lot for 2000 places and a children's game space. It will be managed again by ADMIC group, which opened a new Monoprix for food in Hamra in 2003.[53] But if Cairo is taking over the lead in the numbers of Malls, the area of grand Beirut has the total sum of 71 super and hypermarkets, some of these with a long

---

[48] Ashrafieh opened after the success it had with its branch in Dbaye under the direction of Robert Fadel. It took a while to take off economically, probably because the rent of the shops is so high, ranging between 800 and 1500 $ per m2. Guillaume Boudisseau "Les nouveaux rois du shopping", *Le Commerce du Levant*, Octobre 2004, (pp. 60–65), p. 60.

[49] www.abc.com.lb

[50] Personal Communication with architect Dolly Debs-Braidi, Kaslik,Lebanon, 24th of January 2005.

[51] Guillaume Boudisseau, "Les Nouveaux rois du shopping", *Le Commerce du Levant*, Octobre 2004, p. 60.

[52] Personal communication with Rashid Massoud, Manager of ABC Ashrafieh, 26 Beirut, January 2005.

[53] Guillaume Boudisseau, "Pas de Monoprix a Hamra", *Le Commerce du Levant*, Aout, 2003, p. 76.

and established tradition of operating in the country.[54] Many however, have questioned the survival of these supermarkets and if they
are not killing the small corner grocer. The locally established ones
like the Bou Khalil, created in 1935 will certainly be threatened by
big names like Spinneys and Monoprix. Besides, that the purchasing power does not look as if it is rapidly expanding when compared to this sudden multiplication of supermarkets. Nonetheless,
these newly erected commercial centres exist alongside the growing
number of street children, ambulant perfume sellers and handicapped
beggars. Poverty is certainly far from being eradicated.

Dubai

The future Middle Eastern landscape seems to be mega projects and
bombastic dreams: the creating one of the largest lakes in the middle of the desert, snow cities implanted in unbearable heat of long
summers, erecting the tallest tower on earth such as the Burj Dubai,
and the Dubai Mall which are to be completed in 2006. The Dubai
Mall will reach nine million square feet of shopping. It boasts that
it is the largest shopping space in the world, to compete with Malaysia's
largest mall so far and "... bigger than Edmonton Mall, Canada,
and much larger than the Mall of America, in Bloomington, St.
Paul, Minnesota".

The Dubai Mall website puts forth its grandiose expectations for
hosting thirty five million visitors, "... 3.2 billion consumers armed
with a collective GDP of US $18.3 trillion will be knocking on our
door". This is what one gets on the Dubai Mall website a dream
world with an aquarium of glass tunnels to wander in, an artificial
lake of 4.3 million square meters, underground parking for 16,000
cars, hotels, private residences, cinemas and entertainment sites, the
largest gold *suk* (market) on earth, and one million square feet of
leading fashions.[55] All this is under the auspices of the gigantic group
Emaar that is a public joint stock company with a capital of US$
6 billion. The company also has ten major real estate projects, which

---

[54] Guillaume Boudisseau, "Le combat des chefs", *Le Commerce du Levant*, Octobre
2004, pp. 68–70, p. 69.
[55] "EMAAR Announces 'The Dubai Mall', The World's Largest Shopping Centre".
http://www.emaar.com.

include Dubai Marina, Arabian Ranches (including Gazelle), Emirates Hills, the Meadows, the Springs, the Lakes (including Hattan Homes), the Greens and the EMAAR Towers in downtown Dubai.

Dubai has also recently announced the creation of the largest shopping centre in the world by the Majid Al-Futtaym group. The project of the mall of the Emirates is an $850 million investment. The mall will measure over 6.5 million square feet in an area of 2.4 million square feet. It will include 350 shops, a huge hypermarket, and a 12-screen cinema, parking for over 7000 cars and will include the world biggest ski resort with real snow. Already Dubai is been labelled as the "Shopping capital of the Middle East" with approximately twenty-five gigantic shopping centres. The Majid al Futtaim group has experienced in recent years an amazing growth through retail and shopping centre activity, which began with opening the largest mall in Dubai, the Deira city. They have also exclusive franchise for the French Carrefour in the Gulf.[56] The Chief executive officer of Majid al-Futtaim is an Australian who revived the largest shopping centre in Europe, the Bluewater Mall in South of London.

There is also the Mall of Arabia, which is part of a $5 billion project launched again by the government with a giant entertainment centre, parks and museums. If you click on the advertisements of these three malls, each will advertise that theirs as the largest in the world, meaning that Dubai has achieved the highest records when it comes to malls. Emaar, the government owned real estate giant, seems to be competing with the al-Futtaim group when it announced, shortly after the Futtaim group's decision, its own Dubai mega-mall which will be built near the tallest tower in the world erected by Emaar. Emaar's Dubai mall expects over thirty-five million visitors in the first year[57] a number that seems to be over-inflated considering that Dubai consists of a tiny population. One can only guess that the number of foreign workers who will do the job will certainly to increase. The analysts have already predicted the expected

---

[56] The Majid al-Futtaim group runs several projects in Egypt, among which is Carrefour as will be explained later. The group also owns malls in the neighbouring emirates of Ajman and Sharjah and in Muscat. "Dubai's Greatest Shopping Mall Race. The Majid al-Futtaim Group and Emaar Properties are competing to Build Dubai's Best and Biggest Shopping Mall." United Arab Emirates, Thursday, February 12–2004. http://www.ameinfo.com/news/detailed/p. 4.

[57] Ibid., p. 1.

failure of such projects due to over construction and over supply. They brought up the simple fact that:

> Dubai with its population of under 1 million already has four times as much shopping are per capita as the United States. With Dubai's even greater expansion on the way, trouble seems inevitable[58]

The Virtual City and its Double

The success story of the city of Dubai and its recent gigantic expansion in the desert is entirely different from millenary Cairo, its bazaars, its Islamic city and the bordering modern downtown. Although it is possible to make analogies between Dubai and Egypt's newly constructed gated communities and satellite cities in the desert, Dubai seems to be the future model for Egypt. Emaar, again, plans a L.E. 1 million to build a smart village business and leisure district in Cairo. The project will include a convention centre, a hotel and a commercial centre at the Cairo Heights (The Moqattam). According to the *Business Times Magazine*, Emmar has so far been quite secretive about the project, which is a joint venture between Emaar Misr and the state owned Al-Nasr Housing and Development Company.[59] How are these mega-projects then changing Cairo's landscape?

Janet Abu Lughod's *Tale of Two Cities*[60] brilliantly pointed to the dichotomies between the modern Western downtown grid created by Khedive Ismail to boast a modern image versus the old Islamic Cairo. To what extent is this analysis still applicable? Abu Lughod was basically interested in the idea of the "dual city" as a legacy of the colonial past and the increasing "nativization" and the blending of the two patterns. How far have these two patterns blended? Do we now have a "dual city" where the modern Western city has been imposed juxtaposed on the old medina, the *Casbah*, or the Islamic city? Janet Abu Lughod[61] vividly reveals the contradictions in the relationship between these two spaces: the mysterious "old" city opposed to the grid, open and rationalized, modern space. This thesis

---

[58] Ibid., p. 3.

[59] Ahmed Namatalla, "Pay No Attention to the man Behind the Curtain", *Business Times*, December 2005, p. 56.

[60] Janet Abu-Lughod "Tale of Two cities: The Origins of Modern Cairo" *Comparative Studies in Society and History* 7 (4) 1965, pp. 429–457.

[61] Ibid.

is extensively developed in her book *Cairo 1001 Years of the City Victorious*,[62] when by the end of nineteenth century, Cairo developed into two separate communities, revealing discontinuity. The native pre-industrial city was juxtaposed to the colonial city, the architecture, lifestyle related to the *harat* and *durub* (narrow alleys), was left aside and *rond point*, *maydans* and grid-iron street pattern adopted. The contrasts between the two "symbiotic communities" of Egyptians and foreigners were sharpened.[63] Cairo's history during the second half the nineteenth century as Abu Lughod noted became the history of the new Western city.

Zeynep Celik[64] pointed to the imagined gendered sensuality of the *Casbah* of Algiers. In colonial literature, as well as in the eyes of French architects and colonial administrators, the *Casbah* became identified with a single, undifferentiated and sensual woman.[65] This image was probably associated with the difficulty of penetrating the mysterious space of that old and tortuous part of the town. Celik notes again, that French intellectuals, the military and the administrative officers have made the Algerian woman as the "key symbol of the colony's cultural identity".[66] Could we thus extend the spatial dichotomy to a consumer oriented modern city versus the world of slums and marginalized shantytowns?

Nancy Young Reynolds' study of the circulation of commodities from 1907–1961 provides an extensive history of the birth of Egyptian department stores, which owes much to Egyptian Jews. Reynolds argued that the circulation of commodities entailed much more than the simple dichotomy between "traditional" and "modern", and the Islamic city versus the Western city.[67] Goods acquired meaning in their movement among groups, between modern stores and traditional bazaars. Furthermore, through tracing some of the biographies of the founders of department stores like the Cicurels and the Sednaouis, she draws our attention to the fact that they grew out

---

[62] Janet Abu-Lughod, *Cairo 1001 Years of the City Victorious*, Princeton University Press, 1971.

[63] Janet Abu-Lughod, p. 98.

[64] Zeynap Z. Celik, *Urban Forms and Colonial Confrontations, Algiers under French Rule*, Berkeley, University of California Press, 1997.

[65] Celik, 1997: 22.

[66] Ibid., 22.

[67] Nancy Young Reynolds, *Commodity Communities: Interweavings of Market Cultures, Consumption Practices, and Social Power in Egypt, 1907–1961*, Ph.D. submitted at the Department of History Stanford University, 2003, p. 4.

of small-scale commerce in the old city.[68] The *baladi*/European or modern/traditional European/Islamic city dichotomy is strongly questioned. Reynolds considers that the concept of hybridization, and the interweaving of varying publics using different markets coexisted.

For the sake of speculation, can we say that today – if the duality is still valid – the spatial dichotomy has been transformed into consumer-middle class residential areas versus huge slums? What do we think of downtown today? Downtown, which foreigners mainly occupied in colonial times, has become more and more depopulated and invaded in the night by different publics than those of the morning. The downtown morning public might include state employees, bureaucrats, bankers, lawyers and housewives; at night the downtown streets are occupied by *baladi*, lower classes. The public space is dominantly male, ambulant salesmen and women, street children (who are constantly picked up by the police and tortured) and beggars who occupy the streets. This is however, going hand in hand with a revival of downtown intellectual life symbolized in coffeehouses, art galleries, bars, and hotels. Several intellectuals have moved down and renovated the old flats. Downtown is becoming a colourful mix of everything. The demarcation line between the slums of Dar el-Salam, which are considered as a very densely populated area, and the residential quarter of Ma'adi is just one street. The slums of the quarter of Mit-'Oqba are in close proximity with the residential quarter of Mohandessin which means that there is no clear cut segregating line between residential and poor areas. Only in the satellite cities and beach resorts can the upper middle class people enjoy the total seclusion and protection from the "riff-raff" and rampant poor.

The problem of class will certainly be exacerbated by the sheer increase in numbers and by the pervasiveness of corruption. It seems to me that the only group that can actively resist such drastic changes are the rich. Take for example the space of the Gezira club in the well to do island of Zamalek, which is considered to be one of the last remaining few green areas of Cairo. The government's intention to turn every spot in a shopping area and a garage resulted into a series of petitions by local residents who finally managed to stop a nearby mega project. The project to build a 24,500 square metre parking area for 1500 cars was presented by former Prime

---

[68] Ibid., p. 115.

Minister Kamal al-Ganzuri. The residents expressed resistance because this would intrude on the last remaining green spot, and shopping malls are spread all over the place.[69] Did the Zamalek residents win because they had access to influential circles and are considered to be part of the establishment? Or is it a temporary victory, since rumours spread again that, indeed, the project might still materialize. The Gezira club, a relic of British colonial presence, represents one of the last surviving spaces which has, so far, escaped the abstruse destruction, a sad fate which did not spare Cairo's abundant colonial monuments.

---

[69] Lydia Samir, "Residents Victorious", *Cairo Times*, 12–21 May, 2003, p. 11.

CHAPTER TWO

CONSUMER STUDIES IN THE MIDDLE EAST: THE BLIND SPOT

The greed for consumption, an extreme form of what Freud called the "oral recep- tive character", is becoming the dominant psychic force in present-day industrial- ized society. Homo consumens is under the illusion of happiness, while unconsciously he suffers from his boredom and passivity. The more power he has over machines, the more powerless he becomes as a human being, the more he consumes, the more he becomes a slave to the ever increasing needs which the industrial system creates and manipulates. He mistakes thrill and excitement for joy and happiness and material comfort for aliveness; satisfied greed becomes the meaning of life, the striv- ing for it a new religion. The freedom to consume becomes the essence of human freedom.

Erich Fromm, *On Disobedience and Other Essays*
Routledge and Kegan Paul, London, Melbourne and Henley, 1984, p. 18.

It has been argued that sociology has neglected consumption because founding fathers such as Karl Marx concentrated on production.[1] However, in recent years, contemporary Western social sciences have shown a growing interest in consumerism, which has become a field on its own right.[2] Departments of cultural studies are gaining pop- ularity in North America and Europe, but this interest has not yet reached our part of the world. Even though a pioneering work like Jean Baudrillard's *The Consumer Society*,[3] which made an extremely pessimistic statement about the future of "garbage-can sociology" and the waste society, it succeeded in opening a new field framing on

---

[1] Steven Miles, *Consumerism as a Way of Life*, Sage Publications, 1998.

[2] To cite a few leading works: Mike Featherstone, *Consumer Culture and Postmodernism*, London, Sage Publications, 1991 and Mike Featherstone (editor), *The Body Modification*, London, Sage Publications, 2000. Jean Baudrillard, *The Consumer Society, Myths and Structures*, Sage Publications, 1998. Steward Ewen: *All Consuming Images, The Politics of Style in Contemporary Culture*, Basic Books, 1988. Steven Miles, *Consumerism as a Way of Life*, London, Sage Publications, 1998. Michael Miller, *The Bon Marché, Bourgeois Culture and the Department Store 1869–1920*, Princeton University Press, 1981. George Ritzer, *The McDonaldization Thesis*, London, Sage Publications, 1998.

[3] Jean Baudrillard, *The Consumer Society*, London, Sage Publications, 1998.

the notion of "hyper-reality". Baudrillard's thesis is that simulation and counterfeit, kitsch, which is closely related to mass-production as a simulated object, will soon pervade all social relations. "Kitsch offers an aesthetic of simulation, of objects that reproduce, imitate, ape and repeat".[4] Baudrillard argued that gadgets and simulated objects will dominate the broader society and that uselessness and fakery will overwhelm all social and sexual relations. Sexuality will also be offered for consumption and will be emptied of any meaning.

Baudrillard was in fact a fine disciple of the Frankfurt school, with whom he shared a bleak and pessimistic view of the future of the "culture industry". Theodor Adorno and Erich Fromm had envisioned an apocalyptic end, with over production and the banalisation of culture. The Frankfurt school, more specifically Horkheimer in the *Dialectics of Enlightenment*, expressed utter pessimism about the culture industry. Horkheimer pointed to the ironic celebration of the individual in the age of the quantitative increase of commodities. The enlightenment dream did not fulfil its promise of liberation and came to a dead end with the holocaust. The promise also ended because the premise that "machines doing men's work has now come true", and it is "also true that men are acting more and more like machines".[5] So if one were a true follower of Horkheimer-Adorno, the point would be that the simulation of choice, the hyper-reality created by advertising the commodity, and the imposition of the rules of the market is nothing but "the subversion of individuality by technology in the 'one dimensional society' of enslaved consumers and mass culture audiences".[6]

Social scientists have recently looked at consumerism as "a way of life", which has strongly pervaded everyday activities. "Style" and lifestyle strongly influence everyday life and these have become ways of constructing self-identity. The effect of mass society is that it develops unlimited desires. "People were not only offered what they needed but also what they desired, while simultaneously 'wants' actively became 'needs'".[7] The symbolic value of goods was then given a growing social significance. In recent years, since the notion of class became more blurred and complex in Western societies, fine dis-

---

[4] George Ritzer, Introduction to Jean Baudrillard, *The Consumer Society*, p. 12.
[5] Cited from Bert Adams and R.A. Sydie, *Contemporary Sociological Theory*, Thousand Oaks, Pine Forge Press, Sage 2002, p. 69.
[6] Marcuse 1964 cited from Bert Adams and R.A. Sydie, p. 69.
[7] Steven Miles, p. 7.

tinction took other forms. Peter Saunders argues that the notion of class is no longer important, but rather the differences in access to consumption.[8] Bourdieu argues that consumption is a way of establishing variations between social groups. The superiority of the dominant groups or classes is revealed through the appropriation of high culture and high consumption.[9] In *Consumerism as a Way of Life*, Steven Miles attempts to counterbalance the pros and cons of consumerism. He provides a rich summary of both the sceptics and the optimists who see that consumerism could entail democratizing effects, encourage innovative initiatives and potentials for creativity, and foster more conscious consumers' associations. Looking at the fields of design, consuming spaces and places, technology, fashion, sport and music, Miles proposes the idea of the "consuming paradox" as an arena of conflict and tensions. But he sees it as multi-dimensional because the arena of agency and structure are contested. Consumerism can also provide in everyday life a sense of stability in an unstable world following Ulrich Beck's theorization on risk society.[10]

That Egyptians have changed their consumer habits is evident, but no Arab sociologist has gone through the painful process of analyzing these transformations. Yet this is worth looking into in the Middle East; consumer studies are still mistakenly considered as a trivial field by Arab academics. There is no comparison with, say, Indian or Southeast Asian social scientists, which have undertaken serious research on the matter. No doubt, the sociology of consumerism in the Middle East is still to come. An exception are the recent works (nevertheless, still in the English language) of Deniz Kandiyoti and Ayse Saktanber on Turkey[11] and Walter Armbrust's

---

[8] Ibid., p 21.

[9] Ibid.

[10] The German sociologist Ulrich Beck developed the notion of risk society and related it to globalization. Global warming, environmental pollution are manufactured, "man-made risks" which instigated further new choices for individuals. Beck argues that there is no simple recipe to handle such new problems; risk becomes a negotiable matter that puts more pressure on individuals. The over-production of information leads to increasingly more difficult choices on the individual and institutional level. Risk is no longer restricted to environment, but to sexual relations. For example, with the erosion of traditions, marriage, with increasing choice has become a risky endeavour. The insecurity of jobs leads to an unpredictability in planning one's life. Thus personal biographies have become much less "fixed". See Anthony Giddens, *Sociology*, Polity, 2001, 4th edition, p. 68.

[11] Deniz Kandiyoti and Ayse Saktanber, *Fragments of Culture, The Everyday of Modern Turkey*, London and New York, I.B Tauris, 2002, see also Walter Armbrust, *Mass*

edited volume, which both deal pertinently with consumer culture and modernity. But, I did not come across any in depth sociological study in the Arabic language, which tackles the issue of the cultural effects of globalization on Egyptian consumerist attitudes.

Consumer culture for many Arab intellectuals has systematic negative connotations and associations with notions of foreign intrusion, "cultural invasion" the destruction of indigenous values and modes of living, and of Americanisation. The idea that consumerism is mainly imposed by an outside force has wide currency in the Arab world, not only among the left, but among Islamists and nationalists too. The underground Islamist movements during the late seventies refused to have television sets and lived in simple "Islamic" communes as a protest against the frantic, intrusive consumer culture of *infitah*. The relationship between Arab and western culture is a key issue of our times. Sonja Hegasy clarified her view in an article in the website Open Democracy:[12] "Fear and Loathing: Arab cultures need a Strategy of Resistance". There, she charges Arab intellectuals and the Arab press of having succumbed to a culture of victimhood, "A passivity and cultural pessimism, which is its own worst enemy". In her critique of the Egyptian leftist intellectual and anti-globalization activist Sherif Hetata, a renowned Egyptian novelist and medical doctor, Sonja Hegazy takes issue with this view. Invoking the Frankfurt School, she says at one point:

> We might conclude from rereading Horkheimer and Adorno that advertising and television artificially create needs, as a means of compensating for alienation. But for Hetata, global Americanisation is solely responsible, with its quest for ever-increasing numbers of consumers . . .

In Hegasy's view, Hetata fails to understand that consumerism also brings increased choice. She cites the peasants who today can decide whether to play Elvis Presley or Cheb Khaled at their wedding. It is true to say that we have seen some degree of choice, and the flowering of a new hybrid culture in Egypt. But I would argue that

---

Mediations, New Approaches to Popular Culture in the Middle East and Beyond, Berkeley, University of California Press, 2002.

[12] Sonja Hegasy, "Fear and Loathing: Arab cultures need a Strategy of Resistance" *Open Democracy* http://www.open democracy.net/articles/view.jsp?id =1059. See and my response to it. I have reproduced here some passages of my response in "Who is afraid of Disneyfication? A response to Sonja Hegasy", *Open Democracy*, 23/10/2003, http://www.opendemocracy.net/home/index.jsp.

Hetata is all too faithful to the Frankfurt School in his pessimism about globalization. If there is a criticism to be made of the School (and of Adorno and Horkeimer's *Dialectics of Enlightenment* in particular) it lies in their utter pessimism vis-à-vis the culture industry.

Here again, Hegasy misreads Hetata. The latter, a veteran Marxist, consistently applies a class-based analysis. For example, his anti-globalization writings make clear that his concern is with the alliance between Arab governments, corrupt elites and the World Bank, rather than the North-South divides. In his view, the policies (such as structural adjustment) of these established plunderers of the public domain have eradicated neither poverty nor unemployment. The local bourgeoisie is not spared in this critique. Elsewhere, Hetata endorses an interaction between the Egyptian anti-globalization movement and their European colleagues in coordinating protest movements against neoliberalism, social injustice and the marginalization of the unemployed. He would be the last one to be taxed with "westoxification".

Of course, some arguments of the anti-globalization movement about culture and consumerism are simplistic and should be challenged. But they have succeeded in creating an effective global web network. They belong to a wider movement, which does not believe that free trade offers magical solutions to poverty and global inequality. Nor can all Egyptian leftist intellectuals be characterized as anti-globalizers just because many of them militate for a network for global justice.

The view of consumerism as an outside imposition is quite popular in the Middle East. It partners the notion of "cultural invasion", originated by French intellectuals, with Americanization. All evils stem from the materialist west, which confronts the purity and spiritualism of the east. Indian intellectuals adopted this familiar discourse of Arab intellectuals in colonial times, too, as did Iranians leftists and Islamists before the 1979 revolution.

The governments of Singapore, Malaysia, and Indonesia have often invoked the "curse of Westernisation", as Chua Beng Huat calls it, in order to defend their markets. More importantly, they use it to justify their authoritarian regimes. As he writes:

> The political differences are often discursively formulated, in Asia, in terms of the 'Otherness' of the West; thereby creating the space for a discourse of cultural 'difference' between the 'East' and the 'West', in which the latter is criticized as an 'unhealthy' cultural penetration into

'wholesome' cultures of the former. . . . The bridgehead of this 'insid-
ious invasion' is supposedly in the 'Western culture' that is inscribed
in products imported from the West.[13]

Chua Beng Huat's sharp analysis on Southeast Asia is extremely useful when applied to the Middle Eastern context. It is possible to conclude that for many left-oriented intellectuals, Islamists, and nationalists
the "Westoxification" discourse needs further reflection in relation to
the newly ascending classes and their positioning towards the old
"cosmopolitan classes".

In general terms, it has been argued that globalization implies the
"promotion or invention of difference and variety".[14] Robertson and
Khondker raise the point that for many Third World intellectuals,
globalization has been synonymous with Americanization. Since the
late 1980s, a large body of literature, concerned with global versus
indigenous knowledge and about the interaction and intricate dialec-
tical relationship between the global and the local, has developed
and expanded.[15] Whether the particular emerges against – or is complementary to – the universal and whether the weight of "local truth"
may be part and parcel of the global cultural condition, have been
themes well elaborated by Roland Robertson.[16] On the other hand,
Pieterse saw that quite often globalization can be seen as a process
of hybridization which needs to be theorized rather than celebrated.[17]
The case of Egypt teaches us that what we are witnessing is a process
of hybridity in consumerism whereby a McDonald's, a shopping mall
or a consumer brand is recycled according to local tastes. A Wimpy
or a McDonald's in Singapore is Asianized and adapted to local
culinary tastes and in Cairo it is Egyptianized. It is the creation of

---

[13] Chua Beng Huat, "Consuming Asians: Ideas and Issues", in: *Consumption in Asia, Life Styles and Identities*, ed. Chua Beng Huat, London, Routledge, 2000, p. 12.
[14] Roland Robertson and Habib Haque khondker, "Discourses of Globalization: Preliminary Considerations" *International Sociology*, 1998, 13 (1), pp. 25–40.
[15] Martin Albrow and Elizabeth King, *Globalization, Knowledge and Society*, Readings from International Sociology, London Sage, 1990; Mike Featherstone, . . . 1990; Roland Robertson, *Globalization, Social Theory and Global Culture*, London, Sage, 1992.
[16] Roland Robertson, ibid.
[17] Cited in Ayse S. Caglar, "Hyphenated Identities and the Limits of Culture" pp. 169–86, in: P. Webner and T. Modood (eds). *Debating Cultural Hybridity: Multi-Cultural Identities and the Politics of Anti-Racism*. London and New York: Zed Books 1997.

something new, having to do with an imagined representation of an American culture fusing with invented Egyptian artefacts. This is not a novel argument. What interests us is how the hybridization of tastes and reifications of Egyptian cultural symbols are marketed locally. For instance, one often observes the phenomenon of mis-spelled American names on consumer goods. The fashion of using Western names that are then Arabicized and misspelled dates back to the late 1970's and 1980's. Recycling a consumer good means adapting it to local tastes. One can mention as an example here Baskin-Robbins at the World Trade Centre in Cairo, which is sell-ing entirely different goods under this brand. This often produces a cacophony of tastes.

Hybridity might be an interesting concept when applied to con-sumer culture. In fact, it is appealing if one looks at consumption from a multicultural perspective.[18] Here Egyptian or Southeast Asian shopping centres become a fascinating anthropological laboratory. This is where everything is recycled, piled up, metamorphosed and put together in a new form. It is possible to argue that Southeast Asia and Egypt have been witnessing a form of hybridity in mass culture and the everyday habits of the rising middle classes, which coincides with a discourse about purity.

Most interesting, are the recent sociological studies undertaken by Southeast Asian scholars on hybridity in food in Singapore. Beng Huat and Rajah present here a stimulating study about the hybridiza-tion of food that "may be seen mistakenly as pure cuisine".[19] They point to the changing perceptions of what is considered as either pure or hybrid in Fujian and Guangdong, Peranakan and Indian food. Furthermore, they observe the fusion of Chinese cuisine with Malays food, and relate it to the Islamization of Chinese food. The process of "imagined cuisines" becomes associated with ethnic identities and the markers that one also identifies through dress and language.

Although this invention of cuisine in the Singaporean case owes a lot to the external impact of tourism and the promotion of a cos-mopolitan and friendly image of the island, it seems to have devel-oped its own dynamic. Chuah Beng Huat's intelligent reflections on

---

[18] Ayse S. Caglar, 1997: 182.
[19] Chua Beng Huat and Anandah Rajah, "Hybridity, Ethnicity and Food in Singapore", *Working paper No. 133, Department of Sociology, National University of Singapore*, 1996, p. 4.

consumer culture in Asia are useful in helping to re-think the impact
of consumer culture from a new perspective. Beng Huat argues that
consumerism for youth in Asia may be a generational form of resistance to their parents, who were brought up to be frugal and to
save. These thoughts on consumer culture stimulate the comparative perspective.

I searched for the equivalent literature on consumer culture in
Egypt and found that it is still influenced by Marxist and dependency theories, which can be illuminating for explaining macro-level
change rather than the effects of "globalism", or cases in the Third
World. In fact, interdisciplinary studies are what is most lacking in
Egypt. The economist Galal Amin's recent book, *Matha hadatha lil-
masriyying* (*Whatever Happened to the Egyptians*),[20] which won the State
prize in 1998, is relevant in this context. Amin, who is an economist, endeavours to explain changes since the *infitah* (open door policy, economic liberalization), which led to Egypt's shift in loyalty
from the Soviet Union to the world capitalist system. Amin's study
is a semiautobiographical nostalgic account of how he experienced
his own childhood and youth in contrast to the decadent present.
Amin recalls the alterations in lifestyle, the changes that maids, housekeepers, women and the members of his family have undergone, to
generalize and quite often theorize about the major structural changes,
which occurred in the 1980's and 1990's.

Amin's style is witty and his observations are certainly very insightful in understanding transformation in today's Egypt. Nonetheless,
what is disturbing about Galal Amin's analysis, is his moralistic tone
and especially his nostalgia for a golden past. Amin seems to be
most concerned about the "frightening" social mobility and class
transformation due to the *infitah* policies and migration. This one can
only agree with, but perhaps somewhat disturbing is the way he
passes harsh judgments on these rising classes. Amin interprets the
phenomenon of conspicuous consumption among the Egyptian middle classes as attempts to conceal their "real" class origin. In this he
seems to be in accord with the discourse of the previous declining
upper classes, which called the peoples who emerged during the
Nasser regime *parvenus*. Interestingly enough, the condemnation of
the *parvenus* seems to have filtered through and become a floating

---

[20] *Whatever Happened to the Egyptians? Changes in Egyptian Society from 1950 to the
Present*, Cairo: The American University in Cairo Press, 2000.

category. Many in Egypt today have an obsession about these unnamed ones who stole privileges. Similarly, it has become a sport for the *nouveaux riches* in Egypt to buy and appropriate houses and furniture from the socially declining old class, to dress and decorate houses in pre-Nasser revolution style, to claim that they belong to good families, and to accuse others of being *parvenus*. It has become fashionable in Egypt to talk about this rampant "riff-raff" as implicated in one's own declining economic standards and as a self-defence mechanism. This accusation against the *parvenus*, so present in Amin's tone, is very similar to the discourse of the decadent, old, so-called aristocracy and their lament for their paradise lost. It seems that Amin is worried about social climbing, the spread of decadent culture (*al-fan al habit*),[21] and decaying moral and social norms. In this he joins religious preachers' condemnation of youth. According to Amin, this decadent culture has led to the flowering of unproductive investment, such as the proliferation of ugly brick houses with inadequate water supplies and sewerage, and taxis (an individualistic solution for unemployment that does nothing to improve productivity) in the countryside. Amin forgets that one of the paradoxes of *infitah* and peasant migration is that it has allowed peasants, for the first time in history, to obtain passports and thereby possess both formal identity cards and passports.

True, migration was undertaken under appalling conditions, but it gave peasants mobility, access to the cash economy and liberated them from the old bonds of the *'Izbah* system (the equivalent of the Latin American *hacienda*). One can only agree with Amin's alarming predictions concerning culture, his critique of individualism and Americanization. But his vision is tainted with a strong bias against the newly rising classes as *nouveau riches*, which, although true, nonetheless requires further reflection. His comments on the spread of the notion of fashion and the Western style through the market economy and his condemnation of open-door policies ignore the fact that Western fashions were introduced more than a century ago in Egypt. His condemnatory tone is disturbing in that it entails a nostalgic vision of the past as beautiful and ordered versus the present as decadent and invaded by social climbers. The old upper classes, according to Amin, were more refined and humane. Again, this view

---

[21] Here *al-fan al-habit* could be popular music, theatre shows and popular singers.

may be valid, but is a statement that presents problems for a social scientist who, rather than condemning as decadent art, films or mass culture, attempts to understand what is popular and what is *etat*-ized or invented tradition. One can only wonder why Amin, who is a professor at the American University in Cairo – viewed by some as a foreign "implanted" institution – adopts such attitudes. Is it some kind of self-justification for his privileged status as an American University professor?

In fact, the phenomenon of brick houses in the countryside could indeed be seen as a form of what the German sociologist Norbert Elias would define as a "civilizing process" for Egyptian peasants. Put aside the extremely ugly[22] and unhygienic way red brick construction is taking place, often disregarding sewage and running water, it has, nonetheless, unintended "modernizing" effects. Amin's righteous tone about consumerism, forgets that, it might represent a real improvement of the life of the poor, as well as being a way out for working-class youth to express protest. Consumerism, but also, strolling in clean, modern and air-conditioned spaces, it could be argued, provides a sense of elevation. The economist Amin appears to be trying to become interdisciplinary, but despises the field of sociological investigation in the domain of cultural studies, despite its rich insights about consumer, mass and popular cultures.

Galal Amin's most recent book *'asr al-jamahir al ghafira, The Era of Abundant Masses*,[23] translated as *Whatever Else Happened to The Egyptians?*[24] follows the logic of his first work. One can make the same critique, that it still remains a much debatable work from a sociological point of view. Amin's book consists mainly of scanty comments, which are mainly based on a nostalgic and personal view about the social transformations, which took place since his childhood, rather than providing an in-depth sociological analysis. It is written in a journalistic style to address a larger public. Amin refers to the major changes by mentioning the intrusion of the supermarket in Egyptian lifestyles, the impact of globalization on tourism, the changes in lifestyles and fashion among Egyptians. Other themes such as love, television and the telephone are also tackled from a rather personal perspective.

---

[22] It is possible to conclude that a whole tradition of peasant mud brick housing is disappearing in the countryside in favour of "modern", unfinished – to evade taxes – red brick multi-storey buildings, which are destroying agricultural land.
[23] Published by Dar al-Shuruq, Cairo, 2003.
[24] Published by The American University in Cairo Press, 2004.

Globalization and Landscapes Compared

When referring to the reshaping of landscapes through globalization, Arjun Appadurai[25] provides us with a stimulating outline of complex, overlapping and disjunctive landscapes. Inspired by Appadurai's visions on globalization, it might be interesting to look at both Cairo and Kuala Lumpur from a comparative perspective as cities where such disjunctions occur and various "scapes" are being reshaped and remodelled. Kuala Lumpur today is a fast-growing metropolis with skyscrapers including the two twin Petronas, the tallest towers in the world, and the longest supermarkets in Southeast Asia. The town is eating the jungle. Jokes about Mahathir's vision allude to the phallic symbolism of such an endeavour. Flying over Kuala Lumpur, the town looks like an endless construction camp with vast expanding new housing estates and condominiums. The feeling of eternal construction camps extends to the countryside, where the effects of logging seem devastating.

The government boasts of Kuala Lumpur's new twin towers as the symbol of Asian success. This is a point, which Mahathir also brings into play, especially since the financial crisis, to symbolize Malaysia's quick recovery.[26] The lavish, post-modern five-star hotels become spaces in which to escape the heat, suffocation from car exhausts, and the hardship of hunting desperately for taxis (especially during monsoon rains). Inventive architecture can also be found in Islamic institutions (for instance, the national mosque, the *Pusat Islam* [Islamic Centre], the Bank *Bumi Putra* and the main post office), all of which have been designed in a grandiose Islamic style. Through the reshaping of landscapes, *flâneur*-ing in the open air, which is one of the attractions of any town, becomes nearly impossible, with the growing number of cars and highways. In Malaysia, trees are constantly chopped down and the jungle is rapidly disappearing.

Cool, fresh air is available only in shopping malls. On weekends, extended middle-class families of all ethnicities – Malays, Chinese and Indian – in their ethnic clothes (Islamic attire of all varieties,

---

[25] Arjun Appadurai, "Disjunction and Difference in the Global Cultural Economy", *Theory, Culture and Society*, 1990, 7: 295–310.

[26] This point was raised in relation to speculations about Malaysia's possibility of overcoming the crisis. See Mark Landler "Has Malaysia's Leader Won His Risky Gamble?" *International Herald Tribune*, 4–5 September 1999.

saris, sarongs and the robes of Buddhist monks) fill these spaces, mingling with people wearing mini-skirts, shorts and sandals. The crowds frequent the Deli France, Kentucky Fried Chicken, McDonald's and Chinese restaurants. They enjoy shopping, window-shopping or the movies. Huge screens with video clips of violent scenes[27] are displayed everywhere, children's games and performances such as the Chinese Lion dance during the Chinese New Year and other dances take place in these shopping malls. These spaces can contain extremely noisy crowds of young people.[28] The breaking of the fast during the month of Ramadan among young Malays couples might take place in a McDonald's. Dates are eaten first to mark the breaking of the fast, following the tradition of the Prophet Muhammad. Dances and celebrations of the Chinese New Year take place in the shopping malls and Malays, Indian and Chinese festivities are also celebrated in these super-modern settings. One could interpret these events as an aspect of "folkorization of culture", which goes hand in hand with the growing "*etat*-ization" of Malays.

The Public Sphere and Public Spaces

We can notice two trends amongst Arab and Middle Eastern social scientists when they discuss the "public sphere". One position seems to support the idea that there is a newly emerging form of "Islamic public sphere" *Islamische Öffentlichkeit* as Reinhard Schulze has argued in response to the work of Jürgen Habermas.[29] According to some social scientists, which borrow a Habermasian theory of communication approach, this "new" and "emerging" public sphere could lead to further democratization of the society. On the other hand, some critics seem to dismiss the idea of linking the new "public sphere" with the burgeoning of democracy.

---

[27] During my stay in Kuala Lumpur in 1996, the films of James Bond and Batman were on the market. I regularly frequented the shopping mall Jaya Jusco, in the area of Bandar Utama. It was stunning to observe the constant, non-stop repetition of clips of films, which lasted for hours in the halls of the mall. Certainly, such pictures attracted large numbers of families and children.

[28] The same phenomenon of youth and consumer culture could be observed in Indonesia, with the difference however, that social unrest seems to be more likely in Indonesia than in Malaysia.

[29] Cited from Armando Salvatore and Dale F. Eickleman, Editors "Preface" in: *Public Islam and the Common Good*, Brill, Leiden, 2004, xiv.

Habermas traced the historical development of the decline of the public sphere in the European context. His main question concerned the social conditions, which instigated "a rational critical debate about public issues conducted by private persons willing to let arguments and not statuses determine decisions".[30] His focus was mainly on the public discourse and the power of communicative action in regulating human life between the state power and the market economies. He, furthermore, conceived the public sphere as an impersonal locus of authority.[31] The bourgeois public sphere is understood as a practice of rational critical discourse on political matters. Here "print capitalism" and the role of the press in spreading critical reasoning and rational arguments is crucial for the idea of the public versus private interests.

Social scientists who followed Habermas argue that the emerging sense of public in the Muslim world is due to the expanding role of the media and the communication systems ranging from the press and broadcast media to the fax and the Internet. Al-Jazeera channel, the various satellite channels and the broad spectrum of Arabic newspapers and magazines that are published in the Western world and distributed in the Middle East are good examples of such transformations. Dale Eickelman and Jon Anderson see these technological transformations as leading to new forms of participation in public engagement in the name of religion.[32] Could one speak of the emergence of a new public consciousness regarding gender and youth issues in Egypt for instance?

After the success of the Iranian revolution an apologetic trend towards a new form of "Islamic feminism" was celebrated among social scientists. It has often been argued that the Iranian revolution has in fact encouraged a stronger participation of militant and strong women in the public space. The veneration of Islamic feminism was meant to have enhanced the public visibility of active and strong veiled women.[33] Quite often such a position attempted to relate the

---

[30] Craig Calhoun, "Introduction: Habermas and The Public Sphere", in: *Habermas and the Public Sphere*, Craig Calhoun (ed.), Cambridge: MIT Press, 1992, pp. 1–46, p. 1.

[31] Ibid., p. 8.

[32] Dale Eickelman and Jon W. Anderson, "Redefining Muslim Publics" in: *New Media in the Muslim World: The Emerging Public Sphere*, edited by Dale F. Eickelman and Jon W. Anderson, Bloommington, Indianapolis: Indiana University Press, 1999.

[33] Khosrokhavar and Roy lump together and criticise contemporary social scientists promoting the Islamic feminist trend in one basket, namely, Faribah Adelkhah,

issue of the growing Islamic groups and their occupation of the media
and public spheres as leading to a further enhancement of civil society and dialogue. Ferhad Khosrokhavar and Olivier Roy who argue
that the public participation and visibility of women went hand in
hand with the consolidation of further conservative laws and regulations concerning gender segregation have criticized this position.
For them, the position of women has in fact worsened and public
space has become much more codified, rigidified and controlled.

In Egypt, Armando Salvatore sees that there is an emergent modern public sphere and "public Islam" in modern day Egypt. He discusses the example of Mustafa Mahmud as belonging to the reformist
discourse. During the Sadat era, Mustafa Mahmud has constructed
a mosque that included a clinic that later expanded into social work.
Furthermore, he has been a successful television star with his program al-ʿilm wal iman (science and faith). Salvatore defines Mahmud
as the "principle generator of public moral authority" and he points
to his commitment to the welfare of the community.[34] He mentions
his "rectitude" and "commitment to the welfare of the community",
as becoming the script of "public virtue". If Salvatore's analysis is
right, it is figures like Mahmud who would be the promoters of the
democratization of society. They would supposedly enhance – in reference to Habermas – any sort of purposeful communication among
various segments of the Egyptian society.

One can only agree with the project of Eickelman and Salvatore,
which rightly aims at highlighting the significance of public reasoning in Muslim culture such as for example, in Islamic jurisprudence.
Their challenging and stimulating theoretical project also points to
the established traditions of public spaces. The edited volume by
Salvatore and Eickelman *Public Islam and the Common Good*[35] con-
vincingly demonstrates that one can speak of a public sphere that
was redefined and reshaped during the nineteenth century Ottoman
Empire. This explains why consumer culture, the birth of women's
magazines and department stores in Turkey have been closely related

---

Azadeh Kian-Thieaut, Yavari d'Hellencourt, Chahla Chafiq and Nilüfer Göle. Ferhad
Khosrokhavar and Olivier Roy, *Iran: comment sortir d'une révolution religieuse*, Paris: édi-
tions du Seuil, 1999, pp. 144–145.

[34] Armando Salvatore, "Public Islam and the Nation-State in Egypt", *ISIM
Newsletter*, no. 8. September 2001, p. 20.

[35] Armando Salvatore and Dale F. Eickelman, (editors) *Public Islam and the Common
Good*, Brill, Leiden-Boston, 2004.

to the construction of the new Turkish modern woman; much as the outcome of such a theoretical reflection leads to discover the significance of coffeehouses in promoting public culture.[36] Indeed, one can only agree with Salvatore/Eickelman that "there is no singular public Islam, but rather a multiplicity of overlapping forms of practice and discourse . . ."[37]

However, I have reservations about Salvatore's concept of a balanced notion of public Islam and the association of Mahmud's public Islam with reformism. My concern is that Salvatore has unfortunately missed the context of Mahmud's ideological perspective. In his analysis Salvatore did not mention that the rise of Mustafa Mahmud's popularity owed much to Sadat's instrumentalization of religion. Mahmud's role in the state religious discourse was used to counteract both the communists and opponent Islamists in the early seventies. The fact that Mahmud is a veteran communist raised deontological questions among secular intellectuals concerning his intellectual honesty. When Sadat launched a smear campaign against the secular forces, figures like Mahmud were certainly utilized by the regime's propaganda machinery. In fact, Mahmud's "public Islam" is far from being "subject to increasing differentiation vis-à-vis the state"; rather it originated from within the state's Islamic discourse. Mahmud's television program *al-'ilm wal-iman* was part and parcel of the official state Islamization of the seventies which later went out of control. Combining faith with science was the favourite motto of the late "faithful" president *al-ra'is al-mu'min*, who was a victim of the over-religiosity that dominated the political discourse.

Along with his co-author, Dale Eickelman, Salvatore argued that Mahmud by articulating the scholarly discourse of the *'ulama* to the wider audience is contributing to the re-intellectualization of Islam through his television programs.[38] At a certain point Mustafa Mahmud and the late popular tele-preacher, Sheikh Sha'rawi are lumped together since both "make of a double billing of complementary

---

[36] I am referring here to the contributions in the same volume of Cengiz Kirli on Coffeehouses during 19th Century Ottoman Empire and Elisabeth B. Frierson on Gender and Consumption in Turkey.

[37] Armando Salvatore and Dale Eickelman, Preface, *Public Islam and the Common Good* (xxii).

[38] Dale Eickelman and Armando Salvatore, "The Public Sphere and Muslim Identities", *Arch.europ.socio.*, XLIII, 1 (2002), pp. 92–115, (2003), p. 110.

personalities in Egypt".[39] They are seen as been rather similar and
reinforcing each other, never really departing from traditional *ʿulama*.
Mahmud is contrasted with Gamal ʿAbdel Nasser who according to
Salvatore and Eickelman spoke to audiences, while Mahmud spoke
with them.[40]

I have serious doubts about interpreting Sheikh Shaʿrawi as a pro-
moter of an enlightened, rational Islam. Even less convincing is his
role in promoting a "public sphere", which would generate a space
for dialogue, negotiation and therefore a forum for democracy. For
secular liberal intellectuals like the philosopher Fuʾad Zakariyya,
Sheikh Shaʿrawi and Mustafa Mahmud are the best examples of
agents of the "petro-Islam" ideology, which flourished in the seventies. It stemmed from the growing Saudi Arabization of Egyptian
society through international migration and the mounting Islamic
tide, which also coincided with the growing influence of the *pax-
Americana*. Some have argued that Islamism was given a free hand
by the Sadat regime, to dismantle the nationalist movement. Both
Shaʿrawi and Mahmud have been involved in dubious financial deal-
ings. Both also had long established close relations to Saudi Arabian
circles. In the late eighties, Sheikh Shaʿrawi became known for his
repeated blessing of the doubtful "Islamic investment companies"
such as the al-Saʿad investment group and al-Hoda Egypt. These
ended up in a huge fraud scandal, cheating millions of investors
through proposing up to 40 percent (*halal*) Islamic returns on their
investments. When Sheikh Shaʿrawi was criticized by the late philosopher Zaki Naguib Mahmud and the novelist Youssef Idriss, these
two underwent a torrent of aggressive verbal attacks from Shaʿrawi's
followers.

Michael Warner, characterizing what a "public" would be, which
seems to be a vague and ambiguous notion, borrows from Nancy
Frazer the notion of counter publics, alternative publics and subaltern counter publics.[41] These counter publics, which are mostly sub-
ordinated social groups like women, workers and people of colour,
are defined as such because, according to Nancy Frazer they "for-
mulate oppositional interpretations of their identities, interests and

---

[39] Ibid., p. 111.
[40] Ibid.
[41] Michael Warner, "Publics and Counterpublics", in: *Public Culture*, 2002, 14 (1),
1–90, p. 85.

needs".[42] The problem with both Mustafa Mahmud and Sheikh Sha'rawi is that their discourses are far from addressing oppositional counter publics. Sheikh Sha'rawi's vision of the world hardly relates to any subaltern oppositional worldview. Ironically, he was appointed during Sadat's regime as Minister of Endowments and his Friday tele-preaching was supported by the government as a tactic working parallel with the violent and harsh suppression of the oppositional underground Islamist group. A more realistic position can be traced in Peter van der Veer's article, also published in the Salvatore/Eickelman volume. Van der Veer, in discussing the concepts of civil society and the public sphere in the Indian subcontinent context and through raising the question whether the *Tablighi jama'at* are participating in civil society and are critical of the state, prefers to remain ambiguous to any clear cut reply.[43]

I would like to be adventurous by citing Sonallah Ibrahim's novel *Zaat*.[44] I consider this novel a landmark in contemporary Egyptian literature. Zaat brilliantly combined fiction with minute documentation of the changing social transformations especially the consumer habits of Egyptians since the coming of the open door policy. Sonallah Ibrahim gathered newspapers clips, which included some of Sha'rawi's sayings, which revealed how reactionary and misogynistic he was. I need not comment on these utterances because they speak for themselves.

Sheikh Sha'rawi:

> If you see a building, for example, which earns its owner a lot of money, you shouldn't envy the man. Rather you should pray for him because he has earned his money honestly. He hasn't exploited anyone because he has put food in the bellies and clothes on the backs of the poorest workers.[45]

Sheikh Sha'raw says the following about the relationship between lslam, communism, and capitalism

---

[42] Ibid.

[43] Peter van der Veer, "Secrecy and Publicity in the South Asian Public Arena", in: *Public Islam and the Common Good*, Edited by Armando Salvatore and Dale F. Eickelman, Brill, Leiden-Boston, 2004, p. 42.

[44] Published by The American University in Cairo, 2001.

[45] Ibid., p. 21.

> The enmity between Islam and Atheism is insurmountable, whereas
> the difference between Islam and Christianity or Judaism is a difference
> in the concept of the nature of Allah.[46]

Sheikh Metwalli Sha'rawi warns shareholders in the Faisal Islamic
Bank that the enemies of Islam are conspiring to destroy the bank.[47]

A woman must wear the *hegab* (head cover) so that a man will
not doubt the paternity of his children.[48]

Those people who go to sleep to the music of Beethoven do not
know Allah.[49]

Sheikh Mitwalli Sha'rawi's grandchildren deposit their money with
el Rayyan as an expression of their trust in the company.[50]

Sheikh Metwalli Sha'rawi in an interview with Kuwaiti newspaper Al-Siyasa:

> I refused to use cars that al Hoda Egypt owned in my journeys to
> and from the company, which I used to visit regularly in order to
> offer advice. I preferred to use the private cars belonging to the com-
> pany's owners so that there would be no suspicion of misuse of the
> depositors's money.[51]
> ... Women working insults the pride and dignity of men.[52]
> ... Women have been forced to go to work because, unfortunately,
> manhood is in the decline.[53]

Sheikh Metwalli Sha'rawi talking on television:

> I haven't read a single book in forty years except the Quran.[54]

For those interested in media and consumer culture, it is possible to
argue that the Sha'rawi effect represents the perfect example of
Marshall McLuhan's celebrated sentence "the medium is the message". One can interpret Sha'rawi's success as due to the fact that
he was an entertainer and an astute actor. He was a skilful hypno-
tizer of masses through his *habitus* and dress. Several critical leftist
and secular intellectuals like Zakarriya have doubted the content of

---

[46] Ibid., p. 24.
[47] Ibid., p. 29.
[48] Ibid., p. 39.
[49] Ibid., p. 96.
[50] Ibid., p. 262.
[51] Ibid., p. 267.
[52] Ibid., p. 292.
[53] Ibid., p. 293.
[54] Ibid., p. 300.

his sermons. The audience were bewildered by his great skills as a successful performer. Egyptians loved to watch him on television, thinking that this could be equal to performing a religious ritual. One can draw an analogy with Ayse Öncü's work on the "packaging of Islam for consumption" on television in Turkey and its "issuetization" to target multiple audiences.[55]

I read Zubaida as counter argument to Salvatore and Eickelman. Sami Zubaida, in trying to demystify the monolithic view of the Muslim World, seems to use the term "public life" to argue that Islamism through appropriating Islam for modernity, seems to "impose religious authority on culture and society. Central quests in this respect are the moralization of public space, the imposition of ritual observance, and the censorship of the cultural and entertainment product".[56] Furthermore, if enlightenment has failed to fulfil its promise in the twentieth century, with the barbarian atrocities of the Nazis, as the Frankfurt School has claimed, there is yet one positive point, which is often forgotten, namely, that it made it clear that the separation between politics and religion is essential to escape the evident danger of despotism. Why is it then that all the so-called promoters and pioneers of the public sphere, who also appear to be spokesmen of democracy, such as Mustafa Mahmud or The Azharite Sheikh Youssef al-Qaradawi, (who provides *fatwas* on the satellite channel al-Jazeera and has close connections with the Gulf sheikhs) are strong advocates of a conservative religious world view? Why is it that the Habermasian ideal speech community once it pertains to our part of the world should then be carried out by men of religion who are closely related to corrupt regimes?

Mahmud and al-Qaradawi are the best examples of the Islamic incorporation of conservative worldviews. Sheikh Al-Qaradawi has been involved in recent years in large scale business and Islamic banking. Many think that his involvement in al-Jazeera is ultimately serving the interests of the Gulf States. Several of his *fatwas* reveal a strong class bias. Take for instance, his fatwa on *Misyar* marriage. *Misyar* is the ambulant contract marriage, which has become widespread in recent years among middle-class spinsters in Saudi Arabia. The advantage of this contract marriage is that the husband is freed

---

[55] Cited from Peter Van der Veer, p. 40.
[56] Sami Zubaida, "Religious Authority and Public Life", *ISIM Newsletter* 11/02, December, p. 19.

from the financial burden of supporting the wife.[57] This marriage
has been often seen as the solution for professional middle-class
women who accept the status of "secondary", but economically independent wives. The spread of this contract has been explained by
the increasing number of aged "spinsters". This sort of contract is
a middle way solution. Al-Qaradawi's approval of such a contract
is certainly one way of pleasing the Saudis. He expressed reservations about ʿurfi marriage, a growing practice among Egyptians. It is
one way for widows to circuit the state and remarry without officially
registering the second marriage and thus continue to receive the pen-
sions of their former husband. ʿUrfi has also spread in recent years
among young students in Egyptian university campuses.

Why is it that Salvatore and Eickelman concentrated on the conservative official protagonists of the religious discourse and neglected
the liberal secular intellectuals like al-Qimni, Mohammed S. Al-
ʿAshmawi, Hussein Ahmed Amin? What about the late Farag Fuda
whose life was ended by the Islamist extremists? Did the case of the
philosophy professor Nasr Hamid Abu Zayd, who was declared an
apostate and forced to divorce his wife, result in raising serious issues
in the public sphere about individual freedom and democracy? Gone
are the days of "progressives" such as Sheikh Suʿad Galal, Sheikh
Shaltut, and Mohammed Ahmed Khalafallah. Why is it that the late
Sheikh Khalil ʿAbdel Kerim, who is indeed a controversial figure
through his courageous attempts to provide a stimulating, thorough
documented historical interpretation of early Islamic history, has not
been taken into consideration?[58] It seems to me that for Salvatore
and Eickelman the public sphere is equated with the "mediatic
effects". Media religious stars and tele-preachers, in my understanding, symbolize a clear-cut imported phenomenon from America. Yet
the authors ignore the fact that the medium of tele-preaching is a
one way, passive means of communication. They interpret tele-
preaching in a way that leads to what Habermas defined as "dis-
cursive interaction".[59]

---

[57] See http://islamonline.net/livefatwa/arabic/browse.asp?hGuestID=RagT8g
http://islamonline.net/livefatwa/arabic/fatwaDisplay.asp?hFatwaID=43623.
[58] See Khalil Abd al-Kerim, *Quraish minal al-qabila ilal-dawla al-markajiyya* (Quraish,
from The Tribe to the Centralised State), Sina lil-nashr. Second edition, 1997.
[59] I refer here to Fawwaz Traboulsi's inspiring reading of Habermas' "Public
Spheres and Urban Space: A Critical Comparative Approach" *Fifth Mediterranean*

Traboulsi, in his critical reading of Habermas concerning the difficulty of applying the concept of the public sphere in the Middle Eastern context, reminds us that while the public sphere entails a bourgeois element, the non-bourgeois subaltern classes is a constant threat. Furthermore, Habermas, again according to Traboulsi, warns against "anti-democratic", and "populist movements", which would confuse the distinction between the state and civil society.[60] I see no problem in being simplistic. I wish to reduce the media stars, Sha'rawi and Mahmud to strait forward demagogic populists, to reverse the argument of Slavatore/Eickelman. Traboulsi again reverses the perspective by reminding us that the recent intellectual production on democratization in the Arab world tends to focus on the *absence* of democracy, instead of trying to understand the *presence* of the existing authoritarian and despotic regimes.[61] This brings me to the recent book of Habermas, *Der Gespaltene Westen*,[62] where he argues that 15 February 2003 is a historical landmark in the birth of a European public sphere. That day witnessed the largest and most significant mass demonstrations in London, Rome, Madrid, Barcelona, Berlin and Paris, against the American invasion of Iraq.[63]

The next question that comes to mind: why is it that the Arab street kept silent? It is again very simple; on 20 March a massive demonstration took place in Cairo. After the several successive demonstrations against the Iraq war, 800–1,500 people were detained. Some were tortured. Created by some 200 activists and leftist intellectuals in July 2002, the Anti-Globalisation Egyptian Group (AGEG) has, like all human rights organizations and NGOs in Egypt, been closely monitored by the government. Some of its members have been subjected to police threats, harassment and internal security monitoring of their meetings. This tells us that participation in an anti-war demonstration in Cairo has different repercussions from joining a demonstration in Berlin.

Anti-war expressions in Egypt have a long history of culminating in violent police repression, jailing, torture, long detentions in inhumane

---

Social and Political Research Meeting, Florence Montecatini Terme. 24–28 March 2004. Workshop X.

[60] Traboulsi, p. 11.

[61] Ibid., p. 6.

[62] Juergen Habermas, *Der gespaltene Westen*, Frankfurt, Edition Suhrkamp 2004.

[63] Ibid., 'Der 15 Februar oder: Was die Europaer verbindet' in: *Der gespaltene Westen*, p. 44.

conditions, and the deportation of non-Egyptian demonstrators. The rights of all the marginalized and excluded, as well as political dissidents, are violated. I am not confident that efforts by global activists against torture and other abuses in our part of the world will do anything to improve this situation. The technology, which documents these events, is a double-edged sword as well. Videotape may be a fantastic tool for documenting anti-war demonstrations for the international media, but it also caters to the internal security police. The images that feed worldwide audiences also provide the forces of internal suppression with a worrying source of information. Democracy has become a catchword, an icon that the US wants to impose by invading countries and inflicting terror by interfering in local politics. Democracy and reform became the agenda of the Egyptian government after it was dictated by the US, providing a justification for the continuation of martial law.

The Emerging of the Public Sphere and "Spaces"

Juergen Habermas identifies the emergence of the bourgeois public sphere in the eighteenth century as closely intertwined with the "development of institutional bases", which were the meeting places, journals and networks of relationships.[64] Habermas mentions the significance the 3000 coffee houses in London in the eighteenth century, the journals of opinion, the salons in France, the table societies in Germany that are all ultimately physical spaces where opinions and ideas were exchanged.[65] Habermas' notion of public sphere was criticized on various levels, on the grounds that he focused on the bourgeois public sphere and discarded the proletariat, and that he was concerned with the form rather than with historical accuracy.[66] On this point Peter Golding argues:

> What, in fact, is the public sphere? Descriptions necessarily resort to spatial or physical terminology. Is it a place – the coffeehouses, salons,

---

[64] Craig Calhoun . . ., p. 12.

[65] Craig Calhoun, ibid.

[66] Peter Golding, "The Mass Media and the Public Sphere: The Crisis of Information in the Information Society" in: *Debating the Future of the Public Sphere* (eds.) Stephen Edgell, Sandra Walklate and Gareth Williams. Brookfield: Avebury, 1995, pp. 25–40, p. 28.

and meeting places of early urban capitalist society? The struggle to get a handle on a vision of something described as the space within, which rational and universalistic political discourse could occur between the private realms of civil society and family, and the realm of the state and court public authority is not helped by the essentially non-social notion of a sphere. Literally? Clearly not.[67]

While partly disagreeing with Salvatore and Eickelman, their merit is that they highlighted the importance of the transformations in the Muslim world, especially during the nineteenth century, and the intensity of "the creation of a the variety of explicit and implicit Muslim forms of civility and publicness".[68] It is evident that for two centuries, Egypt has closely emulated Western public spaces, but these did not necessarily foster a civil society or an important political power. Or, at least, if these spaces did have elements of a burgeoning civil society, the ultimate power was always in the hands of the omnipotent state and the army, which had absolute control over such institutions.

The public sphere has developed as the natural outcome of the material conditions that led to the emergence of new public spaces in European cities that were associated with the growth of mercantile capitalism in the seventeenth century. Urban sociologists, in looking at the emergence of European towns as centres of commerce and exchange, and as a locus for leisure and intellectualism, long ago commented on the emergence of public spaces, exemplified in public or pleasure gardens, promenades and *cours*, alleys, coffeehouses, theatres, opera houses, salons, race courses, and later on department stores and *grands magazins* as forms of civility and urbanization.[69] These spaces were the opportunity for "society", the "polite society" or the *beau monde* to parade itself in the eighteenth century city.[70] We were also told that "society" became a crucial constituent of the cities. Equally, coffeehouses played an important role in the flourishing of science in Europe; the first known coffeehouses in England opened in Oxford in 1650 and moved to London a few years later.[71] In Paris, it was a Levantine who opened the first coffeehouse. There

---

[67] Pp. 28–29.
[68] Armando Salvatore and Dale F. Eickelman, 2004, Preface, xviii.
[69] Mark Girouard, *Cities & People: A Social and Architectural History*, New Haven and London: Yale University Press, 1985.
[70] Ibid., p. 181.
[71] Ibid., p. 207.

were 300 coffeehouses in Paris by 1716, 1800 by 1788 and 4,000 by 1807.[72]

Since the middle of the nineteenth century, Khedive Ismail's endeavour to modernize – which meant to Westernize – Cairo, led to the creation of wide boulevards. The modern grid planned downtown inspired by Haussmannian ideas, clearly distinguished it from the old circular and mysterious Islamic city. Certainly as André Raymond has argued, it led to the creation of a double city.[73] Ismail' s admiration of the West led to an abundance of architectural emulations, such as the reproduction of the Bois de Boulogne in the Azbakiyya gardens by Barillet-Deschamps.[74] The old Opera House was an emulation of the Italian *La Scala* in Milan. However, parks, public gardens, old coffee houses such as the Indian tea house, Lapas, Groppi, and many others, theatres (the old Opera House, *al-masrah al-qawmi*, (The National Theatre), the Balloon theatre and others have undergone a decline during the last two decades, if not a disappearance from public life.

While some public spaces, such as *baladi qahwas* (popular coffeehouses) clubs, bars, hotels, have survived extremely well, other spaces have surfaced in recent years, such as shopping malls (which are considered as semi-public spaces) as well as modern coffeeshops. If the glorious days of the colonial grand hotels were during the period after the First World War, these have nearly all disappeared with the exception, perhaps, of the Cosmopolitan Hotel (inaugurated as the Metropolitan hotel in 1928 and restored in 1990). There are two versions concerning the Shepheard's Hotel. According to Joseph Fitchett, a Victorian businessman, Samuel Shepheard established it in 1841 and it became one of the most established hotels in colonial times.[75] The more prosaic story is one in which Samuel Shepheard came to Egypt after having escaped the drudgery of apprenticeship to a pastry cook and "landed somewhat fortuitously in Egypt in 1842, having been put ashore there in consequence of a minor mutiny".[76] After working for several years in the hotel business,

---

[72] Ibid.

[73] Andre Raymond, *Cairo, City of History*, Harvard University Press/AUC Press, Cairo, 2001, p. 305

[74] Ibid., p. 312

[75] Joseph Fitchett, "Rendez-vous at the Shepheard's" in: *Masr al-Mahrusa, Impressions of Egypt, Grand Hotels of Egypt*, Vol. XVIII – March 2002, pp. 103–121, p. 114.

[76] Janet Abu Lughod, *Cairo 1001 of the City Victorious*, p. 100.

Samuel Shepheard met Khedive 'Abbas who gave him a grant to build a hotel. The site granted turned out to be the palace of Muhammad Bey al-Alfi, which overlooked the Azbakiyya Lake. Over the next century, three Shepheard's Hotels were constructed in various areas. The third Shepheard's Hotel was burnt in the 1952 riots leading to the revolution while the fourth and last version is located today along the Nile near the Kasr al-Nil bridge.[77] The Mena House Hotel, the Winter Palace, the Semiramis (originally built in 1886), the Continental (1860), the Grand Hotel Royal, the Grand Continental Hotel (Ibrahim Pasha Square), the Hotel Gezira Palace, (originally built to receive Empress Eugenie), the Savoy Hotel in Soliman Pasha street and the National Hotel became magnificent magnets for travellers, writers and artists who aspired to discover the mysterious Orient.[78] International chain hotels such as the Hilton, the Sheraton, Sofitel, Meridien, Movenpick, and many other chains have replaced the colonial style grand hotels today.

The Tahrir Hilton was a landmark of the achievements of the revolution. Its modern architecture is a good example of a Bauhaus adaptation to Cairo. Inaugurated in 1959, it quickly became the favourite place for the 1960's bourgeoisie and new rising classes; they met at its coffeeshop, and celebrated fancy weddings there. In the 1970's the Taverne, the Pizzeria and coffeeshop were considered special outings for the well to do Egyptians, where they felt cosmopolitan by intermingling with the passing tourists. Michel de Grece wrote a sardonic comment on grand oriental hotels of the Middle East; here he spoke about the Hilton Tahrir:

> My favourite of all the family is the old Nile Hilton in Cairo, which I have staunchly supported for more than two decades. This hotel commenced in lamentable style, for in its early years an African diplomat, having decided to stay at the hotel on his wedding night, ate and consumed his bride there, an event that provoked a stir in the world. Sad to say, occidental rigor has now ousted charming local ways. No longer can one slip a modest tip the concierge, as in the old days, and obtain at a moment's notice as many rooms as one may desire, with the hotel packed out and every bed reserved one year in advance.[79]

---

[77] Janet Abu Lughod, *Cairo 1001 of the City Victorious . . .*, pp. 100–101.
[78] Ibid.
[79] Michel de Grece, "Grand Oriental Hotels" in: *Masr al-Mahrusa, Impressions of Egypt, Grand Hotels of Egypt*, Vol. XVIII – March 2002, pp. 8–10, p. 10.

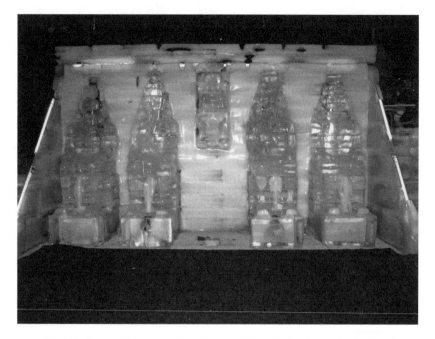

Fig. 12. Snow City, Nasr City. Pharaos Temple. Today a dead place.

The *grands magasins* (department stores) in Egypt have contributed since the early twenties to the idea of the modern "new woman" who goes out on her own to purchase her clothes. Nancy Reynolds argues that: "Part of this new prescription of women nurturing the family and its status included a newly articulated role for women in consumption and provisioning – 'women shopping in person' – an image perhaps most famous now from nationalist and feminist leader Huda Sha'rawi's first shopping trip to an Alexandria department store where she was protected by a screen in order to review goods in a semi-private space".[80]

Since the beginning of the twentieth century, the public space where the Egyptian *beau monde* paraded included private clubs such as the Gezira Sporting Club, the Heliopolis and Alexandria Sporting Clubs, the Ahli and Shooting Clubs, many of these were created for colonial administrators. But one can argue that the nature of the public spaces changed during this time. We have witnessed the dis-

---

[80] Nancy Y. Reynolds, "Sharikat al-Bayt al-Masri: Domesticating Commerce in Egypt 1931–1956" *Arab Studies Journal*, Fall 1999/Spring 2000. pp. 75–119. p. 82.

appearance and destruction of certain public spaces, which were considered to be landmarks of the ancient regime: the Azbakiyya gardens, the bourgeois coffeehouses such as Groppi's, Lapas, the Indian tea and the *grands magasins* after state nationalization.

The Middle East has been witnessing the emergence of new public spaces such as the semi-public spaces of shopping malls, modern coffeeshops, hyperspaces, amusement parks, folkloric tents and belly dancing in international hotels, and snow cities in the desert. In discussions of the public sphere, these public spaces are seen as "modern" ones while ignoring, for instance, traditional coffeehouses, which are spread throughout the Ottoman Empire and existed in the Middle East well before they did in Europe. The coffeehouses were introduced in Istanbul in the mid-sixteenth century[81] and these were crucial spaces for not only socializing and spending time, but for gathering information and spying on the people for the authorities. The spy reports called *jurnals* are valuable sources revealing the public sentiments of the time. "Informers were mainly stationed in coffeehouses, a perfect locale for the informer to 'steal information' in the form of rumours . . ."[82]

Nelly Hanna links the significance of the coffeehouse with the perpetuation of both oral and literary traditions. Coffeehouses started to become popular in the urban setting of the Ottoman Empire, early as the middle of the sixteenth century, and continued to flourish in the seventeenth and eighteenth centuries. Cairene coffeehouses catered mainly to the well to do middle classes. It would also seem that the coffeehouses were the domain of popular culture and entertainment, "such as games with animals, vulgar displays, male dancers dressed up as females, drugs such as *hashish* and opium".[83] Coffeehouses also provided a space for humorous shows, comedies and musical performances. They also seem to have given impetus to literary forms such as storytelling and poetry. There existed a guild of storytelling and Hanna reports of a storyteller or *hakawati* in 1068/1657 in Sulimaniyya coffeehouse of Bulaq. The storytellers had a high level of literary knowledge and sophistication. It was also a meeting place

---

[81] Cengiz Kirli, "Coffeehouses: Public Opinion in The Nineteenth-Century Ottoman Empire" in: *Public Islam and the Common Good*, Armando Salvatore and Dale Eickelman (editors) Brill, Leiden-Boston, 2004, p. 75.

[82] Cengiz Kirli, p. 78.

[83] Nelly Hanna, *In Praise of Books*, The American University in Cairo Press, 2004, p. 66.

for religious conversations and
Sufi networks, for reading poetry
and for hashish consumption.[84]

Why, then, did not these traditional or old spaces develop
into a modern public sphere? If
we accept Eickelman and Salvatore's thesis that the public sphere
can be prompted by religious
groups and institutions, then in
the Islamic culture, the mosque
could also be seen as one "traditional" space where preaching,
politics and public matters were
discussed and decisions undertaken. The recent Islamic revival
proved that it still plays a vital
role in mass mobilization. At
a certain point private funded
mosques came under severe scru-
tiny from the government be-

Fig. 13. Benzion Ad. From *Le Réveil de
l'Egypte*, 1937.

cause they were suspected of supporting fundamentalist anti-state
sentiments. But what one can see is that there is a "disjunction"
between what is viewed as the traditional "spaces" such as popular
coffeehouses and mosques and the newly created spaces. The social
scientist is exploring this new public sphere as it relates to modern
systems of communication, to fit in with a Habermasian outlook
based on the historical evolution of Western enlightenment. But what
seems to be the major urban reshaping of the cities of the Middle
East is taking place with the aim of promoting a consumerist gentrified
lifestyle.

Les Grands Magasins: *Forgotten Early Egyptian Consumerism*

Recent theories of globalization tend to regard consumer culture as
a recent phenomenon. Consumer studies generally focused on the
impact of mass culture upon the European working classes in the

---

[84] Ibid., pp. 66–68.

1960's and 1970's in Europe and the United States. Cultural studies has been interested in issues of mass media and the impact of American mass culture on European working classes from a neo-Marxist point of view. It could be insightful to apply cultural studies debates to earlier colonial upper-class lifestyles. In fact, very few such studies have been undertaken. It is often forgotten that European lifestyles and fashions were introduced to Egypt in the middle of the nineteenth century. Max Rodenbeck reminds us of the fusion and interactive aspects of the *khawagat* culture of Cairo[85] by stating that by 1910 an eighth of the city's 7 million people were foreigners. At this time, we are told, "the 'rich Cairene' lived like a Parisian".[86] It is no coincidence that the emergence of these new lifestyles paralleled the birth of department stores, which "catered to the new tastes with the latest fashions from Paris and the catalogues of Christophle, Louis Vuitton and Mappin and Webb".[87]

In recent years, various valuable studies about department stores in the West have appeared. To mention a few, the significant work of Michael Miller on the *Bon Marché* in Paris,[88] in which he traces the history of a business of the family Boucicaut who founded the *magasin*. Miller's main thesis stresses the role of paternalistic relations in the functioning of such a bourgeois institution and how it was used to control and organize the work force. He draws analogies with Japan to enhance the idea that industrial relations in certain times lead to the restructuring of traditions, by "rephrasing" feudal loyalties. In other words, how *Gemeinschaft* values have been regenerated for the enhancement of bourgeois capitalist values.[89] His analysis of the gender roles, and how young saleswomen have been experiencing a situation of a totalized institutional control, is revealing. Bill Lancaster's *The Department Stores: A Social History*[90] is another crucial study. The introduction provides a comprehensive summary of the works undertaken on department stores and *grands magasins*

---

[85] The term *khawagat* is used by Egyptians to define foreigners living in Egypt. It included Levantines, Greeks and Italians of Egypt. It contains a touch of irony.

[86] Max Rodenbeck, *Cairo The City Victorious*, Cairo, The American University in Cairo Press 1999, p. 176.

[87] Rodenbeck, 1999, p. 184.

[88] Michael B. Miller, *The Bon Marché: Bourgeois Culture and Department Store, 1869–1920*, Princeton University Press, 1981.

[89] Ibid., p. 11.

[90] Bill Lancaster, *The Department Stores: A social History*, Leicester University Press, London and New York, 1995.

and the history of retailing in
modern times. Lancaster looks
at British department stores and
relates them to the larger process
of retailing in Britain. Astonishingly, the creation of department stores in Egypt coincides
with the period of their birth in
Europe in the last part of the
nineteenth century. Nancy Young
Reynolds has finally filled the
immense lacunae on Egyptian
department stores. Reynolds takes
up Miller's thesis on the significance of the family enterprise
and applies it to the Egyptian
case, more specifically to the
Chemla Department Stores whose
owners were the sons of an
Arab-Jewish olive oil producer

Fig. 14. Benzion Ad. From *Le Réveil de
l'Egypte*, 1937.

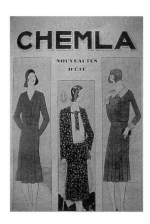

Fig. 15. Chemla Ad.
Courtesy *al-Risalla*,
Sednaoui Magazine.

from Tunis. The family came from Tunis
to Cairo in 1907 to open a shop in Bulaq
Street. During its early days, the family
business did not seem to be doing well
and it suffered from debts until the
inflation caused by the First World War.
The various brothers of the family divided
their activities between Paris and Cairo.
As the business expanded, cousins and
even the daughters, who ended up marrying different heads of departments, were
involved in the activities of the store. The
children and wives, according to Reynolds
again acted as "living advertisements" by
wearing the dresses made by the store.[91]

---

[91] Nancy Reynolds, "Sharikat al-Bayt al-Masri: Domesticating Commerce in Egypt,
1931–1956", *Arab Studies Journal*, VII, no. 2 and VIII no. 1 (Fall 1999/Spring 200):
75–107, pp. 84–85.

For example, at Clement's wedding (one of the Chemla brothers), which was a grand social affair, the company manufactured special stylish black jackets and striped pants for employees who could not afford fancy outfits to wear, since 'almost all employees had begun with the (brothers), as soon as they began to have employees, (and) they followed them always. When the store ascended, they too, their situation ascended, such that it was very important that the employees attended their marriage.' As one Chemla child remembered it, the business – its owners, employees, and customers – was 'vraiment comme une grande famille.'[92]

The impact of European architects in Europeanizing Cairo, much like Italianising Alexandria,[93] and reinterpreting Islamic architecture by reinventing the neo-Mamlouk style as the Italian architect Mario Rossi (1897–1961) was far from negligible in creating hybrid styles.[94] The department store stood as the symbol of the modern city and modern interactions.[95] Here as elsewhere, the architecture revealed the pervasiveness of European influence. For example, Tiring Department Store in al-ʿAtaba al-Khadra was designed by Oskar Horowitz (b. 1881, d. before 13 November 1927), an Austrian architect who studied in Vienna and was in Cairo between 1913 and 1915. Tiring was a daughter branch of the one established by Victor Tiring and Frères in Vienna. The company did not survive long and was liquidated in 1920.[96] Rudolf Agstner, who wrote about Austrian architects in Cairo during 1869–1914, describes Tiring as follows:

> Tiring's department store covers an area of 1,235 Square meters, and has six floors. The building is crowned by a cupola, on top of which 4 Herculean figures are holding a globe . . ., reason enough to think

---

[92] Nancy Reynolds, p. 85.

[93] See Simonetta Ciranna, "Italian Architects and Holy Space in Egypt" in: *Le Caire-Alexandrie, Architectures europeennes, 1850–1950*, pp. 49–57, and Mohamed Fouad Awad, Cristina Pallini "The Italianisation of Alexandria an Analogy of Practice", pp. 89–104, sous la direction de Mercedes Volait. Etudes Urbaines, 5. CEDEJ-IFAO, 2001.

[94] Rossi was chief architect at the Ministry of Waqfs from 1929 until 1955 and he designed 260 mosques. This tells us to what extent Egypt underwent European influences. Ahmed Sidky, "L'Oeuvre de Mario Rossi Au Ministère des Waqfs: Une reinterpretation italienne de l'architecture islamique" in: *Le Caire-Alexandrie . . .* 2001, pp. 71–76, p. 63

[95] Even though Nancy Young Reynolds argues that the dichotomy tradition/modern is erroneous and she well demonstrates that many of the *grands magasins* owners started in the old traditional bazaar sector.

[96] Rudolf Agstner, "Dream and Reality: Austrian Architects in Egypt: 1869–1914" in: *Le Caire-Alexandrie, Architectures europeennes, 1850–1950*, sous la direction de Mercedes Volait. Etudes Urbaines, 5. CEDEJ-IFAO, 2001, pp. 141–160, p. 150.

Fig. 16. Tiring Grand Magasin.

of "Tiring" as Cairo's only practical joke. Tiring is certainly one of
the most imposing buildings in Cairo.[97]

The Tiring building has survived the massive devastation of the city
of Cairo. It still remains in the ʿAtaba quarter, close to the demarcation line between the new European city and the old bazaar of
Khan al-Khalili. The area around Tiring has since been transformed
into a *baladi* market filled with ambulant carts, selling textiles and
all sorts of items. It is one of the most densely populated markets
in Cairo, where one can hardly walk in normal working days. Tiring
itself is now subdivided into hundreds of tiny, shabby and cheap
looking shops. (See picture) Orasdi-Back Department Store (1908–1909),
today turned into the Omar Effendi store in ʿAbdel ʿAziz Street was
built by Raoul Brandon. It has been heavily influenced by French
Neo-baroque style.[98] The Sednaoui Store (1913) was designed by

---

[97] M. Scharabi, cited from Rudolf Agstner p. 151.
[98] This is the view of Mohamed Scharabi, *Kairo Stadt und Architektur im Zeitalter des
Europäischen Kolonialismus*, Verlag Ernst Wasmuth Tübingen, 1989, p. 260.

Fig. 17. Gattengno Grand Magasin

Georges Parcq; both architects were French.[99] Magasin Gattengno, previously the Bon marché, borrowed traditional elements from Venetian architecture.[100] The architecture of Ades grand magasin reveals a strong Art Deco influence.[101]

If the department store owes its existence to the changes in the production system whereby the factory produced more goods more efficiently, as argued by Sennett,[102] the birth of Egyptian department stores is closely linked with the flowering of Egyptian Jewish capitalism. Jewish capitalism became powerful in Egypt by the end of the nineteenth century. Like many other foreigners, Jews were invited since the reign of Mohammed Ali to contribute in the economy. The Jews contributed in creating banks and their impact was to be

---

[99] André Raymond, (editor), *The Glory of Cairo, An Illustrated History*, AUC Press, 2002 403.

[100] Mohamed Scharabi . . ., p. 250.

[101] Mohamed Scharabi . . ., p. 235.

[102] Cited in Peter Corrigan, *The Sociology of Consumption: An Introduction*, London: Sage Publications, 1997, p. 50.

felt in the Egyptian National Bank of Egypt, Egyptian Credit Foncier, Bank Misr. The Mosseiris created their own bank. They were also Jewish families involved in philanthropic work and they dominated the business world. Names such as the Cattauis, the Cicurels and the Mosseiris often recur in the world of finance.[103] Evidently, they were the main motor in the birth of the department store in Egypt. Some of these stores in Cairo already existed in the 1880s. *Les grands magasins* and commercial houses carried names such as Ades, Chalons, Chemla, Hannaux, Levi-Benzion, Cicurel (Italian), Orosdi-Back, Simon-Artz, Chalons, Cohenca, Morums, Oreco, Pontremoli, (Salon Vert), Simon-Arzt, and Rivoli.[104] Members of the Jewish *grande* bourgeoisie owned almost all of these stores. The only exceptions were the Syrian Sednaoui brothers, Samaan and Selim Sednaoui, who settled in Egypt at the end of the 19th century. They came to Cairo via Damascus, but were originally from Sedenaya and Maaloula. The Sednaoui stores, we are told, in contrast to the other stores, which were in the centre of town, were established away from the town centre, in Sharia Khazindar. The Sednaoui *magasin* was meant to be a replica of the Galeries Lafayette of Paris.[105]

What distinguished the Cicurel Stores were their European character and the extensive number of French-speaking Jewish staff.[106] French signs are still to be found in elevators and in advertisements. The founder Moreno Cicurel migrated from Izmir in the mid-nineteenth century. The Cicurel family held Italian passports. This department store was opened in 1909, in the centre of the European section, on the present day 26th July Street. In contrast to the location of Cicurel department store, in the popular quarter of Muski Street, a member of the Hannaux family founded in 1887 a haberdashery and a toyshop. It later expanded into a fashion store called Au Petit Bazaar to be later sold to Moreno Cicurel who was a former employee of Hannaux. Les *Grands Magasins* Cicurel et Oreco

---

[103] Victor D. Sanua, "The Contributions of Sephardic Jews to The Economic and Industrial Development of Egypt" *Foundation for the Advancement of Sephardic Studies and Culture*, http://www.sephadicstudies.org/contributions-jews-egypt.html.

[104] See Historical Society of Jews From Egypt. Department Stores Founded and owned by Jews in Cairo, Egypt: http://www.hsje.org/depstores.htm.

[105] Samir Ra'afat, "Sednaoui", *Cairo Times*, 29 May, 1997.

[106] Joel Beinin, *The Dispersion of Egyptian Jewry: Culture, Politics and the Formation of a Modern Diaspora*, Berkeley: University of California Press, 1998, p. 22.

grew into the major department chain with branches in Alexandria and Isma'iliyya.[107]

Beinin, in *The Dispersion of Egyptian Jewry* (1998), considers that Egyptian bourgeois Jews, because of their cosmopolitanism, seem to have adapted very well to the Egyptian nationalist discourse. Beinin maintains that Jews were perceived as "different from" Muslims and Christians, and yet "the same as" their non-Jewish neighbours. Concerning the Cicurel department stores Beinin writes that:

> To protest the re-arrest and deportation of Sa'd Zaghlul to Seychelles, the Wafd called on Egyptians to purchase only at 'national stores' in 1921–22. The Cicurel Department store near Cairo's Opera Square was specified as an approved shop. In a 1948 memorandum submitted to the ministry of Commerce, the Cicurel Form described itself as 'one of the pillars of our Egyptian national economic Independence'.[108]

However, Nancy Young Reynolds insists on the fact that although department stores were the "emblem of Jewish culture in the Middle East", the employees came from different mixed backgrounds. "Native Egyptian Muslim and Coptic men and women worked on store floors with salesclerks who were local Jews, Southern (and at times Northern and central Europeans, and other ethnic groups from the old boundaries of the Ottoman Empire."[109] After the Arab–Israeli war of 1948 a massive migration of Jews took place. With the nationalization policies of Nasser, many members of the foreign communities left, ending the era of cosmopolitanism that was oriented towards European culture.

For many older-generation Cairenes, department stores evoke nostalgia for refined tastes and images of fashionable, upper-class women being attended to by skilled saleswomen and men. Amina El-Lozi, a well to do Egyptian who is in her mid-seventies, recalls that in the forties she had her dresses made by Madame Rosette, who was employed as a *couturiere* at Sednaoui department store. Amina El-Lozi was her client until the nationalization of the store. Sednaoui was also famous for its imported dresses and the excellent organization of the shop.[110] The staff became known for their good manners.

---

[107] Gudrun Kraemer, *The Jews in Modern Egypt, 1914–1952*, I.B. Tauris and Co. Ltd., London, 1989, p. 44.
[108] Joel Beinin, p. 21.
[109] Nancy Young Reynolds, p. 211.
[110] Interview with Amina El Lozi, Zamalek, 11 November 2004.

Fig. 18. Omar Affandi, Orasdi Back, Abdel Aziz Street.

Fig. 19. Omar Affandi, Orasdi Back, Abdel Aziz Street.

The experience of shopping in such stores was in itself a form of elevation.

In the sixties the department stores were nationalized. Hannaux and Salon Vert were Egyptianized. Of the surviving Egyptian department stores in today's downtown Cairo, Omar Effendi and Salon Vert, seem still to be faring well and catering for a large middle class. Sednaoui's 'Ataba and Chemla have both been recently stylishly renovated. For the generation of the sixties and seventies, school uniforms were still purchased from Department stores. Each school sent its pupils to a specific store. Cheap "castor" cloth to make night dresses and pyjamas, blankets, sheets, heaters and fans were equally purchased at department stores.

According to the most recent Egypt Almanac, in 1996, the government announced that it would put up for sale its *grands magasins* (Omar Effendi, Hannaux, Benzion, Ades, Rivoli, Sednaoui, Cicurel) to an investor. These stores remain potentially interesting financially, since Omar Effendi alone has eighty-two outlets all over Egypt and owns 108.000m2 of retail space. The attempted sale was rather a failure, there after the government renovated the stores. It seems however, that this did not improve the financial situation since the retail market continued to decline. In year 2000 Omar Effendi made L.E. 661 million in sales, while in 2000 it dropped to L.E. 463 million. One main reason, it seems, is that many middle-class Egyptians now prefer to shop in boutiques. Omar Effendi is still being offered for sale for around L.E. 300 million.[111] This is the view of the recent Almanac on the decline of department stores. It might be true that for clothes and fashionable items, Egyptians prefer to frequent small shops and fancy boutiques. But for consumer durables such as refrigerators, electric heaters, kitchen items, toasters, fans, plates, sheets, and electrical items, Omar Effendi and Salon Vert remain as the best address, which does not explain the financial decay. Corruption here might be the answer.

Today, globalization has become the catchword, replacing the older notion of cosmopolitanism. One clear manifestation is the proliferation of Chinese, Indian, Thai and Argentinean restaurants, while international and Asian food and imported goods from all over the globe have become available in Egyptian stores and supermarkets.

---

[111] *Egypt Almanac, The Encyclopedia of Modern Egypt*, 2003, Egypto-file LTD.L.L.C. Wilmington. USA, p. 180.

Cosmopolitan culture, epitomized in colonial culture, the department store, and private clubs, compared to globalization, was more restricted to the small elite. The contemporary neo-liberal ideology, which is paired with globalization, did increase class cleavages. However, mass culture simulates a semblance of democratizing tastes that can blur the effects of class and economic disparities

The Social Life of Malls

'Malls' In its original meaning refer to the tracts for strolling. Now most of the malls are shopping malls, tracts to stroll while you shop and to shop while you stroll. The merchandisers sniffed while you stroll. The merchandisers sniffed out the attraction and seductive power of strollers' habits and set about moulding them into life. Parisian arcades have been promoted retrospectively to the bridgeheads of the times to come: the post-modern world islands in the modern sea. Shopping malls make the world (or the carefully walled-off, electronically monitored and closely guarded part of it) safe for life-as-strolling.[112]

(Bauman, 1996: 27)

Hyperspaces such as stations, airports and shopping malls have attracted increasing attention from urban sociologists in recent years.[113] These public spaces, similar to those the French sociologist Isaac Joseph defines as *éspaces de passage* or *lieux-mouvement*, have inspired urban sociologists to re-think the notion of space as a sphere of communication and meeting. Isaac Joseph asks us to study such spaces from a micro-sociological or Goffmanian interactive sociology perspective. Another fascinating study, which looks at British shopping malls, is *Shopping, Place and Identity*.[114] Miller et al. argue that shopping does not merely reproduce identities, but provides an active and independent component of identity construction. The study provides new insights about how to theorize and link ethnicity and consumption through the different uses of public space. It highlights the

---

[112] Zygmunt Bauman, "From Pilgrim to Tourist – or a Short History of Identity" in S. Hall and P. Du Gay (eds) *Questions of Cultural Identity*, London, Sage, 1996, pp. 18–36. p. 27.

[113] Robert Schields, "Social Spacialization and the Built Environment: The West Edmonton Mall", *Environment and Planning: Society and Space*, 1989, 7, pp. 147–164. Isaac Joseph, "Les competences de rassemblement une ethnographie des lieux publics", *Enquetes*, 4, 1996, pp. 107–22.

[114] Daniel Miller, Peter Jackson, Nigel Trift, Beverley Holbrook and Micheal Rowlands, *Shopping, Place and Identity*, London, Routledge, 1998.

importance of space and place for consumer identities as well as the cultural practices of shopping. Moreover, it reminds us how these new geographies are constantly creating new forms of shopping and lifestyle. It also emphasizes the need to look at shopping malls from the perspective of shop workers and how shopping influences sexuality and social relations.[115] Inspired by the works of the French sociologist Michel Maffesoli, Ricardo Ferreira Freitas[116] produced a monograph in which he compared various shopping centres in Brazil with the Parisian Forum des Halles. Freitas often uses the notion of *imaginaire* about the internal reshaping of the space. The shopping centre, according to Freitas, symbolizes the ideal city. This space is protected from pollution and nature. As a simulated space, notions such as the "copy", the "recycled" or the "virtual", become significant.

In Brazil, paralleling the rise of violence over the last two decades, shopping centres have increased from one in 1980 to nineteen in 1995 as a way of providing non-violent monitored space. In Rio, they talk about the Barrashopping (73,906 square metres) as the largest shopping centre in Latin America, as a place associated with a "humanizing" space without violence.[117] Zygmunt Bauman reminds us that it was Walter Benjamin who invented the *flâneur* as the symbolic figure of the modern city. Through associating the new space of the malls with *flâneur*-ing,[118] Bauman tells us that shopping malls make the world – "carefully walled-off, electronically monitored and closely guarded" – "safe for life-as-strolling". The names of Walter Benjamin and Georg Simmel constantly reappear in the literature of the city, emphasizing the stranger and loneliness as the inspiration for the reinvention of spaces; they initiated discussion of wandering in modern cathedrals and empires of consumption. Mike Featherstone[119] reworks Benjamin's concept of *flâneurie* through its multifarious dimensions and argues that the *flâneur* is not just a stroller in the city; his

---

[115] For a gendered spaced perspective, with the focus on the notion of woman walker, see Meaghan Morris, "Things to do with Shopping Centres" in S. During (ed.) *The Cultural Studies Reader*, 2nd ed. London and New York: Routledge, 1993, pp. 391–410.

[116] Ricardo Ferreira Freitas, *Centres commerciaux: lies urbaines de la post-modernité*, Paris l'Harmattan, 1996.

[117] Freitas, 1996, p. 95.

[118] Bauman, 1996, p. 95.

[119] Mike Featherstone, "The Flaneur, the City and the Virtual Public Life", *Urban Studies*, 1998, 35(5–6): 909–25, 910.

or her *flâneurie* is also a "method of reading texts" and "for reading the traces of the city".

Benjamin tells us that the traces of the city, which need investigating are hieroglyphic signs, signs and broken images, which draw attention to gendered spaces, such as the *grands magasins*, dominated by women.[120] Thus, shopping can be seen as another form of *flâneurie*, a mobile gaze closely associated with women, in contrast to the suggestion that the subject of the city is exclusively male.[121] The process of the feminization of the *flâneur* can be linked to the rise of the department store, which was an attempt to move the street into the interior. This work builds upon the important writings of Janet Wolff, Elizabeth Wilson and Mica Nava,[122] who discuss and dispute the nature of the emergent women's public sphere in nineteenth-century England and France. Mica Nava, in particular, strongly emphasizes the ways in which women developed their own form of cosmopolitan public space in department stores such as Selfridges in London. How much is Bauman's observations appropriate for understanding the changes taking place in the Third World? Could unexpected uses of spaces in the Third World by youth and women be a new field for social investigation?

There is much theorizing about how consumer habits and forms of socializing have taken place in the Western world. There have also been debates in recent years about the multiple and alternative modernities of non-Western societies. This would suggest the need for further reflection about the variegated and differential impact of consumer culture on Third World societies. Certainly, in recent years there have been a large number of studies concerned with the impact of consumerism, relating it to identity construction and globalization. One could mention Jonathan Friedman's work on Congolese appro-

---

[120] Featherstone, 1998, Bech, 1999.

[121] R. Bowlby, *Just Looking*, London, Methuen, 1985. Anne Friedberg *Window Shopping: Cinema and the Postmodern*. Berkeley, University of California Press, 1993. Henning Bech "Citysex, Representing Lust in Public" in Mike Featherstone (ed.) *Love and Eroticism*, London, Sage, 1999.

[122] Janet Wolff, "The Invisible Flaneuse: Women and the Literature of Modernity", *Theory, Culture and Society*, 1985, 2(3): 37–46, Elizabeth Wilson, "The Invisible Flaneur", *New Left Review*, 1992, 191: 90–116; *The Contradictions of Culture*, London, Sage, 2001. Mica Nava, "Modernity's Disavowal: Women, the City and the Department Store" in M. Nava and A. O'Shea (eds) *Modern Times: Reflections on a Century of English Modernity*, London, Routledge, 1996, Mica Nava," Cosmopolitan Modernity: Everyday Imaginaries and the Allure of Difference" *Theory, Culture and Society*, (Forthcoming).

priation of French fashion, referred to as *la sape* (from the French verb *se saper*), and the impact of dressing elegantly and lifestyle among youth in Bacongo[123] *Consumption and Everyday Life* is another work which discusses the issue of appropriation of consumerism among both the European working classes and in different Third World countries such as in Trinidad.[124]

A New Public Sphere

American shopping malls have kept sociologists busy from the mid-1980s on. Many would argue that the topic has become old-fashioned, especially as American shopping malls are suffering a significant decline. Dead shopping malls are described today as littering the landscape; nearly one in five US malls standing in the 1990's will be out of business by the end of 2001. We are also reminded that in 1960 there were 3,000 shopping centres in the United States, whereas there are now nearly 40,000 malls.[125] As Meaghan Morris[126] noted in her study on Australian shopping malls, it is change in the city, the managing of change and the changing role of shopping centres, which is worthy of attention.

The Southeast Asian and the Egyptian cases tell us that shopping malls are today increasingly flourishing and expanding. In this context, we should perhaps be reminded that the Mahathir government in Malaysia has boasted for years of the fact that it has built the largest shopping malls in Southeast Asia. I would argue that shopping malls in Egypt would become a new field of sociological investigation. In the shopping malls, an interesting hybridization of tastes, and entirely different conceptions of space and ways of spending leisure are in the making. Although shopping malls are an American invention, they do not necessarily fulfil the same functions in the Middle East or in Southeast Asia. Featherstone tells us that shopping entails a multiplicity of operations "ranging from shopping for necessities, to shopping around (window shopping) to recreational

---

[123] Jonathan Friedman, *Cultural Identity and Global Process*, London, Sage, 1994.
[124] Hugh Mackay (ed.) *Consumption and Everyday Life*, London, Sage, 1997.
[125] *International Herald Tribune*, 3 January 2000.
[126] Meaghan Morris, "Things to do with Shopping Centres" in: S. During (ed.) *The Cultural Studies Reader*, 2nd Edition, London and New York: Routledge, 1993.

shopping (spending time in the city, walking in the streets taking in sights, moving in and out of department stores, shops in public spaces)".[127]

In Egypt, for instance, due to the shortage of public gardens, the newly built malls might not be spaces for shopping, but rather for youth to socialize and mix in groups. The government has recently encouraged the construction of public gardens but, to the disappointment of everyone, these green spaces are fenced off and forbidden to the public on the pretext that Egyptians are unable to behave in public and cause no end of littering. Shopping malls could represent a new space for the study of youth culture in Cairo. That malls are gendered spaces is a recurrent theme in consumer studies, but that malls could be viewed as offering social mobility and access to cash for lower class, young saleswomen, through diffusing an image of the "modern", presentable and fashionable salesperson, needs further research. It is the contrast, coexistence and fusion between Islamic attire (albeit already Westernized, turned fashionable) and Western dress that is of interest.

But there are rising as well as declining shopping malls in Cairo. Cairo, similar to the US is not spared from dead shopping malls. There are *baladi, shaʿ abi, biʾa* (all meaning popular) shopping malls, there are "family oriented" malls, and also very "chic", fancy ones. There also is a paradox in Cairo's malls. On the one hand, the sheer number of malls constructed in the last decade (around 30) reveal that it they are becoming a popular institution. According to the survey I conducted in 2003, these malls included the following: in Madinat Nasr district; Tiba Mall, al-ʿAquad Mall, Geneina Mall, Wonderland Mall, Al-Sarag Mall, City Centre, Group Centre, al-Horeya Mall (Heliopolis); in downtown Cairo; Talʿat Harb Mall, and the Bustan Centre. Along the Cornish al-Nil is the Arkadia Mall, the Hilton Ramses and Hilton Tahrir Malls as well as the World Trade Centre, in Bulaq. Farther away from central Cairo in Maʿadi one can find the al-Maʿadi Grand Mall, Bandar Mall, and Town Centre, Maʿadi. Finally, al-Yamama Centre in Zamalek, the Cairo Mall, near the Pyramids in Guizeh, the Mustafa Centre, the Florida Mall, (Masaken Sheraton), the First Mall in Giza, the Al-Amir Mall in Shubra and the Al-Binyan Mall in Zaytoun quarter comprise the

---

[127] Mike Featherstone, "The Flaneur, The City and the Virtual Public Life", *Urban Studies*, 1998, 35(5–6), pp. 909–25, p. 916.

remaining malls in the greater Cairo area. The most recently created City Stars mall with 400 shops, four hotels with a total of 1200 rooms is so far the biggest mall ever constructed in Cairo.

According to one businessman, the life span of malls is very short, ranging from eighteen to twenty-four months, as less than 20 percent of all Egyptians can afford to shop in malls.[128] Thus many of these fancy malls have been described today as "ghost towns", deserted areas. Take for instance, the World Trade Centre (WTC) in Bulaq and the First Mall in Giza. These started as very classy malls, both of them constructed near five stars hotels, the Hilton and the (WTC). However, today they are losing their popularity because they are too expensive, as they aim at well to do elites. Complaints about poor management were another reason that explains why these enterprises haved failed. However, dying malls do not contradict the fact that companies such as Orascom and others are doing financially well and flourishing as contractors. In 2005, the same is happening now to the First Mall, which first charged the rent in US dollars[129] and had to reduce its rent recently. Yamama in Zamalek and Bustan Centre, located downtown face the same sad fate. If shopkeepers declare bankruptcy, it is practically impossible for managers of malls to collect the unpaid rent, and the only resort is to throw these shopkeepers out.[130]

I revisited some of these malls in 2005, after conducting my first research in 1999. The complaints seemed to be the same, a frightening economic recession and practically no purchasing power available. Second, the malls have been badly managed. At the Yamama Centre, after failing to collect the rent and losing great amounts of money, the management evicted three entire floors of shopkeepers. In 2004, they redesigned the mall with a new concept, aiming at turning it into an amusement and leisure time mall. The Saudi owner

---

[128] Nadia Mostafa, "Retail goes Wild", *Business Today*, June 2003, p. 61.

[129] Several Malls collected the rent in US dollars, but when the Egyptian pound fell drastically down, the rent had to be fixed according to the pound.

[130] In relation to this topic, *Rosa al-Youssef* for instance stated that in year 2000, there were 50 thousand court cases of declared bankruptcy. Of these cases, some 38 thousand cases had sentences issued concerning bankruptcy. According to *Rosa al-Youssef* these were used as an alibi to escape from paying bank loans. The rate of bankruptcy in small projects had reached in year 2000 the number of 30%. See Gamal Taye', "rigal al-a'mal yushhirun iflassahum lil-taharrub min sadad al-qurud" (Businessmen Declare Bankruptcy to Escape Paying Loans) *Rosa-al Youssef*. 24/2:2/3/ 2001 no. 3794, p. 20.

invested massively in building four cinemas, an Internet cafe, classy
restaurants and a children's games section in the hope that this new
conception will bring customers. A fitness centre which functions
well, replaced some of the evicted shopkeepers.[131] However, as with
many other malls, Yamama Centre suffered great losses because the
shop renters abstained from paying the rent and electricity. The
managers had to sue these on court, which cost the Saudi owner a
fortune. "We knew that we will never get the money of the unpaid
rent back, but at least the shops renters were evicted", said the managers. The mall was redecorated last year from top to down with
bright coloured paintings, kitsch Arabian-oriental camels and deserts
landscapes done by the students from the Faculty of Arts. A huge,
frightening, (possibly a Poseidon or a flying Pegasus) statue has been
put at the atrium and the upgrading of the mall seems to be working
by attracting the Zamalekites to the highly professional and well-
equipped fitness centre. Thus, the customers are a mix of students,
Zamlekites, and wealthy Saudis with vulgar taste (from the point
of view of Zamalekites). However, the project of "gentrifying" the
Yamama centre is still under construction and insecurity is reigning
because the managers seem to face administrative problems in regards
to the government's attempt to obtain a license for a Cineplex and
an Internet café.

When the World Trade Centre was still functioning, in some of
its restaurants, the *muhagabbat* (women wearing the Islamic attire) and
men who wore *galabeyyas* (the popular male long robe) were forbidden to enter, thus also excluding the wealthy Gulf clientele. In the
First Mall, if a branded pair of boots can cost 5,000 Egyptian pounds
(One Dollar = L.E. 6. 25), it is evident that these shopping malls
have no future among the masses of Cairo. But different new malls
are emerging and seem to be doing very well. For example, the
Arkadia Mall on the Cornish al-Nil, near the World Trade Centre,
the malls of Madinat Nasr and the mall of Tal'at Harb in Downtown.

To summarise, it is evident that the notion of the public space
and its maintenance evokes different meanings culturally and socially.
One of the reasons why so many malls died, according to the managers, is because these failed to collect from shop renters the charges

---

[131] Interview with Ashraf Abu 'Aref and Ahmed al-Sukkary, managers of the
Yamama Centre, 14 March, 2005.

for the public utilities of the mall. Some said that the clause on public utilities was not clearly defined in the contract. Obviously, the
fact that this is a new form of a "semi-public space" seems to raise
questions about who is responsible for what. Clearly, if public gardens are to be permanently closed, using the excuse that the public is uncontrollable, these public spaces devoid of a public become
sites for mere visual consumption. The embellishment of the city,
through gardens and painting the facades in downtown, seems to be
done in an effort to counterbalance the "fear of tarnishing the country's image", a fear which has increased among officials due the
global tourist gaze.

CHAPTER THREE

MEMORIES

Benjamin (Walter Bejamin) regards everything he chooses to recall in his past as prophetic of the future, because the work of memory (reading oneself backwards, he called it) collapses time. There is no chronological ordering of his reminiscences, for which he disavows the name of autobiography, because time is irrelevant.

Susan Sontag, *Under the Sign of Saturn*, Farrar. Strauss. Giroux, New York, 1980, p. 115.

This chapter is an effort to weave contemporary sociological observations with my past childhood memories. I confess that this "demarche" is definitely based on my nostalgic vision of the past. This autobiographical exploration is meant to provide clues and illustrations of past consumer practices. The ruse of memory is that it is often subject to betrayal. Nostalgia means that affirmative memories tend to

Fig. 20. Sednaoui, Ceiling.

be magnified, while naturally dis-
graceful events are systematically
erased from our consciousness. I
am conscious that the past is em-
bellished at the expense of the
decadent present, a natural effect
of nostalgia. I nevertheless con-
solidate the nostalgic mood with
magazine and newspapers documentation, in addition to interviews with middle-upper class
women who are today in their
early seventies. What I next attempt is a portrayal of the practices
of certain members of the Cairene
upper middle classes. I recognize
many of practices described here
have filtered through to the lower
middle classes. In spite of my criticism of Galal Amin's positions, I
would like to emulate his strategy

Fig. 21. Radio Transistor Ad.
Akher Saʿah

Fig. 22. Al-Nasr Company Ad.
Al-Mussawar 13–5–1966.

of grounding his work on personal
experience, which will be exposed
as a collage of themes.

The Ideal and Nasr Companies

The generation from the 1960's
can recall that they grew up in
households possessing locally produced consumer durables manufactured by the nationalized *Ideal*
company. The *Ideal* national company produced complete metal
kitchens, stoves, fridges, metal cupboards, beds and desks and even
toys that were perhaps aesthetically unattractive. Nonetheless, one
could agree that these consumer

durables were functional and practical. A visit to the Bauhaus Museum in Tiergarten, Berlin, which opened in 1979, is inspiring if one wants to understand how the *Ideal* company carbon copied functional and well designed desks, cupboards, lamps, ashtrays, tea pots, chairs and tables (originally produced in the 1930s). Clinics, beds and furniture for hospitals were again emulated from Bauhaus[1] to look as if this was an indigenous Egyptian style. I discovered that I grew up with chairs and tables, which were based on designs by Marcel Breuer, one of leading figures of Bauhaus in the mid-twenties in Dessau.[2] These were locally produced. I always thought as a child that they were genuine Egyptian inventions. Bauhaus furniture was well adapted to our household needs. It mixed well with the old style furniture of my family. I also recall relatives and classmates' tables, desks made of metal, and kitchens with "Formica" work tops. These were solid and easy to clean items. Canaltex plastic floors were often found in hospitals and government offices and in many houses. Again the genius of Bauhaus was that it promoted the idea of producing good-looking items with inexpensive material. It encouraged the idea of using inexpensive affordable instalments.

El-Nasr Company produced all sizes of Egyptian televisions, including portable and transistor televisions. *Sharikat al-delta al-sina'iyyah, Ideal* Company was the regime's symbol of success. In 1966 *Akher Sa'ah* magazine[3] displayed a propagandistic article with a picture of Nasser

---

[1] Bauhaus is considered as one of the most significant architectural schools of the twentieth century. It was established in Weimar in 1919. The German architect Walter Gropius is considered to be the chief founder. However, after it creation, the movement was fought by the right wing conservatives who considered Gropius's philosophy too revolutionary or rather as supporting communism. Bauhaus later flourished in Dessau, it became a landmark of modern functional architecture. It aspired at simple and clear forms. Large surfaces of glass were introduced to enhance transparency and the interplay with light. Bauhaus was extremely powerful in inventing functional furniture, wonderful carpet patterns, fabrics, ceramics, glass, designs and photography. The movement was fought by Nazis who closed the Bauhaus. Most of its protagonists migrated to the US where Bauhaus flourished and experienced success. Susanna Partsch, *Kunst-Epochen 20. Jahrhundert*, Reclam, 2002, pp. 86–91.

[2] For a comprehensive study of the Bauhaus movement see *Experiment Bauhaus. Das Bauhaus-Archiv Berlin* (West) zu Gast im Bauhaus Dessau, Herausgeber Bauhaus Archiv, Museum für Gestaltung, 1988.

[3] *Akhir Sa'ah*, "President Gamal Abdel Nasser and the Industrial Fair in 1966" (al-ra'is Gamal 'Abdel Naser wal ma'rad al-sina'i fi 1966), 9–2, 1966, pp. 2–3, no. 1633.

visiting the fair, which boasted the company's triumph in conquering African markets in Dakar, Senegal and in Lagos, Nigeria. The subtitle of the article boasted that the markets all over the world had been competing for *Ideal* fridges and air conditioners. We are then informed that *Ideal* fridges were even sold to Eastern Germany.

The company proved so successful in multiplying its capital to eighty times after the revolution. *Sharikat al-delta al-sinaʿiyyah*, *Ideal* Company started in 1962 as a merger between *sharikat al delta al-tuggariyya* and *sharikat al-taʿdin*. The parent company was founded in 1920 starting with a capital of 20 thousand pounds. *Ideal* company started producing the first

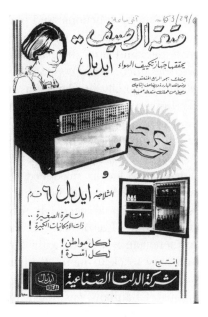

Fig. 23. Ideal Ad.
Akher Saʿah 29–6–1966.

refrigerators in 1954, (probably the first fridges ever produced in the

Fig. 24. El-Nasr Ad.
Televisions Al-Mussawar, 3 June 1966.

Middle East), and air conditioners followed in 1956. The company had by then expanded into three large factories with a capital reaching 1,600,000,000 Egyptian pounds.

These locally produced consumer items were considered to be the pride of the "Public Sector" and were sold in nationalized *grands magasins* such as Hannaux, Sednaoui, Chemla and Tarbishi. They also took over various previous companies and expanded them. *Al-Mussawar* magazine reported on the Nasser's visit to the *Ideal* company stand at the 1966 industrial fair, boasting again that it exports its products to twenty-five countries.[4] In the same issue, Nasser is pictured visiting factories such as the *Nasr* car factory, the Egyptian transistors and electricity Company and the military industries. All these goods were purchasable on installment. In 1966 *Akher Sa'ah* published a special report entitled "*Why did taqsit* (the installments) *Return?*" Under the earlier system the consumers could have purchased the items without making any payment for two years, which caused many financial problems for consumers (and producers). The government had blocked the system of payment in instalments a year earlier but then reintro-

Fig. 25. Fiat Ad.
Al-Mussawar, 24 December 1967.

Fig. 26. Fiat Ad.
Al-Mussawar, 24 Feb. 1967.

duced it with a few changes. The government's argument was that it wanted to encourage people to buy goods, which were not moving. Again, according to the government there might have been the problem of distributing certain goods, such as fridges, which were not competitive for export. In that case installments would be one way of getting rid of surplus production. Therefore, it was decided to open the *taqsit* system on fridges, televisions, stoves and washing machines. The new regulation required an advance payment of 20 percent of the price of the goods purchased.[5]

---

[4] *Al-Mussawar*, 4 February, 1966, no. 2156, pp. 2–15.
[5] Ali al-Magharabi, "limatha 'aad al-bay' bil-taqsit" (Why Did the Instalment

Middle-class families drove locally assembled "Fiats" constructed by the *Nasr* Company. The tiny *Ramses* car, a close imitation of the Italian "Topolino" was the first truly Egyptian, locally produced car. The *Ramses*' logo consisted of a drawing of the conquering Pharaoh Ramses on his chariot and was advertised as the first wholly 100 percent Arab car ever produced. The *Ramses* did not last long, but at least the attempt was undertaken. One had to reserve in advance to purchase the *Nasr* cars. It often took more than a year to obtain delivery of the car. In the early 80's, after many tribulations and contradictory statements made by government officials, *Nasr* Company was sold to the American company General Motors. For many this was seen a conscious betrayal of the philosophy of "import substitution" and the fostering of indigenous industrial development which was basically a defiant stand by the nationalists post-colonial countries in response to the arrogant "colonial" West. I quote here again Sonallah Ibrahim's novel *Zaat*, which lists a revealing historical moment in newspaper clips:

> The Egyptian press announces that the contract for the one hundred percent Egyptian motorcar had been signed with the American company General Motors.
> The American government stipulates that 200 million dollars of aid money be allocated to guarantee the new investments of General Motors in Egypt.
> The Egyptian Industry Minister: "Egypt has not signed a contract with General Motors".
> Youssef Wali, Secretary of the National Democratic Party: "We have signed the contract with General Motors".
> The Egyptian Industry Minister reconfirms; "We have not signed."
> General Motors announces in the American press: "The contract has been signed."
> Experts at the Egyptian Industry Ministry: "The General Motors contract means that the millions of pounds spent on developing the Egyptian motor company Nasr (public sector) will have gone down the drain, and that a quarter of a century of experience assembling the Italian Fiat will have been wasted. Everything has turned upside down".[6]

One can conclude that the death of *Nasr* Company, like many public sector companies was the result of growing foreign intervention

---

System Return Back?) *Akher Saʿah* (19/10/1966, no. 1669, p. 5). *Akher Saʿah* prepared a special report on Why did *taqsit* Return?
  [6] Sonallah Ibrahim *Zaat*, AUC Press, 2004, p. 69.

combined with internal support. *Infitah* became synonymous to the death of the
public sector companies that
went hand in hand with privatization and corruption.
Moheb Zaki summarizes the
Infitah period as follows:

> It was only natural that an
> *infitah* that impeded serious
> industrial investment and
> left most of the 'socialist'
> institutions in place would
> fuel corruption, as the pri-
> vate sector manoeuvred to

Fig. 27. Ideal Ad.
Akher Saʿah 29–6–1966.

obtain a share of the import licenses, quotas, and privileged contracts
disturbed at the discretion of underpaid state officials. . . . With great
opportunities for mutual enrichment offered by the system, strong links
were soon forged between the state bureaucracy and a considerable a
segment of the business community. The 'crony capitalism', which
developed succeeded in "Alienating not only potential losers in the
reform process but also potential winner. By the end of the 1970's
corruption had become so prevalent that it appeared as though it 'had
to large extent been institutionalized'.[7]

Galal Amin suggests that the government investments in the 1960's
and 1970's were directed mainly to the new middle class. These
". . . were beyond the reach of a good proportion-say 40 percent or
more of the population".[8] One can thus conclude that if the Nasser
regime did satisfy the needs of the urban middle classes, consumer
durable goods failed to reach the peasants and the poorer classes.
Despite the successive agrarian reforms, destitute, seasonal peasants
continued to live under wretched conditions. The spread of television,
cars, fans, fridges and the red brick constructions in the countryside,
which revealed access to cash, did not take place before the mid
seventies. This was due to the massive peasant migration to the Gulf
countries, Jordan and Iraq. Migration was one major source of bringing in the country hard currency and the importation of consumer

---

[7] Moheb Zaki, *Egyptian Business Elites*, p. 91.
[8] Galal Amin, *Whatever Else Happened to the Egyptians*, p. 140.

goods. Whole villages witnessed
the desertion in large numbers of
the male population.

Bauhaus

Bauhaus architecture, like Bauhaus
household goods, was a German
invention born out of a situation
of scarcity. As such, its revolutionary, modernist and functional
outlook was adopted by the Nasser
regime in order to solve the housing problem for the needy. This
is understandable, as Bauhaus's
universalist philosophy was
inspired by non-Western civilizations, for example by African art[9]

Fig. 28. *Radio sha'abi, al-Mussawar.*
2–10, 1964.

and handicraft (in pottery and carpets). This must have been extremely
appealing to the new regime, which aspired for a break from the
former feudalist tastes and "decadent" art. Furthermore, Bauhaus in
Germany aspired at uniting art with craft and this was certainly a
very attractive philosophy.

European Bauhaus architects were geniuses in inventing a futuristic transparent architecture, with economical spaces in the form of
small flats organized in clear-cut blocks. These spaces were designed
for the modern small household. Perhaps also the futuristic, utopian
aspect of such architecture fitted well with the newly independent
nations aspiring for change. This idea was seen as functional and
operative in a "developing" nation like Egypt. *Al-masaken al-sha'biyya,*
the popular housing, could have been a replica – but much worse
maintained – of the German social housing.

It should be made clear that Bauhaus philosophy and techniques
were exported to Egypt well before the Nasser revolution as a natural extension of the cosmopolitan culture, which dominated the for-

---

[9] Marcel Breuer designed an African inspired chair, which is in the Berlin
Bauhaus Museum.

ties amongst which a trend advocating modernity was heard. First, the period between 1908 and 1931 witnessed the government sending many students to France and England (Liverpool) to study architecture and Beaux-arts.[10] Second, the school of engineering in Egypt was re-organized in 1925 under the auspices of a Swiss expert, Professor Potterat who was then the Dean of the Polytechnicum in Zurich. He also brought to Egypt three Swiss professors who taught at that school. Lastly, the Egyptian market before the 1952 revolution was heavily dominated by foreign architects and companies which were highly competitive to their Egyptian homologues[11] Many architects saw in modernism a clever solution to the acute social question such as Sayyed Karim the founder of al-'Imara magazine who raised the crucial problem of reforming the Egyptian village. The al-'Imara magazine (1939–1959) is an excellent testimony of the modernist trend and a good evidence of the "professionalization" of the Egyptian engineers who by the late 1940's were participating in international congresses. They were also included in a broad network of Arab architects, they produced specialized magazines, and they created a syndicate in 1946.[12] Mercedes Volait argued that until 1945, both Levantine (like Antoine Salim Nahhas, Albert Khouri, Albert Zananiri, Max Edrei, Charles Ayrout), and foreign architects (Max Zollikofer, Georges Parcq, Jacques Hardy, Victor Erlanger, Guiseppe Mazza and many others) were the ones whose projects mostly prevailed in the al-'Imara magazine. After World War Two, increasing space was given to the Egyptian architects.

Commenting on Bauhaus in Egypt, architect Ahmad Hamid, a disciple of the late Hassan Fathi, said the following:

> A very natural coincidence in time and place that Bauhaus techniques were there in Egypt, even before Nasser at the end of monarchic Egypt. What was in Europe was present in Egypt in the forties, maybe with a difference of a couple of years maximum and due to the architects who were working in cosmopolitan Egypt . . . we have names like Antoine Salim Nahas, Max Edrei, Raymond Antonious and Liebermann who were to be considered as the pioneers of adapting Bauhaus to an Egyptian context. Because of cosmopolitanism in Egypt . . . the works

---

[10] Mercedes Volait, l'Architecture moderne en Egypte et la revue al-'imara 1939–1959, CEDEJ, Le Caire, 1988, p. 28.
[11] Mercedes Volait, p. 24.
[12] Mercedes Volait, p. 14.

and latest architectural innovations were present in Europe and Egypt, almost simultaneously . . . there was no *décalage* in time and place between Europe and Egypt . . . Even the famous architect Ali Labib Gabr who constructed Italianate villas for the bourgeois society in the forties, did at the end of his life a fabulous modern piece of architecture, almost Bauhaus in Zamalek.

When the Nasserite regime came to power, because of the remoteness of the relation to the past everything had to be born new. Thus the motto was that we are functionally living like the West exactly. That we were industrialists more than agrarian . . . we can produce weapons. There was this sense like importing the latest from the West like the Mercedes and BMW everything from the West and grafting it to local necessity but I insist, on the local necessity and not tradition . . . All nationalist regimes, every revolution wanted to have nothing with the past . . . When Nehru adopted a new capital he imported Le Corbusier . . .[13]

This change and yet continuity explains why then the Egyptian architects, who were all cosmopolitan by training, would be later given a key role in the nationalist reconstruction. The old Cairo airport, which was the symbol of the national pride of the revolution, was designed by Mustafa Shawqui and Salah Zaytoun, both students of Frank Lloyd Wright. Salah Zaytoun also designed the current American School in Ma'adi (the CAC), which gained fame for its functional architecture. Abu Zayd Rageh had studied at MIT in the USA and Mahmud 'Omar and Sherif No'man at the ETH of Zurich. All these Western trained architects played a paramount role in adapting Bauhaus to the post-colonial reconstruction and needs of the regime.[14] Nasser understood from the Eastern bloc that architecture could not be dissociated from lifestyle. Bauhaus furniture was then imported as a package from the Eastern bloc, more specifically Eastern Germany.[15]

Mohandessin, the *City of Engineers* was then the epitome of beautiful modern Bauhaus architecture in planning, in development and in villa typology. The quarter was planned in the fifties and constructed in the early sixties. It was meant to create a new example, a quarter to house the engineers who were going to build the High Dam, to promote the industries, to provide electricity and the irri-

---

[13] Interview with architect Ahmad Hamid, 15 May 2005.
[14] Ibid.
[15] Ibid.

gation. The engineers were in a way a substitute for the educated university professors. Consequently Mohandesin provided the new paradigm for the new middle classes, symbolized in university professors and the educated middle classes. Mohandessin had a clear planning methodology, with small villas with gardens. According to Hamid, Mohandessin's architecture: "was built in a very

Fig. 29. Zakariyya Mohieddin Villa, the Facade.

remarkable stark, stoic, heroic, cubic structures, no ornaments, no arches. There were no palaces . . . no free standing Prima Donna architects, no Rococo French styling. The villas were much smaller than the earlier ancient regime style. The villas had similar balconies: either circular, rotunda or rectilinear. . . . It was the pride of the nationalist taste. We cannot negate that there was something positive going".[16] Mohandessin was divided into various sections like the city of the officers (*madinat al-zubbat*), another section was allocated for the university professors, while a third space was called *madinat al-iʿlamiyyin* (the City for the media specialists) and *al-sahafiyyin* (the journalists). The purchase of land was then possible via the various syndicates such as the university professors and the engineers' syndicates. Many Ministers of the Nasser regime like Hussein al-Shafeʿi, Zakkariyya Mohi eddin, ad Kamal Eddin Hussayn purchased land and built their villas in the *City of Officers* since they were themselves in the movement of the Free Officers. Today, some of these villas of the *al-thawra* street (the Revolution street) have been sold, torn down and replaced with high-rise buildings (See pictures of Zakariyya Mohi Eddin's Villa). Mohandessin today looks like a chaotic conglomeration of high-rise buildings, with villas and unfinished buildings. Boutiques, shops, restaurants, bakeries, supermarkets and what not have multiplied. Many offices moved from the traditional downtown to Mohandessin because it offered more space, wider streets and better parking facilities. However, Mohandessin is turning to be an ugly quarter, and just as congested as downtown.

---

[16] Ibid.

Gamal Bakry, one of the leading Egyptian architects, who is a follower of Bauhaus, has created a fascinating blend of modern and traditional elements in his design. While considering himself a modernist, Bakry is equally concerned with identity and sustainable architecture. "Architectural endeavours ought to be part of a continuous dialogue between needs, means, site, time and cultural heritage".[17] Bakry tells us that he was "breastfed" with modernity ever since his birth in the cosmopolitan city of Port Said, the city-port where multiple nationalities coexisted together and where an incredible traffic of goods took place. The fact that Bakry grew up in the foreign quarter, *al hay al-afrangi* led him to constantly contrast it with the traditional Arab quarter. Bakry then favoured the European quarter because of its cosmopolitanism and constant movement. Bakry's family was well to do middle class. His father was an accountant and the interior décor of the house he grew up was Art Deco. The fact that he grew up in a city like Port Said must have strongly influenced his outlook and attraction to modernism that according to him did offer excellent solutions for a country like Egypt. For Bakry, Egypt's heritage and traditions are loaded with a dominant religious component, which is often stifling and inflexible. "We only had as a solution modernism". The first building Bakry ever designed in his life was in Port Said. It was completely inspired by one of the Bauhaus founders, Ludwig Mies van der Rohe. Bakry was utterly fascinated by van der Rohe's idea of "anatomical architecture". It was meant to be a minimalist architecture without cosmetics or superfluous decorations. "I borrowed van der Rohe's great idea, not one extra line should be allowed in designing a building."[18] Nevertheless, according to Bakry, he admitted that minimalism is not what Egyptians like. "I was often told when I designed for Egyptians houses that these look for them like hospitals. The architecture is so austere, was their comment. Evidently many do not like my architecture," said Bakry who in his old age (seventy-two years-old) only managed to realize 2 percent of his projects.

However, Bakry's philosophy and the subtle modernism reflected in his work were never meant to be a blind imitation. In fact, most

---

[17] Ashraf Salama, "The Architecture of Gamal Bakry" in *Medina*, issue 21, April 2002, p. 28.
[18] Personal communication with Gamal Bakry, 3 October, 2004. Gamal Bakry's office. Dokki.

of his interior decoration and designs are inspired from local, Pharaonic, Islamic and Bedouin art. Gamal Bakry for instance, designed a wooden chair, which is similar to Marcel Breuer's African chair, but it is inspired by typical Egyptian motifs. It has been on display in one of the London Museums. Gamal Bakry opened a joint office in Berlin with German partners, which they named E + G (Egypt + Germany). The office worked from 1974 to 1992. German architects, for Bakry, were the real masters of modernity and functionality. He owes them his training, his love for Bauhaus furniture and ultimately his success. The joint Egyptian-German office realized many successful projects in Egypt and in Saudi Arabia. Bakry however, believes that the Nasser regime's adoption of Bauhaus was distorted. Officers did not seem to know much about architecture and lacked a visionary outlook, said Bakry.[19] The only exception to that rule was the officer 'Ali Nassar who had a training in architecture and therefore ran successfully *sharikat a-ta'mir wal massakin al-sha'biyya* (The Construction Company and Popular housing). The Nasser period, according to him was the worst period for Egypt's architectural development. The moment all urban construction institutions were taken by the military in 1961, things went wrong because they had little or no knowledge about the profession. "The very next day there was a 50 percent increase in all related prices."[20]

Continuities

Why then dwell on archaeology of the sixties' consumer culture? Many commentators perceive the transition from the Nasser regime to that of Sadat as symbolizing a complete break between two epochs, as two antagonistic philosophies. The popular view maintains that the Nasserite philosophy was based on "socialism", nationalizing and Egyptianizing foreign companies, import substitution and industrialization through state monopoly, as the antithesis of the following epoch, which was characterized by a liberalization of the economy. *Infitah*, or "opening up" was geared towards global markets and intensive foreign investment. Nasser, who never denied his modest origins,

---

[19] Personal communication with Gamal Bakry.
[20] "In the Words of the Architect" (Interview with Gamal Bakry), *Medina*, issue 21, April 2002, p. 12.

maintained rhetoric in support of the poor and destitute. The Revolution's motto was "social justice", the rapprochement of class differences and "self-sufficiency". When Sadat launched the May counter revolutionary attack, he swiftly eliminated the pro-Nasser supporters. The philosophy of socialism and social welfare, which required an omnipresent state, was under attack.

This popular view is evidently mistaken in romanticizing Nasserism. I will argue that the logical outcome of the post colonial stage, as exemplified in Nasser's "state capitalism", had inevitably to lead to the subsequent stage of liberalizing the economy. A closer look at the nature of the capitalist class in Egypt reveals a certain continuity, a perpetuation of alliances typical of family capitalism. Gamal 'Abdel Nasser was right when in a 1956 press interview, he lamented that Egypt was mainly ruled by sixteen families which controlled the closely intertwined political, social and economic domains.[21] These families had produced all the ministers, prime ministers and influential politicians during the monarchy. Astonishingly, several of these powerful families continued to survive and even flourished during Nasser's time, by making alliances with the ascending military classes and the bureaucrats. Several members of the old landed class ended up running the sequestrated and nationalized public sector companies in the early sixties. Sometimes, they became the managers of their own companies after nationalization. This was due to the fact that the military officers who took over lacked the know-how and still had to rely on the expertise of the "ancient regime". For instance, when the *Stella Beer Company* was nationalized, the government appointed 'Omar Foda as the manager, a former "ancient regime" landowner and Ph.D. holder from the US in food technology (completed in 1952). Foda also later became director of Coca Cola and Pepsi Cola companies.[22] His brother Daoud Foda whose company was sequestrated and (who was also the director of the Ford Company), ended up after long years of sequestration becoming a financial director of

---

[21] Samia Sa'id Imam, *man yamluk misr (Who Owns Egypt)*, Dar al-Mustaqbal al-'Arabi, Cairo, 1986, p. 53.

[22] In 1968 'Omar Foda made one of the largest beer export deals with Rumania which brought to Egypt circa $4 million, a significant sum for that period. According to his son, he was given the credit during Nasser's time for having made Stella, Coca-Cola and Pepsi-Cola successful, profit making state companies. (See picture . . .) Personal communication with Joyce Foda and Hussein Foda at Mehri Foda 3 March 2005.

the nationalized Corona, Nadler and Royal and the Hawamdiyyah companies.[23] A certain continuity is also to be observed in the seventies during the open door policy.

As Samia Sa'id Imam has argued, many of the capitalist families that resurfaced during the seventies' open-door policies are nothing but "old wine in new bottles" that is the same pre-1952 families were back again, but with hegemonic power. Many of the members of the old class survived by being given the management of many "nationalized" and later public sector companies during Nasser's time. For example, the Nasserite state allowed many public sector companies to be run by former wealthy families such as 'Othman Ahmed 'Othman, Hassan 'Allam, Mukhtar Ibrahim and al-'Abd.[24] The old classes had forged ties to foreign capital, which eased the task of remerging financially in the seventies. These same families became the major intermediaries and profiteers of the open door policies. Here, also, one should be reminded that many contractors like 'Othman Ahmed 'Othman, the Sawiris family, the Sabbours and others accumulated their wealth by working in Saudi Arabia and Libya well before the *infitah* policy was implemented. In relation to this topic, Saudi and Gulf capital also played an important role during the *infitah* and Mubarak's era of joint projects such as the Four Seasons chain, of which a major share belongs to Prince Walid Bin Talal, the Majid al Futaim group who invested in Carrefour, and the Saudi Sharbatly and Shobokshi families who invested in City Stars.

However, Nasser's project of modernization, although anti-colonial in rhetoric, was yet much caught up in Western mental constructions and stereotypes. Certainly, there was an attempt since the revolution to Egyptianize capitalism as a reaction to the dominant influence of foreign capitalism before 1952. European companies and the *mutamassirun* (people of foreign origin who became residents), together with the landed bourgeoisie were largely controlling the economy. But most specialists of the period agreed that the economy could be designated as "growth without development".[25] On

---

[23] Personal Communication with Mehri Foda, 17 February, 2005.
[24] Samia Sa'id Imam, p. 84.
[25] Moheb Zaki, *Egyptian Business Elites. Their Visions and Investment Behaviour*, Konrad-Adenauer-Stiftung and Arab Centre for Development and Future Research, 1999, p. 47.

the other hand, the radical break with tradition, which predominated amongst the majority of nationalist movements, was taking place propelled by the need for change, to industrialize and modernize. Modernizing meant to import fully Western lifestyles, apparels, architecture, and items, but with attempts at local adaptations and local production. My argument is that Nasser's model of development sustained a large middle class, which developed consumerist lifestyles that were mainly influenced by an amalgamation of both the Western consumerist model and the socialist model. It is true that one had to wait long months before obtaining the subsidized state car, the "Nasr". The nationally produced car was nothing but the local assembly of the successful Italian "Fiat" cars. As will be discussed later, fashion, furniture and partying for the better off classes was modelled according to Western ideals. The Free Officers succeeded in liberating the country from British hegemony. But, apparently, they took over without having a clear-cut ideology that would lead to indigenous development. We should be reminded that at the start of his career, Nasser was an admirer of the US. We are told that he quickly became disappointed when Americans refused to assist him with aid. Thus, the Soviet Union seemed to have been his second choice. Although Egypt received significant aid from the Communist bloc, Nasser was vehemently antagonistic to communism. He manifested it by jailing and torturing large numbers of communists as well as the Muslim Brothers. Following this logic, we are told that the revolution had initially great hopes that the private sector would expand. It announced recurrently that private property would not be affected. But resistance from the old capitalists was felt since no investment in the productive sector had occurred. Samia Said Imam tells us that at the start of the period of the five-year plan of 1960–1965, the private sector was involved in more than 95 percent of the agrarian sector and 90 percent of the industrial sector, while most of the construction and external commerce was in the hands of the private sector. When the regime thought of erecting a public sector, it was originally meant to provide an infrastructure for the expansion of the private sector. However, this did not materialize, for the regime was not ideologically consistent from the start. The attempts of the Nasser regime should rather be understood as "trial and error" endeavours mainly due to the uncooperative and underdeveloped nature of private capitalism, which as

Moheb Zaki argues, was mostly agrarian origin and lacking an adventurous spirit.[26]

The free officers were clearly concerned with the social issue and the toppling of the "ancient regime". Yet, while Nasser's socialist ideals and consecutive agrarian reforms[27] did hamper the power of the previous feudalists, they never really managed to totally eliminate their influence. In fact, many of the old families survived quite well under Nasser. The *'Izba* system[28] with its coercive work measures, exemplified by the *ghafirs* who stood in the field with a stick behind the women and children, continued even under the socialist regime. Ironically, the *tarahil* workers, (homeless, seasonal workers), who were the most destitute class, disappeared only during Sadat's time, when the door for migration to Iraq, Jordan and the oil producing countries was opened. The paradox of the Sadat era is that for the first time in history peasants acquired passports and travelled. This certainly affected labour relations in old *'izbas*, if it did not destroy them. Daily wages soared and for the first time landowners could no longer find workers to toil on their land. At the same time, international migration was, in effect, a modern form of slavery because the Egyptian fellahin were at the total mercy of the local sponsors in the hosting country, and were also subject to passport confiscation and inhuman working conditions. Many ended up fighting in the Iraq-Iran war and thousands disappeared or lost their lives. However, some commentators still see that it liberated them from the old *'izba* system. Peasants travelled and "saw the world".

The sixties consumerism, under Nasser was the result of the expansion of the state projects of industrialization and economic development. A large bureaucratic-technocratic middle class grew up, parallel to the expanding military which was increasingly given civil and political functions in the government. In contrast, the seventies and eighties thus witnessed a wild privation and a sporadic expansion of

---

[26] Ibid., pp. 84–85.

[27] The 1952 revolution restricted first land ownership to 200 feddans; then in 1961 to 100 feddans, finally to 50 Feddans in 1969. The consequence of the reform was the redistribution of 365, 247 feddans to 146, 496 families. See Arthur Goldschmidt and Robert Johnston, *Historical Dictionary of Egypt*, New Revised Edition, The American University in Cairo Press, 2004, p. 229. Entry: Land Reform.

[28] *'Izbas* were large farms which existed before the 1952 revolution with a highly organised coercive labour system. These could be compared to the Latin American *Haciendas*.

socially ascending new middle classes with a new purchasing power.
Analysts see a continuity and re-emergence of the old class of "family capitalists", with the appearance of a new class of parasitic "nouveau riche" capitalists who accumulated wealth through short term
investments in the service sector, mainly in money lending, money
exchange and land speculation.[29]

In a recent study on the contemporary businessmen of Egypt,
Ahmed Thabet argued that neo-liberalism and privatization has led
to encouraging export mainly by allowing businessman to obtain
bank loans.[30] Furthermore, businessmen were given advantages that
exempted them from market competition so that they could buy
public sector companies. In other words, these advantages constituted a form of state protectionism.[31] Structural adjustment meant
increasing financial intervention from international organizations and
donors in which the state plays an intermediate role between these
organizations and the people. But the fact that it is the state or its
banks that are funding the business class with loans means that it
has played an important role in boosting this class so that it can
replace the state in various productive sectors.[32]

The simple fact is that today there is a businessmen's association
in Cairo with some 450 members and another financial association
in Alexandria. That these include members of the National Party,
politicians, bankers and investors[33] tells us that businessmen constitute an increasingly important lobby. Thabet's empirical study revealed
that most of the businessmen preferred to collaborate closely with
the state, which has increasingly come to act like a private company. In addition, many former ministers, their sons and relatives
have turned themselves into businessmen with extended family ties
and marriage alliances within the bureaucratic and state elite and
the business world. Thus, borderlines between the world of business
and the government have become blurred. However, the businessmen as a group, because of their inner rivalries, are far from being
a strong and unified entity. Thabet argues that they are not influential

---

[29] Samia Sa'id Imam, pp. 124–125.
[30] Which led to a massive capital flight.
[31] Ahmed Thabet, *nukhbat rigal al-a'mal fi-misr* (The Elite Businessmen in Egypt)
in: *al-nukhab al-ijtima'iyyah halat al-gaza'ir wa-masr* (Elites in Algeria and Egypt) ed.
Ahmed Zayed and Arous al-Zubair, Madbuli, Cairo, 2005, p. 412.
[32] Ibid., p. 414.
[33] Ibid., p. 417.

in political decision-making. Moreover, the long history of authoritarianism means that the government is likely to overreact to any independent pressure group that might emerge from business circles.[34] It seems that, in retrospect, in spite of the many government facilities, the business class achieved very little because it did not invest in big industries or in the infrastructure, and it failed to boost local industries, instead, it encouraged an atmosphere of *mafiaisation* and recurrence to terror to liquidate competitors.[35] Moheb Zaki argues that businessmen have gained increasing power during the last two decades, but with much ambiguity because the ultimate power holder is an authoritarian regime backed by the army. There seems to be a consensus that the businessmen do not constitute a cohesive or single voice, but are rather divided into factions and conflicting interest groups according to Moheb Zaki. There are conflicts, for instance, between industrialists and importers over the issue of tariff protection for domestic industries.[36]

The class issue, although addressed by the Nasser regime is still poignant and unresolved. The evidence presented here reveals rather a continuity in the transition from Nasser to Sadat's regime, more so a counter-revolution. Galal Amin claims that the regime in the fifties and sixties was generous with the poorer classes because it could rely on foreign aid, either Soviet or American, and thus it never really managed to develop an indigenous model of development, or a genuine perspective on import substitution. Many commentators see that Soviet assistance was benign since the Russian experts departed from Egypt so rapidly without any strings attached. It is difficult to envision such an end to the current American presence in Egypt, which has been connected to Egypt's peace treaty with Israel and its strategic role in the reordering of the world according the doctrine of *Pax-Americana*.

Transformations/Metamorphosis in Continuity

Many belonging to the generation coming to maturity in the '60's would agree that the most drastic change they ever experienced in

---

[34] Ahmed Thabet, p. 422.
[35] Ahmed Thabet, ibid., p. 429.
[36] Moheb Zaki, Egyptian Business Elite . . ., p. 132.

their lifestyle was during Sadat's *infitah* (the open door policy), which revolutionized their consumer habits. It was during Anwar al-Sadat's time that Egyptians discovered the unlimited desires, but also frustrations and deceptions, related to the eternal unfulfilled wishes of consumption. Sadat's shift from alliance with the Soviet Union to the Western world in the early 1970's was symbolized by the policy of the "open door" economic policy (1974). Concretely, this meant further privatization at the expense of destroying the "public sector" and the state monopoly over large-scale industries. Foreign investors were invited to bring in capital. The World Bank and the IMF's increasing intervention in internal Egyptian economic planning decisions followed this.[37] The Nasser regime's achievement in "import substitution" came under attack. Many forget that the discourse of the Nasserist regime was to achieve an indigenous model of development with the motto: "from the needle to the rocket" (*minal – ibra ilal sarukh*) i.e., self-sufficiency to counteract the hegemonic West. The shift from the Nasserist "state capitalist" era to full integration into the world capitalist system went hand in hand with encouraging consumerism as a new lifestyle for Egyptians. This led to an astonishing and swift transformation in the consumption norms and shopping habits of Egyptians.[38] On the one hand, the Nasser regime through its socialist orientation had led to the creation of middle classes with consumerist attitudes, which were "somehow" fulfilled by the expansion of a local production. This went hand in hand with "somehow" isolating the country from international markets (though actually allowing some production).[39] Yet at the same time, the long years of Nasserist ideology, emphasizing massive investment to build up primary industries, encouraged belt-tightening and frugality among these very same middle classes.

For some fortunate Egyptians the *Infitah* transformation was symbolized by boasting of changing from smoking the Egyptian *Cleopatra*,

---

[37] Although Galal Amin argues that the close relationship with the World bank and the IMF only began in the mid seventies, *Whatever Else Happened to he Egyptians*, AUC Press, 2004, p. 118.

[38] I speak here of middle class Egyptians.

[39] The expression "somehow" is used because a thorough reading of the Egyptian newspapers reveals that foreign imported goods were never totally prevented from coming into the country, but availability was restricted to the various elites.

Nefertiti and *Belmont*[40] cigarettes to the American Marlboro and Kent brands which cost double if not triple the price of Egyptian cigarettes, from driving the locally produced "Fiat" and "Nasr" cars to higher status BMW and Mercedes, and from home made clothes to imported clothes. The local Coca-Cola, Randa and Sinalco, all notorious for swimming cockroaches, were replaced with imported cans. In the 1960's *Masr-Cola* had been advertised in *Rose al-Youssef* magazine as the new national beverage, which cost one

Fig. 30. *Al-Mussawar*, 3 June 1966, no. 2173, Cigarettes.

Fig. 31. Nefertiti Cigarette *Akher Sa'ah*, 27 July 1973.

and a half piaster. Even though inflation rocketed during Sadat's time, the number of those who could afford to purchase non-essential goods increased. Many still recall the outrageous commercial *insif hammamac al-qadim* (blow your old bathroom) and replace it with fancy ceramic. It symbolized the coming era of affluence Galal Amin's main argument in *Whatever Else Happened to the Egyptians* is that the 1970's and 1980's witnessed a most impressive rate of growth in the size of the middle class, and a sudden increase

---

[40] Astonishingly, there were several brands of locally produced cigarettes by the Eastern Company. During the sixties the *Al-Musawar* magazine advertised the following brands: *Cleopatra, Nefertiti, Florida, (Shariakat al Nasr lil dukhan wal saga'er). Belmont (Eastern Company), Cairo, 555 filter Kings, Paxton* (a product of *Philip Morris*) and *Simiramis and Craven A.*

in their wealth. Migration and the expansion of intermediary services were two reasons for including larger sections of the society
into the middle class and providing them with new purchasing power.
This went hand in hand with the widening disparity between income
groups and the monopoly of wealth in the hands of a few.[41]

Downtown Shawarbi Street epitomized the height of the "*infitah*
period*". Shawarbi Street displayed all brands of imported clothes,
consumer durables, gadgets and video films that were either smuggled or brought from the free zone trade of the town of Port Said.
The Wimpy food chain became popular and was followed years later
by McDonald's and Kentucky Fried Chicken. Advertisements on television, already existent during Nasser's time but strictly controlled
by the state and unattractive, gained prominence and expanded, with
private businessmen such as Tareq Nur producing hundreds of successful and appealing commercials. The '60s commercials popularized the idea of opening savings accounts, learning how to save water
by properly closing taps,[42] and purchasing Melamine plastic plates
and other Egyptian brands. In the seventies and eighties, commercials had plenty of sexy blonde young women (Western and Egyptian
Western looking) constantly belly dancing or jerking. Women dressed
as peasants, were also used to advertise in a kind of parody of rural
life, certain brands of food, such as animal fat. Commercials, all
financed by private business, multiplied to include hundreds of items
ranging from food, to household goods, to bathrooms and lavish furniture, to mobile phones (in the late '90s, early 2000). In the eighties, *Al-Ahram* newspaper started to advertise the idea of "gated
communities" of villas and condominiums in the desert. The ads
portrayed a small family of four members in the garden of a lavish
two storey villa relaxing by a swimming pool. Golf courses, swimming pools, gyms and saunas were annexes to the villa complex.
Amusement parks were introduced to Egyptians in the late eighties.
In short, the American suburban dream was finally exported to the
Egyptian desert.

---

[41] Galal Amin, *Whatever Else Happened to the Egyptians, From the Revolution to the Age
of Globalization*, AUC Press, 2004, pp. 115, 123.

[42] The commercial consisted of a cartoon representing a typical plump middle
class woman. The song started with: (*sitt thaniyya sayba al mayya tirrukh tirrukh min il
hanafiyya . . . haram ya sit thaniyya*) Madam Thaniyya is letting the water drop and
drop. Shame on you Madam Thaniyya.

But *Infitah* meant further American intervention. Many viewed American aid as creating a direct state of dependency with very pervasive strings attached. The role of the state as responsible for social welfare, for economic intervention, for promoting culture and free education was more than ever challenged. Many analysts described the state in the seventies as having been rendered "absent", "weak" or "soft". The implications of the absent state meant that citizens had to search for individual solutions by migrating to the oil pro- ducing countries. In the eighties some well-placed officials publicly stated that Sadat's policies were only succeeding in transferring financial resources and foreign currency out of the country.[43]

Sonallah Ibrahim's novel *Zaat* is a rich documentation of the trans- formation of consumer habits in the seventies and eighties, which also conveys the high level of corruption and the rotten political and social atmosphere. The newspapers statements related to the *infitah* period in *Zaat* are worth mentioning as a sharp critique of Sadat's policies. For example the then Minister of Finance Dr. Mostafa el- Said declared: "The huge foreign currency reserves that Egypt built up between 1975–1981 have been completely squandered on luxury goods rather than being used to import essential items and produc- tive requirements, or to reduce the country's debt".[44]

The epoch of the seventies, so well described in *Zaat*, will be thus remembered for the emergence of the *nouveau riche* vulgar culture of quick money making, of discriminating, abusing and torturing the working class, of the dissolution of trade unions, of numerous frauds, of smuggling money out of the country, of incidental fires to dis- mantle public sector companies and of massive food poisoning scan- dals. All this was done under the authority, or rather in collaboration with government officials.

Household Consumption

Whereas the previous sections incessantly shifted between the Nasser and Sadat periods with the aim of providing a contrast, to complete the picture, a flashback to the sixties' household consumption is what

---

[43] Statement by Dr. Mustafa el Said, the then Minister of Finance, quoted from Sonallah Ibrahim, *Zaat*, AUC Press, 2004, p. 26.
[44] Sonallah Ibrahim, *Zaat*, p. 37.

follows. Upper and middle class families grew up with one or two brands of bad quality powder soap for clothes, *Rabso* and then *Savo* brands.[45] We had no washing machines and certainly no dishwashers because domestic servants were abundant; at least, this was the case until the early seventies.[46] A washerwoman came once or twice a week. The washerwoman used to sit on the bathroom floor in front of a large basin to wash our clothes. She also performed other tasks for the female members of the family, such as removal of hair from legs and arms, using *halawa* (waxing, made out of cooking lemon and sugar).

Many would also recall the significance of the *namliyya* (a kitchen cupboard that served for storing food items such as rice and oil). Those who had spacious houses had a *karar*, which consisted of a room where large quantities of food, oil, tea, coffee, lentils, rice, soap and other items were stored. The *namliyya* was a typical item in many middle class households; it always had to be locked for fear that the servants would steal. But the point was that one obtained with the ration card large quantities of one brand or another of sugar, tea, soap or rice, when it was available on the market. One feared shortages all the time. The art was then where and how to purchase goods. From time to time, rice, *ishta* (cream) and *fetir mushaltit* (a special peasant pastry) was provided from the countryside. The *namliyya* was later replaced by large freezers and microwaves. The idea of purchasing large quantities of food to be frozen did not become popular, I would say, before the eighties.

My family had plastic "melamine" plates and stainless steal cutlery for everyday use, while the china set and silverware were locked and on display in the salon, only to be used on important occasions. The plastic tablecloth on the dining table was for everyday usage while the embroidered tablecloth was only for guests or rare occasions. But how different would such a practice be from say a German or American housewife of that period? It seems to me again that all this was an import, or an emulation of an American or Western "modern" functional ideal.

---

[45] However, I found in *Akher Saʿah*, 3 August, 1966, no. 1658 an ad for Tide powder, advertised as 'America's Favorite'. p. 32.
[46] Our first Egyptian produced washing machine was semi automatic, which still required a lot of manual work.

Everyone who was an adolescent in the sixties remembers the Egyptian television commercial *ana al-milamin gamed wa-matin* (I am the strong and solid Melamine). Another public sector company, the plastic company *sharikat al-blastic*, produced these plastic plates, boxes and other household goods. Its aim was to promote economical products for newly wed couples.

Fig. 32. Bata Ad.
Akher Sa'ah. 14–6–1966.

Many would remember how the empty whiskey bottles were recycled for cold water. No one ever thought of buying bottles of mineral water, these did not appear until the eighties. Biscuit tins served for multiple purposes, and all sorts of fancy wrapping paper were reused for wrapping presents. Those who possessed rare imported luxury goods were looked upon as the "elite" in the period of the sixties. When my grandfather purchased a television in the early sixties, he made strict rules about when to watch it and to switch it off. He allowed us to watch television for only one hour, or maximum two hours, claiming that more of it would ruin our health. Once the television was switched off, it was carefully covered. At that time, TV programs transmitted only in black and white. Before the intrusion of the satellites, I recall that we listened to BBC World service and later on to Radio Monte Carlo.

Fig. 33. Gil Ad.
Akher Sa'ah, 28–9–1966.

Girls played with the locally produced "Sabrina" dolls. These rather fat and kitschy looking dolls with impossible to comb, disintegrating hair could certainly not compete with the popular Barbie dolls which could not be legally imported but were sold on the black market. But there was always someone in my class, or a wizard cousin who showed off her Barbie doll and thus drew envy and admiration. Lego games, matchbox cars, Batman, Robin and the Bat woman dolls and Superman clothes belonged to the sacred class of imported toys. We grew up with Chinese toupee and mechanical toys, but as children we despised then. Yet today, these toys are considered "antiques" by collectors in the Western world.

Bata shops, selling locally produced shoes, existed everywhere and everybody could purchase the white sports shoes, among other types of shoes. There were two shops downtown, which sold children's clothes, and I recall my mother taking us there twice a year. Notably *Gil* Company made male and female underwear of Egyptian cotton. *Gil* has survived and has gained a good reputation and was even exported to Europe.

Many who experienced the Nasserite era would say that much less money was available, but also much less was spent because there were not enough luxury goods to be purchased by those who could afford them. Fathers saved money for each member of the family in a *daftar tawfir* at the post office (a bank savings book). The *shariqat al-ta'min* (the insurance company) propagated the idea of the importance of having a life insurance and *shariqat al-ta'amin 'amla bulisa li-'amm amin* became a famous Nasserite ad. Frugality and saving were the dominant culture that many grew up with. This being said, it did not apply to everybody as will be discussed in the following chapter.

The state employees adopted an informal uniform that reminded many of similarities in other socialist countries. Many will recall the famous government slogan, *al badla al-sha'biyya ahsan min al-galabeyya*: the popular suit is better than the *galabeyya* (the long peasant robe). Was not this the best example of the regime's imagination of modernization? Away with *baladi* culture? But then what really happened was that lower classes had to be torn apart into two bodies. Two clashing lifestyles? Maybe not. One body, or one outfit was adopted for the outside official world, the trousers, ties and shirts, or the uniform. This was the elevated world of the *affandiyya*. Meanwhile, the *galabeyya* survived very well in the realm of the private sphere, which extended to the popular quarter, the *hara*. Hence, once men returned home, they immediately took off the official attire, to relax in *galabeyyas* in which they felt at ease in the sphere of the local quarter, among the neighbours, at public gatherings and in the coffee house.[47] The space of the quarter, or the dead-end alley is, according to Janet Abu Lughod, interpreted as a semiprivate space, as a the third category between public and private, where a compromise for some freedom of movement for women was given.[48] It is possible to draw a similarity with India in the colonial period when Indians changed clothes according to the occasions in order to maintain "two distinct sartorial identities, an Indian and an European one". According to Emma Tarlo, this enabled "a person to dress according to different and often incompatible standards of cultural correctness."[49] Tarlo then asks if this has led to cultural dualism. Concerning Egypt, it is possible to argue that whatever were the attempts at modernising garments, it seems that the popular world of *galabeyyas* continued to coexist with the *affandiyyas*. But for how long? More and more in the countryside, one observes that young men working on the land are today dressed in jeans and trousers, whereas rural women seem to be more resistant to change. The male *galabeyya*, on the other hand, seems to be related to the life cycle. Increasingly, men who wore trousers in their youth, shift to *galabeyyas* when they get older.

In the late seventies with male migration to the oil producing countries, the *galabeyya* underwent interesting changes. A Saudi Arabian white, semi-transparent *galabeyya* with a high-buttoned collar became popular, in contrast to the traditional peasant *galabeyya* with a low round opaque collar, dark in colour and with ample sleeves. This coincided with a spreading popular image of the rich *hagg* (title given to the pilgrim) who was possibly a rich contractor or an entrepreneur. Another change has been the introduction of the Western shirt collar to the *galabeyya*.

---

[47] The tension between the *galabeyya* and trousers culture is wonderfully depicted Ibrahim Aslan's novel *Nile Sparrows*, AUC Press, 2004. One character, 'Abdel Reheem originating from the countryside dates a Cairene nurse who refuses to go out with him to the cinema in *galabeyya*. The way she expressed her shame and despise of rural culture is beautifully described in the novel.

[48] Janet Abu Lughod, "The Islamic City: Historic Myths, Islamic Essence, and Contemporary Relevance", first Published in *International Journal of Middle East Studies* (1987), I cite it from the: "*The City Reader*" Edited by Richard T. Legates and Frederic Stout, Routledge Urban Reader Series, First Published 1996, Third Edition, 2000, pp. 172–181, p. 178.

[49] Emma Tarlo, Clothing Matters, Dress and Identity in India, The University of Chicago Press, 1996, p. 52.

Those who are nostalgic for this epoch would claim that in fact people were rather satisfied with what they had and less resentful of the continuous unfulfilled expectations of consumerism. Nevertheless, to believe that the fifties and sixties development was mainly based on an indigenous autochthonous worldview would equally be misleading. Ironically enough the increase of consumption during the 1950s and '60s were according to Galal Amin due to: "the revolutionary government resorted to external sources, either through the nationalization of the foreign assets inside of Egypt (such as the Suez Canal or foreign banks and insurance companies) or through foreign loans. It is probably safe to say that it was that sizable flow of foreign resources into Egypt that enabled the Egyptian state in the 1950's and 1960's to show such generosity towards the lowest classes on the social ladder, without at the same time granting them any real say in social affairs of state."[50]

The enemies of Nasser would counter pose him to Sadat by arguing that abundance and display was the major achievement of Sadat, but if this were true why did then the masses riot in 1977 when the IMF ordered that subventions be lifted from basic goods such as bread, oil and soap? Life never became rosy for the poor in the seventies. It needed a tiny increase in prices to pour oil on fire. It so happened with the *intifadat al-haramiyya* (the outbreak of thieves) as Sadat insolently dared to call it. The debate over the financial losses of the public sector and the serial fire incidents of the state factories that caused bankruptcies raised many questions about intentions, which aimed at weakening the role of the state.

Shopping

In the sixties, the women of my family wore short, colourful, fashionable sleeveless dresses, as well as shorts and trousers. The elderly wore bathing suits, while teenage girls wore bikinis. I found pictures of my mother, as well as my grandmother, wearing trousers in the forties and fifties. I found a picture of my grandmother, probably in the thirties or forties posing in a bathing suit. Until the mid-seventies no one seemed to be bothered by the sight of bikinis. Today,

---

[50] Galal Amin, *Whatever Else Happened to the Egyptians*, AUC Press, 2004, p. 141.

these are only to be seen in private beaches such as Agami or others on the north coast. Even at the Gezira club, women very rarely wear bikinis in mixed swimming pools. With the growing Islamization, a special day has been dedicated for women to swim at the Gezira club. It is impossible for men to peep into the swimming pool area, because it is carefully encircled with thick cloth. However, even on that day, one can see women swimming in Islamic bathing suits. These consist of leggings and long sleeves T-shirts, which are worn underneath a bathing suit. An extra skirt tops the whole outfit. These outfits look very uncomfortable in the water. Often water penetrates through these multiple layers of clothes and women then look like blown-up balloons.

الموضة

ثلاث موديلات يقدمها محل لوليتا ٠٠ قامت بتصميمها صاحبة المحـــل ومديرته مـــادام دنيــس قلـــاس ٠٠ الموديلات الثــــلاثة للربيـــع القـــادم والأقمشة المستعملة التيـل الموجاتيـل للفساتيـن المســـــادة ٠٠ والأنابـــاك الفستان من الحرير الطبيعي والبالطومن التيل الموجاتيـل ٠٠

Fig. 34. *Rosa al Youssef.* The page of Madiha, 14 Feb., 1966.

Magazine articles spread information about fashions and shopping for the new ascending Cairene classes. *Tahiyati ila zawgik al-ʿaziz,* "(my) Regards to Your Beloved Husband" was the page signed by Madiha in the weekly *Rosa al Youssef* magazine during the sixties and seventies.[51] Illustrations and sketches of the latest fashions often accompanied the articles from Paris, London and Rome and the latest hairstyles, shoes and accessories. Some of these designs were reproduced directly from Western magazines; others were emulations of Western fashion drawn by Egyptians, foreigners and Levantines living in Cairo. Madiha's topics included descriptions of the latest fashions in Europe, sales and "occasions" and the most stylish Egyptian *maisons de couture* and where to find the most recent inexpensive silk ties and socks,

---

[51] I found the first article of Madiha published in *Rosa-Youssef,* in 18 May 1953 and it was about the best shopping places and the sales of the *grands magasins* downtown. Madiha still writes for *Rosa al-Youssef,* nonetheless, her articles turned to be increasingly political to include news about the *majlis al-shura,* politicians and intellectuals. See *Rosa-al Youssef* 5/6/1995 no. 3495 p. 62. She also wrote acerbic comments on television serials on how un-appropriate the interior decor in houses of the former upper classes and the royal family have been portrayed. See *Rosa al-Youssef,* 29/12/2001–4/1/2002 no. 3838, p. 96.

male sweaters and pyjamas, children's clothes, shoes and what not. Several shops and boutiques were mentioned with precise descriptions of addresses and prices. Madiha extended her investigation to expensive furniture and auctions that sold all sorts of antiques. Benevolent associations, which produced cheap "tricot" dresses and other items, by employing poor young females, were advertised. Precise prices of fabrics, clothes, stockings and many other household items were given, including where to find the most recent imported clothes, perfumes and accessories. Abundant gossip, life histories, scandals, and love affairs about the shop owners, big factory owners, down-

Fig. 35. Sednaoui Ad. Bikini Girl. Akher Sa'ah 27 July 1966.

town boutiques and business families were a source of inspiration for Madiha's articles.[52] She also told us where the best *maison de couture* was to be found, and news about the travels, imports and last sales of the owners. Madiha's page reveal that she was catering to the middle classes which sought a kind of "clever" and economical shopping, but she also points to the luxurious and well do to "informal sector" markets of the declining upper classes. Moreover, Madiha extended her consumer inquiries in the early seventies to good quality restaurants and coffee houses such as the restaurants with attractive views located on the Nile in Ma'adi.[53]

Quite often, her articles seemed to have included several unrelated topics as if they were a flow of disconnected ideas. I took randomly the issue of 18 January 1965, in which Madiha informed the reader about the most recent 'cris' in European (London, Rome and Paris) fashions. Madiha started by saying that with Ramadan just over and Egyptians having spent all their savings on the religious occasion, shopping in Cairo is stagnant, but in Europe sales have started. She described the most recent collection of bikinis and bathing

---

[52] See Madiha, *"tahiyati ila zawgik al-'aziz,* 'hawadit min al-suq'" (Stories from the Suq or market), *Rosa al-Youssef,* 13 October, 1969, no. 2157, pp. 48–49.
[53] Madiha, *Rosa al-Youssef,* 11 October, 1971, no. 3361, pp. 47–49.

Fig. 36. Sednaoui Hall

suits of Coco Chanel, which have finally appeared on European markets. The year's fashion bikinis consisted of silver and golden threads
to produce the "dentelle". The bikini came with a matching cache-
maillot made from an identical fabric. The bikinis are very tiny and
the *dentelle* reveals the most sensitive parts of the body. The latest
craze in Paris was the very short mini-skirts. In Rome, most of the
models wore *dentelle*, transparent dresses which looked as if the wearer
had nothing else on underneath. Madiha then takes us to the Khan
al-Khalili Bazaar to notice its unchanging character over hundreds
of years. The products there have not changed. Madiha picked a
lamp, a copper water pipe. She then describes the gold shops and
the incense, and ends up saying that successful buying in the traditional bazaar depends mainly on cleverness in bargaining. In another
issue Madiha informs the reader about various newly arrived items
in the *grand magasin* Shalon. These include a new purple colour face
powder for blonds and brown powder for brunettes.[54] Jean Patoux,
La Roche, Nina Ricci, Pierre Cardin, Coco Chanel's latest fashions

---

[54] Madiha, "tahiyati ila zawgik al-'aziz", *Rosa al-Youssef*, 31 January, 1966, no.
1964 pp. 38–39.

are also reported in another article entitled "The new fashion and heat".[55] Clearly, *Rosa al-Youssef* magazine was a good source of information of the latest "sales" called in Arabic "okasion" in *Salon Vert* and other *grands magasins*. Summer cloths such as silk, satin, nylon and "mousseline" were announced for sale. Silver plates were sold at the Watchmaker Papazian and many other sales ranging from lipsticks to carpets were advertised. From *Rosa al-Youssef*, one gets the impression that the *grands magasins* that belonged to the public sector, were, up to the late sixties, successful enterprises because these offered big sales of various items. In 1964 *Akher Sa'ah* published an article titled "okasion" with amazing pictures that revealed how packed and well frequented were the sales in the department stores. Thousands of women were rushing to buy cloth, children's toys and bicycles. One picture shows that even traffic policemen took special days off to purchase goods on sale.[56] In 1969, Madiha again informs us that in spite of the quiet sales that year, *sharikat bi' al-masnu'at* (the Textile Company) managed to earn daily around sixty thousand pounds, while the *Salon Vert* daily turnover sale circa L.E. 30 thousand. Cicurel and Hannaux *grands magasins* earned circa L.E. 25 thousand. This is due to the fact that the prices offered were extremely low.[57]

In the issue of 13 July 1964, *Rosa al-Youssef* Magazine[58] advertised that Nussa, the owner of Nussa shops has just arrived from Europe and brought with her the most recent fashions in bathing suits from Christian Dior (the prices are ranging from L.E 8 to 12) and bonnets (ranging from L.E. 5 to 10). A lady from Garden City had opened an atelier for sewing where she trains housewives and middle-class young girls, under the direction of a specialist. The designer and owner of Nur shops has won a diploma from a University in Rome. Nur presented for the exam a dress on the theme of the High Dam made out of silver (Brocard). Nur was amongst the first graduates of this university (which name is not mentioned) and his project was received with great admiration.

Already in 1969, one year before Nasser's death Madiha laments about the creeping free market (*al-suq al-hurra*) that had flooded

[55] Madiha, *Rosa al-Youssef*, 31 February, 1966, no.1967, p. 50.
[56] Hafez Imam, "al-okasiun" (The Sales), *Akher Sa'ah*, 12 February 1964, no. 1529, pp. 12–13.
[57] Madiha, *Rosa al-Youssef*, 17 February, 1969, no. 2133, p. 44.
[58] *Rosa al-Youssef*, 13 July 1964, p. 41.

Cairene shops with imported goods. These goods were being sold for hard currency, and most of them were illegally imported. The shops located in downtown Kasr Al-Nil Street are selling unaffordable expensive refrigerators, whereas Egypt still produces inexpensive, good quality Ideal refrigerators. The down town markets also offered tape recorders, radios, furniture, perfumes, soap, beauty products. Madiha wonders why Egypt should import beauty creams if the country can produce similar good quality products? Why import fancy useless crystal? Watches, on the other hand are a necessity, but hard currency became a luxury for the few. Those who had access to hard currency can afford to travel and thus purchase such goods cheaply overseas. Madiha thus concludes that what is offered in the free market is of little use to the middle class consumer. What Egyptian women need is underwear and bras, the production of which is underdeveloped in Egypt. Bathing suits and women's accessories were also needed. They were too expensive in the black market. Madiha ends her article by urging governmental institutions to interfere in order to control the market. Where is the role of the tax control office or the Ministry of Rationing in defending the public from the black market? Madiha warns the reader-consumer to think twice before overspending in such a small and exploitative black market.[59]

Madiha was right, there were many local beauty products, which were available in the local market. To mention a few: Luna lipsticks, *poudre condensée* of Dr. Payot from Paris, deodorant sticks *Odorono*, Williams Hair spray Taft, and hair tint such as Palette. These were all brands advertised in al-*Mussawar* and *Rosa al-Youssef* in the sixties. Whether these were as good a quality as the imported brands is another issue. This lead me to conclude that, first, the black market had already started before *infitah* times, and, second, that contrary to the idea of tightening the belt, various luxury goods were available, but only for the happy few. From the black market, I would like to return to an earlier phase in consumer culture, to the birth of the *grands magasins* in Egypt. My aim is to highlight the fact that the department stores saw the birth at the beginning of last century and they have been extremely pervasive in reshaping modern business, as it offered to women new spaces for flaneuring and shopping.

---

[59] Madiha, *Rosa al-Youssef*, November 1969, no. 2163, p. 44.

Fashion in the 1960's

A large section of middle-class women purchased the German *Burda* magazine, which included sewing patterns. As well-trained, frugal Egyptian housewives, they possessed *Singer* sewing machines.[60] Every middle class housewife took courses in sewing to keep up with the last fashions in Europe. All aunts had such machines.[61] My mother however, quickly gave up the idea of sewing, which she dreaded and resorted to tailors. Many elderly women are nostalgic for such tailors, and for shoemakers who willingly came to homes to draw the size of the foot. Excellent downtown shoes makers were famous for copying the latest models. The shoes were ready in two weeks and cost L.E. 5. in the 1960's. The most expensive shoemaker in Alexandria charged L.E. 10.[62] Despite the feeling of the older generation that one was deprived of luxurious items,[63] the upper middle classes still survived beautifully and had services that have vanished with mass production and the new consumer culture. Until the late sixties, my mother's female tailor, her shoemaker and my father's male tailor often visited our home. There was another female tailor who also came to our house to make clothes for both my sister and me. All these people spent hours fitting dresses and shoes. This was done over long discussions and socializing with my parents while they were sipping their coffee. My mother's tailor could emulate any complicated sophisticated pattern. Indeed, my mother was proud to have an impeccable emulation of the famed Yves Saint Laurent dress, designed in 1965, which was enthused from a Piet Mondrian painting.[64]

---

[60] Singer sewing machines were introduced in Egypt in 1880–1881, when an office was opend in Cairo. Due to political turmoil and Egypt´s declaration of bankruptcy, the company had to retreat. However, Singer company witnessed a success in the Ottoamn region. See Andrew Godley "Singer in Egypt, 1880–1914. (EBHRC) *Economic and Business History Research Centre Chronicles*, October 2005, Volume 1/Issue 2, pp. 16–18.

[61] For the sake of comparison China's major four big items of consumption during communism were sewing machines, watches, bicycles and radio. These shifted with the integration to the capitalist market to six big items, which were colored TV sets, refrigerators, cameras, electric fans, washing machines and tape recorders. Chengze Simon Fan "Economic Development and the Changing Patterns of Consumption in Urban China" in: *Consumption in Asia: Lifestyles and Identities*" Ed. Chua Beng Huat, London, Routledge, 2000, pp. 82–98, (p. 86).

[62] Interview with ʿAfaf Abaza, 23 November 2004. Zamalek.

[63] This sentiment was expressed by both Amina El-Lozi and ʿAfaf Abaza.

[64] Concerning the Piet Mondrian painting made into a dress by Yves Saint Laurent, see Tracy Tolkien *Schick und Schrill, Klassiker der Designermode*. Knesebeck,

Through a network of female relatives and aunts, some merchant women came to homes to sell (smuggled imported) clothes and other gadgets. These female *tuggar al-shanta* (a literal translation would be coffer traders) or women peddlers, provided fabrics, clothes, perfumes, crèmes, pullovers and underwear. Some of these women came on a monthly regular basis and sold all these imported goods at affordable prices.[65] Some aunts for instance, never went to the *grands magasins* in the 1960's but relied rather on ambulant saleswomen who came to their homes. My mother however, disliked this habit. She stopped it after having received a few visits. She felt that strangers were intruding on her privacy. In contrast, this habit was quite frequent among some of my relatives who kept an open house with a constant procession of such commercial visitors. Nancy Young Reynolds points to the fact that "women peddlers" who brought goods to upper class houses already existed by the end of the nineteenth century, as she concluded from the memoirs of Huda Sha'rawi. These were mainly Coptic, Jewish and Armenian and they charged very high prices.[66]

YVES SAINT LAURENT

Fig. 37. Yves Saint Laurent, 1965 Collection. Courtesy of Tracy Tolkien, p. 71.

Downtown well-reputed *maisons de couture*, where one could purchase the latest fashions in clothes, shoes and handbags, seemed to have survived after the 1952 revolution. If we take *al-Ahram's* special issue of 1959, which surveys the industrial and economic achievements of the country, the whole issue could be interpreted as being a propaganda instrument, which boasted the achievements since independence. Two

---

München 2001, English title *Vintage-The Art of Dressing up*. Pavilion Books Limited, p. 71.

[65] In the seventies, French women came to sell such goods. They seem to have commuted often between France and Egypt. (Personal communication with 'Afaf Abaza, Zamalek, 15 October 2004). Women peddlers still exist today. When I was conducting my interview with 'Afaf Abaza, I luckily experienced such a visit at her place. The woman peddler sold her facial crèmes, a sunglass and an evening dress for her grand daughter, which she could keep for a week before deciding to buy it.

[66] Nancy Young Reynolds, p. 196.

pages are dedicated to *haute couture* in Syria and Egypt (Egypt and Syria
were then united). In the same issue, 'Aziz Sedqi the then Minister
of Industry, wrote an article entitled: "The industrial revolution
achieves self-sufficiency".[67] Another article is dedicated to the uni-
fication between Syria and Egypt.[68] A third article is on the achievements of the agrarian reform by Sayyed Mare'i, the then Minister
of Agriculture and agrarian reform.[69] Mare'i states that 565 thousand
feddans had undergone reform and some other fifty-two thousand *feddans* have already been distributed on peasants. Side by side with
the revolutionary achievements, the ads displayed the development
of heavy industries, and other local industries like the Eastern Tobacco
Company, the textile industries, the car industries, shoes, and sugar
production. These are alongside several pictures of the *grands couturiers*
and their fashion shows. Egyptian designers, we are told, although
all influenced by Parisian fashions, are proud of the fabrics made of
Egyptian cotton. Pierre Clovas, Ivonne Madi, and Salha Aflatoun
are mentioned as being the leading fashion designers of the time.[70]
We are told that Salha Aflatoun[71] worked with the pioneer of Egyptian
capitalism, Tal'at Harb, as a consultant to the textile industries,
which belonged to Bank Misr. The article mentions with pride that
she managed to manufacture locally crêpe de Chine, Satin Marocain
and "rayé Taffeta". Aflatoun was arguing that eccentric models might
be eye catching but they might not sell; good designing implied producing fashion without exaggerations to make it convenient for everybody. But the common denominator of the three designers mentioned
is that they are all inspired by European, or rather French *maisons
de couture*. Salha Aflatoun and Ivonne Madi both travelled to Europe
twice a year to follow fashion shows while Clovas derived his inspiration from the Greek ports and beaches. The fancy *défilés* shown in

---

[67] Dr. 'Aziz Sedqui, *"al-thawra al-sinna'iyya tuhaqiq al-iktifa' al-thati"* (*The Industrial
Revolution achieves self-sufficiency*), *Al-Ahram, Special Issue on The Arab Republic of Egypt*.
July 1959, p. 26.

[68] Ibid., p. 12.

[69] Ibid., p. 22.

[70] *Al-Ahram, Special Issue on The Arab Republic of Egypt*. July 1959, p. 88. With the
Designers of the Southern Region (ma'a musammimi al-azya' fil iqlim al-ganubi).
For Syria (*al-iqlim al-shamali*), see p. 121.

[71] Salha Aflatoun was a divorced mother and a daughter of a Pasha who opened
a boutique in Shawarbi Street in 1935 or 1936. She was the exclusive agent for
Christian Dior, Jacques Fathes and Balmain in Egypt. Nancy Young Reynolds,
Commodity Communities . . ., pp. 194–195.

both Syria and Egypt hardly differed from those in Europe at the time. Is not this an astonishing contradiction with the regime's ideology of self-sufficient, indigenous development and yet once it is dealt with fashion, the Mecca remained Europe, especially Paris.

The image of the working woman in the various other articles in this issue looked identical to any European woman. Sportive young women in shorts, playing handball, tennis and hockey seemed to be the norm.[72] The working women in factories all look modern, unveiled and with short sleeves. Salha Aflatoun created her atelier in 1946 to design, the latest European fashions with Egyptian material. In 1962, Aziza Thabet wrote in *Akher Sa'ah* an article praising the fact that Cairo started to design clothes. She makes the point that it has become possible to reproduce locally the latest European fashion. The article was accompanied by a series of pictures of beautiful bourgeois looking Egyptian models, posing in fancy salons and gardens with fine fashionable clothes, some of which were designed by Salha Aflatoun. Bathing suits, *cache maillots* and light sleeveless dresses were also included in the collection. One could conclude that even though the country was undergoing a so-called "isolationist" policy, the well to do classes seemed to have survived well and managed to have a cosmopolitan and modern look.[73]

Fashion was not spared from politics and it became for the sixties a source of pride for the regime as various articles in *Akher Sa'ah* demonstrate. *Al-qahira tussadir al-muda lil 'alam* (Cairo Exports Fashion to the World) is the title of an article written by Thana' al-Bissi in *Akher Sa'ah* in 1963.[74] For the first time, local Egyptian fashion was to be exported to Paris, London and New York. These capitals were now looking at the Egyptian winter collection, which was shown in Alexandria, which lasted for some ten days. Modern, long décolleté evening dresses were shown. Al-Bissi informs the reader that the young model Raga' al-Geddawi designed her own collection with one special embroidered evening dress which she called Cleopatra. The emphasis was on two things: first, it was possible to design fashionable Western clothes, which were inspired from Egypt's traditions.

---

[72] Ibid., p. 118.

[73] Aziza Thabet, "al-qahira bada'at tusamim azya'iha" (Cairo started to design Clothes" *Akher Sa'ah*, 20 June, 1962, pp. 32–39.

[74] Thana' al-Bissi, *Al-qahira tussadir al-muda lil 'alam* (Cairo Exports Fashion to the World), *Akher Sa'ah*, 18 September 1963, pp. 27–29.

Second, this discovery attracted foreign observers and Western television networks, as if the gaze of the Western 'Other' remained essential for self-esteem among Egyptians. Another article, "European
Clothes from the Cotton of our Country" was written by Ibtissam
al-Hawari,[75] stated that the best known German, French and Italian
designers (their names are not mentioned) have agreed that the best
material for their designer clothes was Egyptian cotton. Even the
evening outfits were made from Egyptian cotton. Nevertheless, all
the pictures accompanying the article could have been cut from any
Western fashion magazine. Ironically, none of the designs displayed
were in cotton. In fact, in the next page, it is explained that chiffon,
silk, shantung and other expensive material were used. Evidently, the
pictures did not seem to have much relation to the contents of the
article. One wonders then why the emphasis was on cotton, if it is
not to praise Egypt's national production, which was ironically one
of the main features of British colonial exploitation. A year later,
Al-Bissi wrote that Cairo exhibits its taste to the world. The new
taste in Egyptian cotton has succeeded in invading international markets. The designs are again European in style, but the models' background consisted of Pharaonic and Islamic settings, such as the
Khayyameyah tents and embroidery, Pharaonic chairs and paintings
and some nineteenth century palaces.[76] It is precisely during these
times that the regime imposed nationalizations and sequestration on
the previous foreign capitalists. In the early sixties Egypt underwent
a closure to enhance import substitution. Imported textiles and many
other items were then rare goods. This explains why the press empha-
sized Egypt's international taste in fashion. The message was that
Egypt could compete internationally. The models looked very European.
One only wonders if this did not betray a schizophrenic state of
mind that bred growing frustrations from closure and distance from
a Western image, which was still highly emulated. A longing for a
distanced, much loved and yet officially loathed European dream?

---

[75] Ibtissam al-Hawari, "azya' urubba min qutn baladna" (European Clothes from
the Cotton of our Country), *Akher Sa'ah*, 16 May, 1962, pp. 31–35.

[76] Thana' al-Bissi, "al-qahira tu'rid thawqaha 'alal-'alam" (Cairo Exhibits its Taste
to the World), *Akher Sa'ah*, June, 1964, no. 1324, pp. 31–33.

The Language of Fashion

Besides the *Burda* magazine several members of my family bought the fashion magazine *Elle*, which we all browsed with great interest. *Elle* set the fashion, provided recipes and new ideas for interior decoration for a whole francophone generation. French was practically the vernacular language used by all the women of the family. French became a gendered language, while the male members of the family spoke Arabic. However, several of my uncles and my father studied law in France and mastered the language. Up to my generation, French was synonymous with good manners, civility and definitively; it was the ticket to a well-matched marriage. My mother and her sister went to a French school. Since this was before the 1952 revolution, the pupils were forbidden to speak Arabic at school. Because my grandfather was conservative, he prevented my mother from obtaining a degree to pursue her studies at the University, a dream she never realised.

Parallel to French, my mother and her sister were both raised by a German "gouvernante", Frau Smidt, who taught them to play the piano, recite Goethe and Schiller and speak a fluent, accent free high German. Thus, they mastered perfectly German and French. They had a French one for a short period until both sisters got married and replaced the German gouvernante. The phenomenon of gouvernantes was typical of the ancient regime upper classes and it became popular, we are told, only since the reign of Khedive Isma'il.[77] Both sisters learned Arabic at home with a private *Qur'an* Azhari teacher, and both ended up with an extremely poor level of writing because the teacher was extremely lax and perhaps careless. For my mother, Arabic was thus the third language, which she started to master when she grew older, mainly through reading the daily newspapers. However, my mother spoke to her father in Arabic since he could not speak French. As adolescents who learnt Arabic at school, both my sister and me constantly made fun of my mother's Arabic writing. My mother's Arabic improved through the years after she inherited land from her father in her forties and started to manage

---

[77] Mona L. Russell, . . ., p. 103. It was even possible to obtain European gouvernantes, piano lessons for daughters and knowledge about the proper schools for girls through the advertisements in various journals and papers at the turn of the last century. Ibid., p. 76.

it. She then spent a long time in the village of origin and quickly learned how to speak the peasant dialect. My sister and I had the privilege of having a Spanish nanny until I was thirteen years old. In 1959 my father had been posted as a diplomat in Barcelona. When the family returned two years later to Cairo followed by two years in Italy, the southern Spanish, Catholic Fidela came to my family when I was a few months old and remained in Cairo until I was thirteen years old. In daily life, I communicated in French with my mother, aunts and my grandmother and switched systematically to Arabic with my father, uncles, my grandfather and the servants. My father on the other hand, had a purely Arabic education at the famed Sa'adiyya School. He learned French when he studied law in France; but he never mastered properly the language. My sister and I spoke to our nanny in Spanish, French and Spanish to my mother until Fidela returned in the early seventies to Spain. Little by little Spanish withered away from our daily life, to only remember a few songs.

My sister and I went to a French Catholic school. The female members of the family from mother's side were francophone, whereas not all the male members were so. In fact my grandfather who, although Westernized in his appearance – he always wore immaculate white shirts, perfectly cut suits, ties, trousers and socks suspenders, silk pyjamas, socks and *robes de chambres*, which were either bought in Europe or handmade at the best tailor downtown – he proudly preserved a peasant dialect, which I guess he used as a power game when my grandmother touched upon a nerve.

Francophone women also had access to *Paris-Match* magazine that was from time to time censored in Egypt because of the political reports on the Middle East. The soap opera "roman photo" such as *Intimité* and *Nous Deux* were widely read, as was *Ici Paris*, a sensationalist paper. It is interesting that the working classes would read such magazines and papers in France, whereas the upper class Egyptian Francophiles appreciated them. Girls were forbidden to read, or to bring these magazines to school, as the Catholic nuns considered them as a decadent and corrupting literature. We were publicly humiliated if a nun discovered these at school. As a result, a wide underground traffic in such magazines developed among the students. In retrospect, these magazines popularized an unintelligent, unreal image of romance, which had its impact on a whole generation of francophone women in Egypt.

My aunts were all a bit "overly" romantic; they had what French would designate as having the tendency to become *fleur blue*. They lived in the past century and they all dreamt of the charming prince who never showed up. Evidently this prince had nothing to do with the husbands they lived with. This conflict between ideal and reality produced extremely neurotic female characters that were mostly either hypochondriac, hysterical, or they developed phobic obsessions about cleanliness. This last obsession ran strongly in the family, even among older male uncles who avoided shaking hands and kissing, fearing the

Fig. 38. Intimité Magazine. February 1987.

transfer of microbes. During an epidemic of Cholera, some members of the family (including my grandmother) required from all visitors, to immerse their hands in a basin of permanganate potassium located by the front door. It then turned into a permanent ritual during the summer. As I grew up, in retrospect, I became increasingly conscious of such a phobia, which my grandmother, her two brothers and some aunts developed. These aunts often complained of their husband's respective treatment towards them. They felt bitter because they had not chosen to marry them.

Books and magazines were circulated among women of the family, both to save money and to provide a shared basis for daily discussion. There also existed a second hand market for such magazines, which were purchased by traders who came to the house. The *roman fleuve*, or roman *a l'eau de rose*, love stories, thrillers like Simenon, Agatha Christi, San Antonio, and literary works by Francoise Sagan, Pearl Buck, Collette, Marcel Proust, Victor Hugo and many other writers were also exchanged among the female members of the family. My mother, who was an avid reader, had a huge library that included French and English novels, German and Spanish history and guidebooks.

I would like to conclude this section by mentioning that my grandmother's first language as a child was Turkish and she then later switched to Arabic and French. This brings me to Mona L. Russell's observations on the multiple languages of the elites at the turn of the last century. She observes that Mohammed Ali expressed himself in Turkish and not Arabic because he belonged to the Ottoman-Egyptian elite.[78] While Turkish remained the language of ruling, Khedive Isma'il encouraged French and Arabic. One can see that if Turkish vanished away[79] the two-track, parallel educational system consolidated by Mohammed Ali and later on by colonial authorities, although weakened during Nasser, still survived. With Sadat's open door policy, the privatization of education once again gave prevalence to foreign languages at the expense of national education and Arabic language.

Readings and Private Lessons

As children we grew up with Grimm's fairy tales and other stories, which my mother read to us in French. All our illustrated books were in French. Our imagination was filled with snow queens, Cinderella, Hansel and Gretel, frog princes, King Arthur, Merlin and the magical swords, dwarfs, gnomes, knights and forests which did not exists in our landscapes. How often I have dreamt of forests, which I missed upon my return to Cairo after Italy. When we were around ten years old, my father brought us Arabic tales from the Arabic "Green Collection". He seemed to be worried about our deplorable level of Arabic language. But the attempt was far from successful because we found Arabic stories unappealing and the language difficult. Father insisted on returning to Egypt with the main aim that we should learn Arabic. We had from early age a *Dar al 'Ulum* teacher, *ustaz* 'Iliwa who was a firm and old *Qur'an* teacher who had taught my parents. I also had a private French teacher, Madame Marcelle, a Levantine who was an excellent teacher and extremely humane. I owed her my love of French language. She was like a family friend and she often spent hours talking to mother before giving me the lesson. In 1968, she became obsessed about the vision of Virgin Mary in Zaitun. Like thousands of people, she spent whole

---

[78] Mona l. Russell, Creating The New Egyptian Woman . . ., p. 4.
[79] By the 1890s Turkish became optional in government schools. Quoted from Mona L. Russell, p. 7.

days in Zaitun until she saw the Virgin. This event as we know happened
immediately after the 1967 defeat, a
collective psychological trauma.[80] Since
the defeat religion and beliefs in the
transcendental gained a growing
significance in the society. One interpretation of the time was that the
causes of 1967 defeat were due to
the irreligiosity of the society.[81] Since
then Madame Marcelle became obsessed by one drive: to leave Egypt.
Two or three years later she migrated
to Canada to follow her two sons. It
is unfortunate to conclude that the
Arabic teachers seemed to do their
best to discourage us from appreci-

Fig. 39. Superman in Arabic.

ating our native language. I am sure that many in my school underwent the same fate. The method of teaching Arabic was stifling and
the topics were boring. Whereas French gave us more space for
thinking and imagination through the illustrations and essay writing.
Like the majority of my class in the secondary level, I had to have
also a private teacher in mathematics and later for my *thanawiyya
amma*, the baccalaureate; I had private lessons in all subjects including history and geography. These private lessons ended up being
shared with two or three other schoolmates. It seems that no one
could escape these lessons and the habit deplored today, so much
was already existent in the early sixties. Private lessons were already
horrendously expensive.

   It is not true that I did not read in Arabic, but what I loved most
were in Arabic comics and thrillers for children. As children we read
the Arabic versions of Mickey Mouse and the Egyptian cartoon
Samir. I collected the Arabic "Superman" comics, which were

---

[80] For the appearance of Virgin Mary in Zaitun see the very inspiring work of
Cynthia Nelson, "Religious Experience, Sacred Symbols and Social Reality" in
Humaniora Islamica, 2, pp. 253–266.
   [81] I could recall frequent discussions among my paternal uncles after 1967 about
the end of the world, further wars by yellow (Asian) invasions and Egypt that will
be destroyed through chaos, floods with the destruction of the High dam. Many of
my uncles, my father and aunts turned towards religion after the defeat.

published in Lebanon and distributed all over the Arab World. The
TV serials of the real American Superman enhanced our admiration for Superman and the fantastic overview of the city New York,
which made us dream about visiting it one day. Batman, Robin and
the joker were all icons, which we grew up with in socialist Egypt.
We also read all sorts of other French cartoons such as *Tintin*, *Spirou*
and *Gaston Lagaffe* in French. We also collected English cartoons in
the summer when salesmen sold them on the beaches of Montazah
(Alex). Later, in the late seventies *Tintin* was translated into Arabic.
As children we loved the illustrated Arab encyclopaedia from *ʿalam
al-maʿrifa*, which was sold as separate parts on a weekly basis in an
alphabetical order. We also read more serious children's French literature, which was mainly published in two collections: *la bibliothèque
rose*, and when we grew older it was *la bibliothèque verte*. Until the
early sixties, adolescents read *La semaine de Suzette*. Those who were
older read *salut les copains*, a magazine of news and pictures about
French singers and stars.

Birthdays

For birthdays, the cook baked chocolate cakes, but the *gateaux*, sandwiches and *petits fours* were brought from Simonds café in Zamalek.
Confetti and toys were given as presents to my classmates. Our birthday party became the occasion for my mother to invite dozens of
aunts and uncles. "Happy Birthday to You" was sung in English
with candles and cake. These were the only words we knew in that
language. We received gifts and my mother conscienciously collected
them before I opened them. The point was to identify who brought
what, so that the child would be reciprocated on equal terms or the
next birthday. Obviously, not all the gifts were of equal value. After
the children were gone, the grownups would continue partying until
late at night. Also for the occasion, every year, my mother hired
from Metro Golden Meyer in Cairo a screen and films, which became
a ritual: animated Walt Disney cartoons; American films such as the
Thief of Baghdad, Ali Baba and the Forty Thieves or Sinbad and
the Flying Carpet, which followed our exposure to Donald Duck,
Mickey Mouse, Snow White and Cinderella. We were introduced
through Hollywood to a fantastic imagined Orient, which culturally

marked us for life. We lived in an Orient that did not resemble the one we saw in those Disney films.[82]

Probably because we had lived in Europe for a long time, my mother bought a Christmas tree every year, which she decorated with cotton to look like snow, balls, candles and angels. We celebrated Christmas by signing in French "Mon beau sapin", by getting presents and by inviting relatives for dinner who, in turn also brought presents. Although Christmas is obviously not in our religious tradition, the fact that all the women in the family had a French Catholic upbringing must have played a role in celebrating it. My mother bought Christmas presents for all my teachers, a habit, which was common among many Muslim families. It was one way for teachers to give us special attention. It sometimes had reverse results. Ramadan was also celebrated with plenty of delicious food, starting with soups, *ful* and finishing with abundant sweets. Until the late sixties, during Ramadan, my grandfather distributed food and a lamb was slaughtered and given away to the poor of the quarter who lined up in front of the house when every servant, *bawab* or grocer knew everyone in Zamalek. The island of the rich was then a wonderful, and spacious quarter, ideal for long strolls along the Nile.

Living in Zamalek

Over and over again, the island of Zamalek has drawn the attention and imagination of several writers and travellers. Edward W. Said speaks of his childhood quarter with nostalgia and tenderness in his autobiography *Out of place (A Memoir)*.[83] Artemis Cooper reminds us that it was the favourite residential place for the English because "its houses and apartments were simpler and airier than those on the east bank".[84] The leftist activist poet Ahmed Fuad Negm wrote an ironic piece on Zamalek, "al-zamalek masalek, masalek" (the labyrinth of Zamalek). It was sung by the late blind Sheikh Imam, (another anti-establishment leftist). Both Sheikh Imam and Negm

---

[82] From time to time some of my relatives organised evenings where ballets, operas and Hollywood films were screened for a large group of invitees.

[83] Published by Alfred Knopf, 1999.

[84] Artemis Cooper, *Cairo in the War, 1939-1945*, Penguin Books, 1989, p. 35.

went to jail between 1968 and 1971 and became known for ridiculing the regime. *The Lady's Dog, kalb assit,* is another sardonic poem by Negm alluding to the true story of Umma Kalthoum's dog, which attacked a poor, young stroller who ended injustly in prison. *The Lady's Dog* was a biting example revealing the arrogance of the Zamalekites. Zamalek was the epitome of the rich and fat bourgeoisie where the poor feel insecure and got lost in its labyrinths and worrying paths.

Samir Ra'afat speaks of the "Three Grand Ladies of Zamalek" to point to the famed landmarks, the Lebon, Union-Vie and the Ali Labib Gabr buildings located near the Gezira Club.[85] Chafika Soliman Hamamsy in her recently published autobiography *Zamalek: The Changing Life of a Cairo Elite 1850–1945,* opens her book by describing the quarter where she was born and grew up. During the 1920s and 1930s Zamalek was a fashionable and quiet quarter for the rich, which was wining over Hilmiya al-Gadida and Munira. Zamalek was a man made island which grew out of accumulated earth thrown to dig canals during the reign of Mohammad 'Ali. In the 1930's Hamamsy describes it as having been the "jewel of the capital" where the British realized its beauty and constructed the Gezira Sporting club.[86] She also notices that there were two areas of Zamalek. What was perceived as the "good side" was in the south with the Gezira club, the Grotto gardens and the Gezira Palace. The north side, the marshland, was the "bad side", which included a few palaces as well as squatters huts.[87] Most striking, the well to do quarter of Zamalek could hardly be visually dissociated from its juxtaposing neighbour, the slowly vanishing popular and *baladi* quarter of Bulaq. Separated only by the Nile River, Bulaq provided and still continues to provide Zamalek with its servants, cooks and lower class workers. Both sides, cultivated perceptions, prejudices, and over magnified imaginations about the *afrangi* (western) high life versus *baladi* life-worlds, revealing much about the intense class polarisation and flagrant spatial and architectural divergence.[88] Fayza Hassan reviewed the recent

---

[85] Samir W. Ra'afat, *Cairo, The Glory Years, Who Built What, When, Why, and For Whom.* Harpocrates, 2003, p. 209.
[86] Chafika Soliman Hamamsy, *Zamalek, The changing Life of a Cairo Elite 1850–1945,* The American University in Cairo, 2005, p. 4.
[87] Ibid., pp. 8–9.
[88] The *Raaqi* (upper class) versus *sha 'bi* (popular) culture is well analysed in Farha Ghannam, "Remaking The Modern . . .", pp. 76–77 and 82–84.

biographies that mention Zamalek as a focal point,[89] to emphaisze the selective and nostaligic tone of this "out of place" generation that had to reinvent the memory of a vanished era.[90] Nostalgia interwoven with decadence is probably the most appropriate impression one gets of Zamalek today.

My maternal grandparents' villa or rather mansion was originally located on the "bad side" of Zamalek, but by the sixties squatters had disappeared to be replaced by wonderful villas, Art Nouveau and modern buildings. I use the word villa because this is how Cairenes used to call it. Our street, called Mohammed Mazhar, was very long and it included several impressive Embassies surrounded by well-kept gardens, the building of the Vatican Embassy and some wonderful Palaces and Gothic villas, which have survived the devastation of modernization and high rise buildings. I experienced the declining grandeur and yet popularization of Zamalek. By the sixties the slow invasion of high-rise, matchbox-like buildings began to replace the villas and the old types of apartments building. Zamalek was still a residential area, but one could notice the new middle class slowly settling in. The architectural disharmony between cheap Bauhaus types of buildings and older constructions was already there. It was exacerbated in the eighties and nineties. We were considered privileged since we were among the happy few who lived in so much space. Most of my friends in the quarter whose parents were middle class (such as teachers, doctors, and engineers) lived in spacious and beautiful flats. The quarter was experiencing an interesting mix between ancient regime and highly placed officials, yet the middle class was moving into the newly built sixties apartments, which were still spacious, but with lower ceilings and modern furniture.

My grandparents' villa is now the Jordanian Embassy, was divided into three spacious separate units, one on each floor; it must have been constructed in the 1940's.[91] Each apartment had large entrées, one round salon and a second inner salon, one dining room and three spacious bedrooms and two bathrooms. My grandparents had an extra fitting room where they dressed and watched television.

---

[89] Jean Said Makdisi's *Teta, Mother and Me*, Edward Said's *Out of Place*, Chafika Soliman Hamamsy's Zanamlek: *The Changing Life of a Cairo Elite*.

[90] Fayza Hassan, "Cairos of the Mind", *Al-Ahram Weekly*, Cairo Review of Books, issue 67, December 2005, 22–28 December 2005, pp. 8–9.

[91] The word villa is used in Arabic.

The salons had arches and large windows, the ceilings were high and the house was airy. Although every apartment had a separate kitchen called the *office*, the main huge kitchen where cooking took place was located in the *badron* or the basement where the servants also lived (see further down the section on servants). The food was transported from the basement to floor one, two and three through a small inner elevator that could carry only a large tray and took endless time to ascend. The villa had a large garden with many exotic trees, which my grandfather must have brought from Lebanon and a large veranda where dinners took place in summer. When my mother got married, my grandmother insisted that her two daughters live in the villa with her. My grandparents lived on the ground floor; my father and mother lived in the second floor while my aunt occupied the third floor. In the mid-sixties my aunt was extremely glad when she moved to Ma'adi to a villa, which her husband built. Our family was then allowed to move between the two upper floors. The spaciousness of this house made it extremely agreeable. We spent the summers upstairs and the winters downstairs. The downstairs "salons" were rarely used.[92] These were only opened for so-called important guests, whom we hardly saw. We were forbidden to enter the sacred space of the salon and if we did, he had better behave, for we would be punished, if we touched any of the ashtrays, "bonbonières", vases, bibelos, embroidered napkins and small tables. The television room on the other hand, was the real used space in daily life. This is where we ate on the floor while watching television, where my father had his afternoon naps and where we played football with other children. During one of these games, I once destroyed a large old family mirror. It cost me a spanking and being locked in my room for a whole day. As kids we enjoyed digging countless holes on the Bauhaus sofa brought from Italy, but my mother, who was evidently much more liberal than my father, after closing her eyes to our artistic experiments on the walls of the living room, quickly became horrified by the devastating outcome and had to stop us from destroying the walls. The discrepancy between the formal, clean and representable downstairs salon and the real, shabby, run down living room always amazed me. My

---

[92] Among the middle and upper classes, the salons are the par excellence, the display room. They were and probably are still always closed and hardly ever used in daily life.

mother often screamed at us, threatening how shameful it would have been if guests would see our "real" living room. For financial reasons my grandparents decided to sell the villa in the early part of the mid-seventies.

Astonishingly, the residential quarter of Zamalek had an extremely busy and lively street life. By the sixties, I recall that there were constantly popular and poor people roaming around for one reason or another. Private cars could have been easily counted and everyone knew whose car is whose. There was an informal taxi station next to our house and the drivers could have been informants for the government as my family believed, since they spent hours observing all movement in the quarter. There was one microbus line with a station just in front of house. Grandfather through his influential contacts managed twice to remove the station, but the government put it back for the third time as an affront until grandfather gave up defying the government. Ambulant salesmen came to the quarter. They shouted the Italian words, *roba vecchia* (old stuff); two words which Egyptians have so well integrated in the Egyptian dialect. For a few piasters, they purchased anything available from old newspapers and magazines, to worn out utensils, to clothes or decrepit furniture. There were also street entertainers with performing monkeys, musicians and *pianola* players, magicians swallowing and spitting fire, singers with orchestras, shadow theatre and puppets players and of course plenty of beggars who came often to Zamalek. I recall my grandfather constantly sending the servants to threaten the crowd of street performers or beggars when they were noisy. Street vendors were a routine; they sold fruits and vegetables, baked *batata* (sweet potato), *tin shoki* (prickly pears), *ful* (beans) and ice cream. I guess that with the invasion of cars, ambulant carts were pushed away. These have been banned, one can still find a few hovering around, but their number has definitely diminished. Today, large trucks collect garbage, but one can still see the miserable looking donkey carts, which are constantly struggling to survive the chaotic streets. The *misaharrati*, who walks all around in quarters shouting about the time for (*imsak* the ceasing of eating), passed during Ramadan to remind us of the fasting time, is still passing.

Today, Zamalek is, like all Cairo, overcrowded and invaded by an amazing number of schools, which makes circulation impossible. When the students come in the early morning and go out in the afternoon, Zamalek reaches a state of paralysis. However, in spite of all the abusive destruction during the last years, the few remaining villas and buildings from the '30s and '40s are a witness of its age-old charm.

The Move to Mohandessin

After several years of searching for a flat we moved to the Mohandessin quarter. The move from Zamalek to a flat in Mohandessin represented for us a totally new era. Departing from the "grandeur" of the villa meant that we had lost status. We were no longer the spoilt privileged of the quarter. We suddenly descended to the middle class, living in a five-storey building among unrelated families. I have previously described Mohandessin as the quarter of the new rising professional classes. Suffice to say here that we moved into a quiet area in Mohandessin, which was a mix of well-designed villas and four- to five-storey buildings. We were amongst the first to move in the building with one engineer, a medical doctor and a pharmacist.

Our quarter was still not completed and half of it consisted of large cultivated plots of agricultural land. One could then observe daily, Bedouins moving with sheep and donkeys to eat from the grass of the public spaces. There were many peasants selling vegetables and fruits from carts. Not very far away, there existed the popular quarter, today a slum known as Bulaq al-Dakrur. It is a ten to fifteen minute walk and you feel as if you are entering another world consisting of *haras* (narrow alleys), children playing in the street, mud brick houses and crammed populations. The two worlds are still so near to each other today. One wonders how these two juxtaposing and shocking class disparities managed to coexist peacefully so far.

There were hardly any shops in our quarter and most of the buildings were still unfinished. One could count the cars parked in the street. There was a government secret agent (*mukhbir*) of the quarter[93] who sold peanuts at the corner, he knew everybody and probably reported all comings and goings. We all knew him and gave him some money every month because he looked poor and shabby and was kind to all of us. The milkman came daily and we purchased our food from the small grocer Saudi who has today turned into

---

[93] This was a frequent practice, which probably started under Nasser.

one of the biggest supermarket chains in Cairo. Today, this quarter has become densely populated, with shops, coffee houses, groceries and thousand of cars. The Bedouins and agricultural land disappeared, to be replaced by crowded, high-rise, ugly, blocks. By the nineties, it has become extremely noisy and car polluted.

However, moving from old bourgeois Zamalek to the new quarter of Mohandessin had a liberating effect. It gave us a sense of being finally liberated from the suffocating control of the authoritarian and conservative grandparents. In the Zamalek villa, after eight o' clock all doors were locked and we were not allowed to go out without the grandparents' permission, neither were we allowed to receive guests or friends. The large dog was then released to frighten outsiders. On the other hand, my memory of Mohandessin consists of happy times and a growing optimism in life. My mother had by then sold the bulky furniture, which she really disliked since the ceilings and rooms were evidently smaller. I recall her delight when she finally got rid of the pompous furniture. We moved into a new flat, which consisted of two flats, merged together. My mother was happy to change her life, after struggling for years in order to obtain her divorce from my father. She had started working before her move from Zamalek. She once told me that she never had one good day in the Zamalek villa and now she was willing to experience something else. My mother then purchased very modern, minimalist furniture, which was crowned with locally made *mashrabiyya* (woodwork), copper and marble tables designed by the interior decorator Nabil Ghali and his wife the jeweller 'Azza Fahmi, who owned the *al-'Ayn* Gallery (see page 210–211). The *al-'Ayn Gallery* was amongst the first to promote local crafts and sell *kelims*, traditional lamps, *masharbiyya* wood work, paintings, *Qur'ans* and many other items, furniture, mirrors, all locally produced, Islamic or Ottoman inspired. It was during this period that my mother, along with her future husband, became interested in modern Egyptian painting. She later ran a gallery downtown with him.

CHAPTER FOUR

THE SIXTIES' LEISURE CLASSES

So far, this is only one side of the story. It would be a great illusion to describe the Nasser era as a mere mediocre emulation of the "socialist" countries. If the official discourse promoted an ideology of scarcity, this far from applied to all. In fact, the view of an economy of scarcity can be dangerously class biased and false. Social distinction survived; it rather took different forms. The bitter critics of Nasserism would say that the palaces, furniture and antiques of the older classes ended by being appropriated through sequestration, or in private sales, and these moving into the hands of the rising officers' class. Previous Pashas[1] specialized in such a trade, were astute in purchasing marvels from the members of the needy declining old class. Every *ancien régime* partisan has a lamenting narrative about having sold silver chandeliers, cutlery or carpets to survive hard days. However, Nasserism expanded consumerist appetites for the new rising middle classes, which certainly created different markets and circulation of goods. Some members of the *ancien régime* I interviewed stated that change in the consumer lifestyle took a longer time than expected before things began to deteriorate. True, the revolution spread a general feeling of insecurity, but restaurants and fine items were available even after the revolution. In the memory of many, it seems that the drastic change in the standards of living was clearly marked with the date of 1961, when nationalizations and the second agrarian reform laws which reduced the size of landownership were applied. This is when the countdown started.[2]

The 1960's advertisements inform us about locally produced air conditioners *(Coldair), Tabrizi-Shirazi* carpets produced in Damanhur by *al-sharika al-ʿarabiyya lil siggad wal mafroushat*, and fancy leather ladies

---

[1] A Wafdist Pasha was known for trading in antiquities and he had access through his contacts to the salons of the old class.

[2] Interviews with ʿAdel ʿAbdel Ghaffar 13 November 2004, and this feeling of deterioration precisely after 1961 was also expressed by ʿAfaf Abaza and Amina al-Lozy.

coats. *Corona* produced Egyptian chocolate Rocket, Nadler, cacao, pudding, and *halwa*. *Ica* Company sold chewing gum. Gramaphone records, glass chandeliers *(Nagaf)*, *Sigal*, metal water heaters, stoves, fridges and pots are all advertised in *al-Mussawar* and *Akher Sa'ah* during the sixties.

One would be astonished at the large variety of brands of watches that were sold in the late sixties. In 1970 *Al-Mussawar and Akhar Sa'ah* had the following brands: Vulcain Switzerland, Camy Watch, Switzerland Felca, Switzerland Cortebert, Nivada's Colorama, diver's watches, Elasto-Fixo and Jupiter. Women complained that they could not get cosmetics like Revlon, which was boycotted because of trade with Israel, or Dior in Cairo but there existed a locally joint venture produced by Max Factor and Elizabeth Arden. In 1970, the year of Nasser's death, *al-Mussawar* advertised various Western cigarette brands such as Marlboro, Benson and Hedges and Craven "A". One could argue that the fact that there were in fact many brands of cigarettes is in itself revealed great diversity.

The *grands magasins* such as Sidnaoui, Tarabishi, Hannaux and Omar Affandi, which were all turned into public sector companies and run by the government, offered plenty of sales "okasiun" of all sorts of household goods. Many of these brands kept the same names as before the 1952 revolution. *Ika* for instance belonged to a Jewish family before it was nationalized. New names such as *Masrcola* appeared next to *Pepsi-cola*. Tide powder soap is advertised near *Rabso*, but *Rabso* was the most available on the market. None of the department stores for instance changed names in spite of the fact that the Jewish and Levantine origin owners had left the country after nationalization.

Many ladies went shopping frequently to Beirut and had private sales at exclusive coffee meetings at their salons. Certainly travel was much more restricted than today but many of the old class knew how to maintain accounts in Switzerland and they managed every year to travel overseas. Until today many stories circulate about these hard times and the art of concealing money when leaving Cairo airport in hidden belts, in underwear and other sensitive parts of the body, since the government allowed Egyptians to leave with only L.E. 5.

The Montazah, the former King Farouk's magnificent resort with its spacious gardens and fields was seized by the new regime. The edge of Simiramis bay was turned into a summer residence for Nasser and his ministers. The other beaches were transformed into private resorts with luxurious expensive summer cabins for the declining

Fig. 40. Simiramis Cabines, Montazah, Alexandria, Picture taken during off season.

aristocracy. Cleopatra and Aida beaches in Montazah hosted the newly rising state bourgeoisies, who could afford a second flat in Alexandria and residences on the edge of the Pyramid road. The new ruling class (the regime's son and daughters) enjoyed motorboats. The rising "crème de la crème" in the late sixties consisted of an alliance of the so-called old class, which to survive opportunistically made marriage and work alliances with the bureaucrats and sons of the "revolution". During summer relatives, acquaintances and friends met on the beach and everybody knew the location of each family's cabin. There were magnificent opulent meals at the end of Simiramis beach. These were known for the succulent cuisine, it was no coincidence they were all overweight. Some members of the family spent the whole morning mobilizing an army of domestic helpers to cook at home and bring in the food. For the snobbish section and the weight watchers, there were afternoon visits for tea and cake in different cabins. Merry gatherings around *'Araq*, Whiskey and *Mezzas* took place at at some former minister's cabin. This is where one could meet prominent journalists, intellectuals and actresses. Drinking went very well with playing cards. They started drinking around noon. Hot political discussions took place there and sometimes these ended unpleasantly. Some women went for a swim perhaps once or twice during the whole summer. The ladies dreadfully feared that they might get sunburnt. They were quite a few of them who came every day to the beach in full makeup, expensive jewelry and dresses. The image I retained was their heavily powdered, whitened faces with shining lipsticks.

There was the counter camp of women who sun bathed, wore simple clothes, walked miles on the beach and staffed the children with tons of sun cream. The so-called intellectuals, who disliked the beach, often complained that it was disgusting to swim in plastic bags and sewage, which was true, went to the coffee shop to play chess, backgammon or just gossip and drink coffee and Pepsi-cola. The adolescent males went fishing and when the harpoons became a fashion, some youngsters showed it off and unfortunate accidents did happen from time to time. Others played racket and socialized on the beach, young girls either shyly showed their bodies or went fishing at the other end of the beach. Flirtatious teens met behind the backs of their parents in the woods or in the vast fruit plantations of Montazah. They also rode in disguise with their boyfriends who drove their fathers'cars. Those who were in their late twenties played bridge and when no one saw them, but everybody knew it, they played poker, betting on a few pounds, emulating the beloved stars of Egyptian cinema.

Montazah hosted beach parties with bands (one was named *Les petits chats* and another *The Black Coats*) airing Frank Sinatra, Charles Aznavour, Claude Francois, and the Beatles. Private dancing parties were frequent. The *soirées dansantes* took place at the Palestine Hotel, another interesting Bauhaus building, which became the symbol of modernization. Time seemed endless. But such parties became a source of discontent and were perceived as the symbol of the decadent leisure class, which had no sensitivity for the dramatic events, which the country was undergoing. *Akher Sa'ah* published three years after the 1967 *naksa* (the six days war with Israel), a sensational article entitled "Hippies Parties . . . Banned in Alexandria . . . by the Governors Command".[3] The several pictures accompanying the article

---

[3] Sa'id Na'mat-Allah, "hafalat al-hibis . . . mamnu' a fil askandariyya . . . bi'amr al muhafiz" (Hippies Parties . . . Banned in Alexandria . . . from the Governor's Command) *Akher Sa'ah*, 23 September 1970, no. 1894, pp. 22–25.

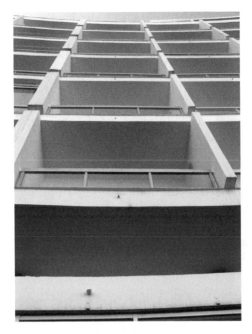

Fig. 41. Hotel Palestine-Alexandria.

show young men and women wildly dancing dressed in sleeveless and short outfits. They looked as if they were in a trance, hardly different from the Western hippies of the time. The subtitle of the article states that a bottle of whiskey was given as a prize to a 14-year-old in one party. The article then goes on to describe the decadent behaviour of youth who typically emulate Western hippies; young girls drew hearts on their cheeks and wore headscarves like gypsies; naked bodies (and promiscuity between sexes). Several pictures of youngsters jerking together are accompanying the article. The article concludes with a citation of the Alexandria governor stating if one of our soldiers would have attended such parties and experienced this debauchery and decadence what would have been his feeling? He went on to say that the country cannot afford to have such parties and these "riff-raff" are not representative of our youth. That was why drastic measures to stop these feasts should be taken, he said.

Once in a while, Hotel Palestine featured in films, portraying the leisure classes' favourite place. These films showed sexy actresses who by today's standards would be too daringly dressed in bikinis. The flair of cosmopolitan Alexandria still survived in its restaurants in the sixties. Restaurant culture was especially spread in Alexandria. One could enjoy the best fish, the most exquisite ice creams, *granita* ice cream, chocolate cakes, and sandwiches of *ful and ta'miyyas*. The old bourgeoisie enjoyed afternoon teas and cakes at the Cecil, the *Beau Rivage* and *San Stefano* hotels. This latter hotel was famous in summer for its open-air popular cinema for youngsters. Then, Agami west of Alexandria became fashionable in the late sixties with its long immaculate sand beaches and few villas. Slowly but surely the classy started to purchase plots of land from the Bedouins and build their own little castles. Everybody was happy in the sixties that one could spend the whole day in a bathing suit, visit friends and neighbour bare-footed. The classy had then discovered "simplicity", which might have not been the case in Montazah, with the made-up ladies in expensive attire. Today, 'Agami turned into another crowded town with high rise building on the beach, thousands of cars driven by spoilt, bad mannered and dangerous youngsters and sewers which blow up systematically in summer. Miasmas, mosquitoes, loud microphones for announcing the call for prayer or lousy Western music in parties, are what I remember most from my last summer in 2001.

The Gezira Club in Cairo was formerly restricted to the British officers was, thanks to the revolution Egyptianized. As a result of nationalization, it became the ideal parading space to show off fashion, cars, dogs and golf playing. Women and young girls wore miniskirts, bikinis and could freely walk in tiny shorts and sleeveless shirts. During the summer, the open cinema screened the latest Western and European films very cheaply. It was the place for dating, flirting and matchmaking. Today, it has become one of the cheapest places to have meals and the only remaining green space in the island of Zamalek. Entire families lunched on Fridays and Sundays.

The middle class outings to the Hilton and Shepheard's hotels and some downtown bars continued to flourish in the sixties. The new rising middle classes of officers and high government officials brought Morano glass and fine crystal from the socialist countries. The appetite for acquiring valuable goods such as carpets, Western furniture, Western landscape paintings, silver cutlery was never hampered by the socialist ideology, even among the members of the revolution. Madiha's page of *Rosa al-Youssef* again informs us in her weekly article that the fashion that year (1961) was the return to antique furniture which she defines *mobilia stile* (styled furniture). The advantage of antique furniture, in contrast to modern was, that it never aged and could last forever, says Madiha. She then informed the reader that that week she had moved around the most lavish and stylish settings by touring the famous downtown antique shops. She first mentions a small shop called al-Leithy, in downtown, and describes its valuable offers, to move to another shop called Anton in Sherifein Street, also located downtown. She then describes how the well-known Pontremoli furniture shop is offering a large *Bahut*[4] and a nearby shop, which offers for sale an *Aubusson*[5] salon belonging to a known upper class socialite. Silverware was sold in private houses and private auctions. Madiha informed us again that there are two permanent auctions, one located in Bulaq and another managed by an upper-class woman in the residential quarter of Zamalek. A range of specialized people (including an "oriental" woman, perhaps she meant to be Indian or Iranian?) specialized in selling secondhand silverware, cutlery, chandeliers, and valuable carpets.[6]

It is true that "Fiat" was the national economical car, but the old classes continued to drive their own old Bentleys, Citrouen, Jaguars and Ford and one could still find quite a few "Mercedes" cars in the sixties.[7] "Where do People go?" was a *Rosa al-Youssef*, tabloid page, signed anonymous, mainly dedicated to gossip. The news targeted the upper leisure classes, embassy circles, socialites, famous actors and visiting Arab and foreign millionaires. Many jokes and nasty comments are made about the Gezira club members who are portrayed as spoilt brats, indulging in partying and drunkenness and

---

[4] The French word "bahut" originally designated a large leather suitcase. During the middle ages bahut was meant to be a wooden suitcase used for travel. Later, it became interchangeably used with "buffet", serving as a cuboard. The most beautiful bahuts are the ones sculptured with leaves and animals, dating from the fifteenth century. The word evolved by the twentieth century to all sorts of "buffets", including modern styles. Bahut, Le *Grand Dictionnaire Encyclopedique Larousse*, 1977.

[5] The Aubusson is a special embroidery on wool or silk which garnished chairs and canapé. It originally started in Aubusson in France as tapestry. During the eighteenth century the manufacture of Aubusson was revived and became a favorite item of the royalty. See *Grand Dictionnaire Encyclopedique Larousse*, Tome 2, 1977, p. 816. According to Mehri Foda, it was believed that good quality Aubussons figured animals and gentry. Personal communication with Mehri Foda, 15 May 2005.

[6] Madiha, *Rosa al-Youssef*, 27 March 1961, no. 1709, no page.

[7] For many years my father drove a Humber. When his car collapsed in the early seventies, he purchased a 125 Fiat. Until the early seventies my grandfaterh owned a Vauxhall that was later replaced by a Fiat.

following collectively insignificant fashions. Lavish parties in villas
and secondary resorts (chalets in the pyramids, Alexandria and
Zamalek etc.), where plenty of whiskey, beer and champaign was
consumed, became the source of gossip. Upper class women and
actresses are portrayed as women of luxury with endless financial
demands. The Shepheard's nightclub events are given a lot of attention. Who married at the famous "One Thousand and one Night"
hall of the Hilton, a famous and costly hall to hire is frequently
mentioned. Miss Spring and Miss Egypt and the most beautiful
woman of a certain residential quarter are often mentioned, which
model will work for which *maison de couture* and who purchased which
expensive car from so and so. For example, information about a
Saudi millionaire who purchased the latest Cadillac (in 1961) is
reported. So and so from Studio Bakr sold his car and purchased a
Mercedes Benz for three thousand L.E. from an Embassy employee,
is reported ironically in the January issue of 1961.[8] So and so sold
his Chevrolet for L.E. 2.000 and purchased a Cadillac (model 1960)
for L.E. 3.000 because he did not like the red colour of his first car
(6 February 1960).[9] Who will be starring in which film and how
much he will be earning. Other amusing news like the Soviet Union
has sent thirty-five cooks to work in the Russian restaurant on Kasr
al-Nil street (Monday 20 March 1961). Nevine Mathlum, the grand-
daughter of the former Prime Minister Hussein Serry has organized
a private fashion show in her house, private because she is still in
morning for her late grandfather.[10]

One could interpret the exaggerations of the tabloid press, with
its spicy ridiculing of the indulgence and leisure of the rich, as revealing the poignant class interaction at the time. *Rosa al-Youssef* was
known in the sixties for its left wing orientation, with its emphasis
on international problems, the Third World, and its often well-doc-
umented articles on African and Southeast Asian liberation and non-
aligned movements. It could also be seen as a form of sarcasm of
the then newly ascending classes, which through access to the press
were given a margin of space to ridicule the ancient regime "decadent"

---

[8] *Ayna yathabul nass* (Where Do People Go?) *Rosa al-Youssef*, January 2, 1961, no.
1699, pp. 40–41.

[9] Ibid. (6 February 1960).

[10] *Ayna yathabul nass* (Where do People go?) *Rosa al-Youssef*, 3 April 1961, no. 1712,
no page.

classes. Nonetheless, a closer look tells us that up until the early sixties the well to do classes had continued to lead a luxurious life.

The old elites frequently complained that the country was "closed" to foreign goods and the regime was clearly anti-Western. But if one recalls carefully Egyptian television, it in fact showed in the sixties, besides the rich and prolific Egyptian films and *musalsalat* (TV serials),[11] plenty of American films. American serials such a Bonanza, the Fugitive, Perry Mason, or Lost in Space were extremely popular, not to mention I love Lucy and Doris Day's films, which were the favourites shows of the women in my family. Hollywood film stars continued to be the ideal for many of our generation very much like our parents. All new Disney shows had to be seen. An audience of youngsters celebrated Elvis Presley's films in Cairo's cinemas by dancing wildly during the screening. It did not take long for some Egyptians to discover the Beatles when a film they acted was shown in Cairo in the sixties. One cousin was a raged fan who boasted her wide collection of the most recent LP's, which she got during her travels. Fashions in dancing changed. Some were proud to perform the large variety starting with the samba, the rumba, tango, the twist, rock 'n roll, jerking and today courses in salsa, tangos and belly dance taught by expatriates are quite popular. Weddings of relatives took place at the Hilton hotel with belly dancers like Nagua Fouad and Soheir Zaki in the sixties and bands, which sang Western music. Everybody enjoyed dancing the twist, later the jerk and Tango. These weddings were ruinous and exhausted the lifelong savings of families, but they seemed to be an unavoidable must for perpetuating alliances, important connections, and the display of the sons and daughters in the marriage market.

Being the centre of Third Worldism Cairo received many international guests and singers from Africa, India and Southeast Asia. Jean Paul Sartre and Simone de Beauvoir, Che Gevara and many others visited the country. Russian films and cheap Russian books were very much available. Weeks celebrating the Yugoslav, German and French cinema was frequently announced in magazines.

---

[11] The whole family watched for years the *musalsal al-qahira wal nass*, which depicted the problems, trepidations, sorrows and happiness of a middle class Cairene family. It was done with great wit and intelligence. *Al-Saquiya* was a peasant saga, which was also very popular in the sixties. As children we also watched every year *al-lilah al-kabira* puppet play.

The Free Officer's sons and daughters were sent to private French catholic schools such as the *Mère de Dieu* and the *Sacré Coeur,* or the *Jésuites* and the *Frères* for boys and Lycées and to English schools like the Victoria College and the Port Said school. The sons and daughters of the old elites and the rising new elites of the revolution frequented the same schools and some were still proud to excel in French and English language often at the expense of ignoring Arabic. But our generation, in contrast to our mothers, learned better Arabic at schools. With nationalism, Arabic was elevated, even though the curricula and the way it was taught left a lot to be desired. In this context, it should be acknowledged that Nasser's three sons did not go to a private language school, neither did they go to an average state school, but to a state school with extra-curricular activities such as singing and dancing for the revolution.[12]

Servants

In spite of Egypt's revolution and the spread of ideas of equity and social justice, yet until the late seventies and early eighties, servants remained cheap labour. The younger these servants were, the worse they were remunerated. Horror stories of young village girls who were subjected to a new form of slavery by ruthless city dwellers were frequent. The abused young female servant, who slept on the kitchen floor, became a "topos" in the literature and films. However, not all servants lived with their employers and many commuted between the popular and well-off areas.

As mentioned before, we had a washerwoman, domestic servants and cooks. My mother never bought food herself. She kept a notebook with the *suffragi* and the cook, which listed every piaster spent. These were sent to purchase goods. Three or four times a week, the milkman used to bring fresh milk, which had to be boiled, and the small grocer in our quarter delivered many items to our home. The bill was paid at the end of the month. The cookery pots were made of copper. Two women used to come every second month to

---

[12] This information is derived from Mona Anis who while revisiting the literature of the 1952 revolution, recalled that she went to the same school of Nasser's sons and was the classmate of the middle son of Nasser. See Mona Anis, "Marginalia: Rendezvous With History", *Al-Ahram Weekly,* 15–17 September 2005, Issue No 760, Books Supplement. http://weekly.ahram.org.eg/2005/760/bo3.htm

"whiten" these pots. If these were not rubbed carefully, they risked turning into poisonous utensils.

Our villa's space consisted really of two separate worlds: the upstairs world, which was where the family resided[13] and the downstairs world, the *badron* or the basement where the servants lived. Our servants consisted of two male *suffragis* who were brought when they were very young from my grandfather's village. They returned every two or three months to their village for a few days. The *bawab* (housekeeper) and his son also slept downstairs. A third *suffragi*, the cook and his son all had their homes in Cairo and so they commuted daily. The dark and to us frightening kitchen was to be found on the other side of the basement. The servants were fed at home and twice a year my grandfather bought them cloth for *galabeyyas*. For official occasions, on Fridays and for serving dinners, the servants wore special stripped *quftans* (caftans) with a large red belt and a tarbush. This army of servants was fascinating to be observed. These were constantly playing cards, socializing, intriguing when my grandparents travelled and of course were part of the very strong network of *Bawabs* and servants that was to be observed in the quarter. Such an army of servants continued until my grandparents decided to sell the villa in the mid-seventies. They then moved into a flat and the domestic workers were reduced to two persons. But as a former *a'yan* or large landowner, I would say that Nasserism did not destroy the lavish life style of my grandparents. On the contrary, it was during Sadat' time that they suffered from inflation and the shortage of workers on the land diminished their income.

Bitaqat al-Tamwin *(Ration Cards) and the Servants*

In 1966, the weekly magazine *Akher Sa'ah* published an interview with the Minister of *Tamwin* (rationed foodstuff) entitled: *Why did I cancel domestic servants from the new ration card (bitaqa)?*[14] The interview was written with the intention of announcing to the citizens that the government had cancelled the old ration cards because these were only

---

[13] As said earlier, my sister and I were cared for by the Spanish nanny who slept in a separate room upstairs.
[14] 'Ali al-Maghrabi, "Interview with the Minister of Rationed Foodstuff 'limatha alghayt al-shagghalin min bitaqat al-tamwin'", (Why Servants were Cancelled from Ration Cards), *Akher Sa'ah* 12–10–1966, no. 1668, p. 6.

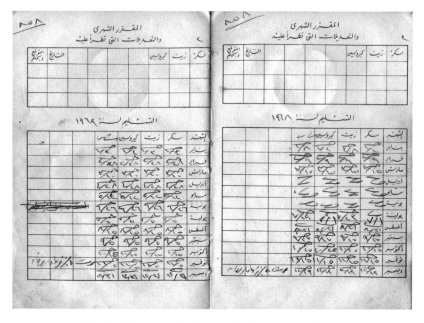

Fig. 42. Ration card. Sugar, oil, Kerosene are listed.

leading to greed and exploitation. The new cards were distributed
with precise information about the exact number of the members of
the family using it. The argument in favour of removing the domestic servants from the ration card was that these new cards include
five million families each consisting of five members. Therefore, if
the government would add to each family one domestic servant, this
would make it one million more who are profiting from the government's subvention. Furthermore, it has been revealed that some
families managed to register many "fictive" servants to obtain more
goods. The article then provides the history of the first *bitaqa* ever
in Egypt, which was launched by the government in 1945. The decision was made after WWII, when the country was suffering from
shortages in sugar, oil and kerosene and 4 million citizens obtained
ration cards. After the 1952 revolution there were many complaints
about the difficulty of obtaining these cards. In 1957 the door was
reopened for citizens to issue new cards and the system installed
(until the sixties) survived for twenty years. For a family of five members the government pays subsidies of six and half pounds yearly.
When the government in 1964 undertook control, it was discovered
that there were 3 million, 670 thousand and 650 (3.670.650) cards

issued. Out of these, 197 thousand cards were under fake names. These consisted of one million and 378 thousand and 724 non-existent names. This meant that the state was paying 2 million pounds for non-existent citizens, i.e. we were raised with the double culture of black markets.

Obviously, domestic servants were a hot issue in the sixties, especially, that they were the ones who stood in queues and brought in food for the household. Many would recall that there was so much trafficking during that period over chicken, soap and oil that the clever servants would then sell in the black market. Mothers, relatives and cousins spent hours on the phone chatting with other female members of the family about where to find what item in the nearest state cooperative (the *gam'iyya*). The domestic servants would be then sent and quite often they would be scolded for not bringing the items. These would often desperately claim that they never reached the head of the queue.

If you look at a *bitaqa* issued in the sixties (see figure 42 . . . issued in 22–7–1967 valid until 21–7–1972), you would find on the last pages some of following instructions: The citizens who were allowed to carry it had to fulfil the following conditions: families. Second, if the person is registered under a family and would like to obtain a separate card, he should provide the valid documents, or if he is not married and he has sufficient documents to prove it. The items are given on monthly basis after signing the card. If the items are not collected until the end of the month, the cardholder looses his right of access to rationed items. The card ceases to be functional if the customer does not use it for three months. The card is valid for five years and is renewable within three month before its expiration. The items subsidized were sugar, oil, kerosene and tea. On the front page of the card, the name of the grocer of the quarter is provided as well as the name and address of the cardholder. The last pages' instructions warn that the holders are not allowed to have more than one card. In case the members of the family change status, it should be notified as well as in case of the death of any member. In case of breaching any of those conditions, a fine of fifty pounds will be imposed.

Today the newly created shopping malls, super and hypermarkets and mega-stores in Egypt have become the symbol of this transformation. Shopping malls are to be found in many towns in the delta and they have spread in the countryside. Ma'adi City centre, which is hosting Egypt's first hypermarket is a witness to this new experience. The less nostalgic would still remember the long queuing in front of the government co-operatives as being the main distributor of oil, soap, rice, meat and chicken, if and when these goods would be available. To purchase these basic products was such an ordeal that Egyptians developed an art intertwined with a great sense of humour in bypassing the long queues. To champion the trespassing of others, or to boast about how to push away the masses was seen as an instinctive reflex, or rather a trait of national cleverness.

Here again the "memory of scarcity" is still alive in the collective consciousness once Egyptians have to queue. I am far from stating that queues have today disappeared. Many fear and rightly so, that queues have exacerbated with the current economic recession. Things got even worse after the flotation of the pound and alarmingly for the basic item of bread. The crisis seems to be exacerbated in the governorates to reach its peak in Beni Souef. Complaints extended to the bad quality and the shrinking size of the loaf of bread. Every day 180 million loaves of bread are sold at five piasters. The recent government proposed to produce a better quality loaf of bread for 10 piasters, but the project proved to be a failure. Apparently, the bakers use subsidized flour to bake more expensive items and thus depriving the destitute from basic bread.[15]

Would the prediction of the corroboration of the *bitaqa* be generalized? What does it mean when long queues for rationed food are reappearing side by side with mushrooming supermarkets *Alfas*, *Carrefours* and *Metros* supermarkets, with most exquisite imported *Delicatessens*. Today, even though basic products are abundantly available in any supermarket in Zamalek or Maʿadi districts, the spectacle of hunger and poverty is haunting the silent majority. Even today there are 40 million citizens who are benefiting from the rationed cards. These cards cover seven items: rice, oil, vegetarian fat, beans, lentils, popular macaroni and tea. One million and 400 thousand tons of wheat to produce bread are subsidized. These items are distributed by some (25–28,000)[16] ration-card-grocers in the 26 governorates. Officials argue that subsidies end up in the black market

---

[15] ʿAbdel Fattah Ibrahim, "ʿaish al-aqalim al-mushkila wal-hall" (The Bread in the Governorates, the Problem and the Solution), *al-Ahram*, 4 December 2004, p. 25.

[16] In the *al-Ahram* issue of 16 November 2004, p. 16, one article provided the number of 25,000 rationed cards grocers while another in the same page stated the number of 28,000 cards.

and these do not seem to reach the poor. The integrity of the specialized rationed cards grocers is constantly put into question. Some officials propose to give money as a replacement to subsidies since the system of the rationed card does not seem to function properly.[17] Many have asked the question: will the government at last cancel the cards after having introduced it 63 years ago?[18] The Minister of the State for Management Development stated that a new pilot project will be established in Suez to use "intelligent" ration cards *al-bitaqat al-thakiyya* to provide subsidized food, which consisted of an updated card which could be used equally at grocers[19] Whether the intelligent ration cards would solve the problem of food shortage, is still an open question. But Cairo's lavish hypermarkets coexisting with the growing pressure on the basic survival item: bread, is indeed the best example that scarcity and waste are the two sides of the same coin. According to the consumerist logic, they will continue to exacerbate, but be parallel to each other.

Boasting Wealth

They live in golden prisons, rather in asylums in the middle of desert. Their villas are located in streets, which are entirely devoid of any social and commercial life and their husbands are in 'real' prisons because they have proven to be thieves.

Their villas are all done by interior decorators. The silent owners have no say about the decoration, style or furniture. They only want to have a ready-made fancy house . . . The way they are surrounded by an army of servants, not even knowing how to turn on the light of their kitchens, which they never visit, gives the impression that they live in a hotel. But they seem to be happy in their first class prison. The most important thing for them is that their neighbours notice their villas and riches. The presence of neighbours is essential. This is why they live in such disturbing vicinity, which contradicts their wealth and status.

. . . There are rarely, if ever books, or magazines. But I have noticed that there are often 'trompe l'œil' commodes and shelves with fake wooden bound books. I once saw a huge painting behind a desk that consisted of drawn shelves filled with books.

(Description of some the villas in the compounds of Qattameyya, Sulaymaniyya Heights and the new satellite cities).

Menha al-Battrawi, freelance writer for *al-Bayt* Magazine (Interior Design and decoration), personal communication 1 November 2004.

---

[17] *al-Ahram*, 16 November 2004, p. 17.
[18] *al-Ahram*, 17 November 2004, p. 1.
[19] *al-Hayat* Sunday 29 August 2004, p. 11.

Conspicuous consumption, as Thorsten Veblen brilliantly argued in the thirties has little to do with satisfying needs or with subsistence. It has rather to do with ranking, with comparing, with envy and with emulation of certain ascending classes in relation to older established one. Veblen also speaks of trickle down effects, which leads to the emulation of fashion and lifestyles. Wealth per se is not significant but it is the evidence of it, such as the exemption from menial work and conspicuous consumption that comes to the forefront. Veblen's analysis is most fascinating because it explains how work is devalued. Idleness becomes a celebrated value because it reveals abundance. Not working is the evidence par excellence of social ranking and wealth. Leisure is then translated as "non-productive consumption of time".[20] Veblen notes that keeping servants then becomes a main characteristic of conspicuous consumption and leisure; it is even better when these servants are superfluous. When Jean Baudrillard spoke of the significance of producing waste in capitalism as constituting the parallel element of scarcity, he was certainly influenced by Veblen who was the first to point to the idea of boasting affluence of time, effort and the waste of goods.[21] The reason why I start this section with Veblen is simply to argue that conspicuous consumption is not a typically Egyptian cultural trait, although it certainly takes a particular cultural and local shape. It is also true that conspicuous consumption has a long history in Egypt. Khedive Isma'il, the designer of modern Cairo, its infrastructure, wide roads, parks, and the Opera House, envisioned changing Egyptian society, with Paris as his ideal. Change and progress were associated with building a large number of lavish palaces, a façade for representation to impress foreign guests and visitors. Isma'il was legendary for conspicuous consumption of jewellery, gadgets, food, western garments and for hiring Egyptian, Italian, French, and Turkish decorators. The new Western consumer patterns spread among the upper classes during his time.[22] It is popularly believed that la Dolce Vita was invented after King Farouk's indulgences and mad spending in Italian casinos. The sumptuous lifestyle of the ancient regime Pashas

---

[20] Thorsten Veblen, *The Theory of the Leisure Class: An Economic Study of Institutions*, The Modern Library, New York, 1934, p. 43.

[21] Ibid., p. 83.

[22] Khedive Isma'il's conspicuous consumption is well described by Mona L. Russell, *Creating The New Egyptian Woman*, . . ., pp. 12–20.

has been abundantly described in novels and in the cinema. The sixties cinema even often inflated stereotypes to demonize the then "withering away" exploitative feudal classes. Thus, if horse breeding, horse gambling and polo were the past time of the *haute volée* forties, today these would considered a bit out of tune (although still practiced by a few) and be replaced by golf playing in Mirage City or in the Qattameyya Club.

However, my concern is sociological. It is rather how the new rich classes have differing ways in which they express conspicuous consumption from the previous Nasserite period. From that perspective, Rokiah Talib's study on the conspicuous consumption of the "new middle class" in Malaysia that emerged in the 1970's out of the policies of *Bumiputrism* (meaning giving priority to the people of the soil. i.e the Malays) is very useful. Malaysia's ethnic specificity, consisting of a large Chinese minority and a Malay majority, followed by Indians, begs further reflection. After the May 1969 ethnic riots, the government launched a new economic policy (NEP) to redistribute wealth among the Malays who were the underprivileged compared to the Chinese who were the most powerful in the capitalist sector. By the mid nineties due to privatization, many Malays and non-Malays entered in multi-million national projects. Talib then describes the changing lifestyles and conspicuous consumption which occurred exemplified in mansions and special hills in Kuala Lumpur where the rich conglomerate, the condominiums of the new middle classes, their feastings and commercialization of weddings and the success of Mercedes, BMW and Harley Davidsons. However, most interesting is that in comparison to the old rich, the new rich do not offer alcohol in their parties because of the Islamic resurgence. They have shifted from Western to Arabized names for their children and parties are accompanied by *Qur'an* recitation. Moreover, Talib remarks that the Malays and Indians have a tendency to use more credit cards than the Chinese, an observation, which reveals a cultural dimension to consumption.[23]

Let us move to Egypt's new conspicuous consumption. One major shift from Nasserism to *Infitah* has been the public boasting of wealth by the ruling class. Compared to Sadat, Nasser was known for having

---

[23] Rokiah Talib, "Malaysia: Power Shifts and the Matrix of Consumption", in *Consumption in Asia Lifestyles and Identities*, Edited by Chua Beng-Huat, Routledge, London, 2000, pp. 35–61.

led quite a modest life style. Neither was he corrupt, nor was he a person who was after private wealth. His wife remained a modest housewife who hardly appeared in public. Nasser never revealed ostentatious inclinations and his hobby was photography, which at his time did not require much consumerism. This observation is not valid for all his ministers and the new rising officers who once in power, had one dream, to emulate the former classes in power.[24] In contrast, many still remember Sadat and his family for his conspicuous consumption, his many residences, helicopters, cars and extravaganza. One could argue that Sadat personally betrayed the very ideals of the 1952 revolution through the marriage alliances of his daughters to sons of the old landed class, the evident enemies of the revolution. One daughter married the son of one of the wealthiest contractors in Egypt and the two others to families belonging to the old feudal class (the Marei' and the 'Abdel Ghaffar families). Sadat loved to pose in different outfits, ranging from the peasant looking "chic" *gallabeyya* in his residence of Munufiyya, to smoking pipe in Western clothes, or posing as an officer with boots. His children shamelessly displayed their multiple cars and their luxuriousness became a source of national gossip.

The Sadat period has been associated with the sudden enrichment of the new classes, the nouveau riches, or the "fat cats". Those who "appeared from nowhere", the "illiterates who became millionaires", the hashish dealers, the *tuggar al shanta*, (suitcase merchants), the "free trade" zone smugglers, the retired army officers turned into arm dealers and the state employees who made millions in "commissions" through government transactions with foreign corporations and multinationals. The construction entrepreneurs who speculated frantically on real estate and later the schoolteachers who became millionaires through private lessons and the medical doctors who followed suit after the privatizing of the medical sector. During Sadat, corruption scandals multiplied. Incidental fires continuously erupted in public sector companies then declared bankrupt. Scandals continued to flourish until today and the best example is the recent case of the runaway businessmen who escaped the country after having taken immense bank loans. In 1999 the central bank report stated that

---

[24] I am not sure that such a description could apply to his ministers, some of whom were known for their greed and aspirations to emulate the lifestyles of the old classes.

these loans have reached L.E. 140 Billion representing 85 percent of its deposits. Businessmen who fled the country with colossal sums became quotidian news. Hatem al-Hawari escaped in 1996 with a loan of L.E. 1.8 (billion) (in Arabic). Rami Lakah, a former member of the People's Assembly, left Egypt after accumulating L.E. 1.4 (billion),[25] Georges Hakim with L.E. 25 million, while Al-Bilidi another businessman fled in 1999 with debts worth L.E. 110 million.[26] According to Ahmed Thabet, the total amount of loans which the businessmen obtained from banks reached L.E. 176 billion of which only 15 percent were invested in Egypt while the remaining amount was transferred to overseas banks. Out of this sum, L.E 73 billion were given to businessmen without any guarantee.[27] These incidents have led to an overrated and inflated negative image about businessmen in Egypt, as if these were systematically associated with government "clientelism" and corruption. It was generalized which according to Ahmed Thabet certainly has affected perceptions of small and middle range businessmen who are not all necessarily corrupt.[28]

If Sadat set the example for boasting wealth, the Mubarak era will be remebered as nothing but the consolidation of crony capitalism and the monopoly of wealth in a handful of families. One hears of the some twenty families,[29] or rather according to Mitchell "the two dozen family – owned enterprises" which own Egypt. Large-scale government corruption scandals became an everyday triviality.

---

[25] According to *Business Today*, Ramy Lakah admitted to have taken loans as much as L.E. 850 million. Lakah holds a double nationality (French-Egyptian). Apparently, this was the source of trouble when in 2000 he defeated a former Minister when he competed on a parliament seat. The parliament members issued then a law banning members who hold two passports in order to discredit Lakah. Ramy Lakah is currently in exile in Paris. *Business Today*, "Businessman in Exile Buys French Newspaper", November 2004, p. 17.

[26] Gamal Taye', "al-Bilidi ra's al-thi'b al-ta'ir allthi akhafa rigal al-am'al al-haribin," (Al-Bilidi the Fleeing Fox who Intimidated the Fugitive Businessmen) in *Rosa al-Youssef*, 19–3–2004, no. 3953.

[27] Ahmed Thabet, *The Business Elites . . .*, p. 430.

[28] Ahmed Thabet, *The Business Elites . . .*, p. 425.

[29] For instance the businessmen who obtained bank loans were the following: Hattem al-Hawari group one L.E. (billion), 460 million and 275, Mohammed Nosseir one billion, 222 million and 160 thousand, Ahmed Ezz, one Billion 250 million and 782 thousand L.E., Hussein Dorra One billion, 23 million 274 thousand, L.E. Ramy Lakah one billion, 448 million 944 thousand, Ibrahim Abul 'Uyoun, One billion, 413 million and 46 thousand, Youssef Allam L.E. 390 million and 890 thousand, Munir Ghabbour and sons 337 million and 611 thousand, Hussam Abul Fetouh 831 million and 373 thousand (in L.E.) quoted from Ahmed Thabet . . ., p. 430.

What happened then in the nineties was the continuation of the sale of the public sector to private companies and the growing inter-connectedness between the private and the public sector. Timothy Mitchell writes that, "in 1999, the government had sold shares in 124 of its 314 non-financial public enterprises".[30] Instead of financing agriculture and industry, or projects to foster employment and edu-cation, the state moved to finance businessmen. Banks proposed tax-free lending with a minimum loan of L.E. one million,[31] which went into the hands of the few capitalists. According to Mitchell, the IMF was the major funding source and factor behind the enrichment of the class of businessmen. It is this emerging culture of the new "financiers" and businessmen, which has set the patterns of con-spicuous consumption and showing off, but also of irresponsible care-lessness towards any civic or public concerns. It is as if the entire country is wide open for theft. Jokes about "first class" Egyptian pris-ons that host previous ministers and businessmen filled the press. The major development activities shifted to land speculation, con-struction companies, tourism and tourist resorts, real estate, food and beverage, and computer and Internet services.[32]

Boasting wealth and distinction take different shades. The new rich like to show the collection of foreign maids they have, a habit that was imported from the oil producing countries. A few years ago it was fashionable to have domestic servants from the Philippines. Fashions change, but it also depends on when the government allows a certain nationality and forbids another from entering the country. Over the years, it became possible to hire Sri Lankan, Somali and Indonesian maids. The government puts sanctions from time to time on one or another nationality as was the case for domestic servants from the Philippines, and so a shift occurred to African maids. If one observes the children's space of the Gezira Club on Fridays, one can see groups of African maids, Southeast Asian and Asian servants, who well-off mothers can exhibit. These domestic servants, while they are remunerated in US dollar are subject to all sorts of modern slavery and drudgery. For sure, it is no longer good to employ Egyptian maids; these are all pickpockets, dirty and lazy, as the Egyptian rich tell us.

---

[30] Timothy Mitchell, p. 280.
[31] Ibid., p. 282.
[32] Ibid., p. 283.

But since the family is one of the most important institutions of support in Egypt, of providing assets and networking, the wedding can be a dangerous, ruinous enterprise, which takes over inflated dimensions. This event is the most important in one's life. To be a princess for a day is the dream advertised. This is the peak of displaying and testing if the chosen partner is really wealthy. This is also the occasion for reciprocating invitations, making business contacts and displaying once again one's daughters in the market of brides. Boasting to have invited important officials and ministers affirms the status of the family. A whole new industry emerged in recent years starting with wedding planners, an American import non-existent in Egypt's seventies, to DJ's who could earn up to L.E. 15 thousand a night, decoration specialists, video film specialists, flower decorators, light system suppliers, fancy wedding dress designers, makeup specialists, wedding magazines to advertise hair dressers, dress makers, photographers; (all of these can charge astronomical prices if they are famous). These magazines also include ads for furniture and interior decoration, the fanciest weddings of Egypt as well as the wide range of various menu price lists in the international hotels where such an event takes place. The prices range between a little more than L.E. 120 to 300 per head taxes excluded. Some wedding planners would only begin to work with a down payment. Other wedding planners are flown to Europe to import the most exquisite goods, exotic flowers, chocolates and caviars and are paid high percentages according to the expenses.[33] Inflated one thousand and one night stories about some wedding planners, famed for bizarre lavish decorations, like putting special perfumes and towels with initials of the brides in the public toilets, hanging shrimps on trees, or decorating entire halls with chocolate and what not are the source of gossip of the Egyptian new rich. One has to add to that, the cost of the *Zaffa* ceremony when the brides are escorted to their seats with musicians, singers and bands. Here again there are several types of *Zaffas*, which include belly dancers carrying chandeliers accompanied with dozens of drummers that is definitively more expensive. Wedding pictures could cost several thousands pounds. But most expensive is the new fashion celebrating a three day wedding in the Red Sea coast, which might double all prices because these are beach

---

[33] See Appendix I. on an estimate of a Wedding budget of a student at the American University in Cairo.

resorts. Since these are far away from
Cairo it is a good excuse for ripping
off customers. *Al-Ahram Weekly* newspaper published a few years ago a list
of the most recent prices of singers,
comedians and belly dancers. The
highest singer earned L.E. 60,000 (Amr
Diab) for one or a few hours performance, belly dancers reached the price
of L.E. 12,000 per performance (Lucy,
Fifi Abdu, while the Argentinean
Asmahan took L.E. 5,000 and the
Russian Nour took L.E. 2,500), comedians earned L.E. 4,000 and DJ, s.
L.E. 4,500.[34]

Fig. 43. Gold's Gym, in Egypt
Today, September 2004.

To belong to the rich means that
besides the Cairo flat, one owns a villa
in a condominium or a gated com-
munity, which is also named a compound. One can possibly own
two secondary residences, even if none of these villas would be used
for more than one or two months a year. But the ideal is to live in
an isolated "compound". It also translates in being a member of the
Qattameyyah Club, which only accepts the crème of the crème
through its unaffordable membership fees, or to belong to the Business
Club in Garden City. To belong to the rich means to train in the
Gold's Gym where all the businessmen go and possibly find a rich
match. To be a member in international hotels who propose an
exclusive atmosphere. It means to launch dreamlike parties with food
flown in from Europe and abundant alcohol. And also to have his/her
stylish house featured in *al-Bayt* magazine.[35] Reports in the press on

---

[34] Tarek Atia, "Open Buffet", *al-Ahram Weekly* online, January 2001, 515. http://
weekly.ahram.org.eg/2001/515/tim1.htm.

[35] *Al-Bayt* magazine is in itself worth pondering upon. Established since now five
years (in 2005) and published by *al-Ahram*, *al-Bayt* magazine is an attempt at advertising the 'new' fancy life-style by displaying houses all over the country and the
work of rising local interior designers and artists. There are moreover, various articles on lavish houses in the Arab world and Europe. *Al-Bayt* not only advertises
houses, but also refined recipes, wood work, table displays, how to acquire antiques,
designing gardens, ceramics, flowers, and the vanishing arts and crafts. The photography is highly professional. A close look can tell that there is a clear interest

who is who, spending colossal amounts on a wedding keep on pop-
ping up.

Branded clothes, shoes and handbags worth thousands of pounds,
owning several cars, goes hand in hand with exotic travels to the
Far East which are competing with the traditional places like Europe
and the US. It means to consume in expensive restaurants, bars and
discos and, hopefully, own a yacht. We are told that the yachting
business in Egypt witnessed a boom during the last two years. It
shifted from European consumers to become an indigenous item of
expenditure.[36] But what is the difference then between a *nouveau riche*
American and an Egyptian? I guess none.

---

among the well to do in interiors and lavish life style. My impression is that there
is no clear cut homogenous life style, but an explosion of styles be it American,
European, French or English, Asian, Southeast, Ottoman, Islamic, Bauhaus, modern or hybrid.

[36] Some Red Sea tourist companies offer weekend Red Sea holidays on a luxury yacht for about $1200–1500 a day. They seem to be successful since these fit
the younger generation tendencies for showing off as some of the agents stated.
There are 400 small yachts in Hurgada and 300 in Sharm al-Sheikh. Moreover,
there are more than 30 luxury yachts, which could reach the cost of $3.5 million
owned mostly by Egyptians and Arabs. See Summer Said, "Lapping it Up: The
Seas are calling a growing number of Egyptians to Luxurious Life on a Yacht-
Owned or Rented", *Business Today*, Novembre, 2004, pp. 84–85.

CHAPTER FIVE

A NEW CONSUMER CULTURE

"It's time we spoke the language of the modern age".
"With real production that will raise Egypt's position up on high".
Mustafa El Beleedy *(one of Egypt's sons)*

"Lancome, Cacharelle, Joval, Wrangler, Guy la Roche, Stefanelle, Van Hausen Made in Egypt by El Beleedy Group"

Sonnalah Ibrahim, Zaat. Translated by Anthony Calderbank, AUC Press, 2001, (p. 311).

This chapter consists of snapshots that attempt to provide a glimpse of the changing habits and consumer lifestyles amongst the middle class and the newly rich Egyptians in the nineties. It might appear as if the chapter has no coherent centre. In fact, it evolves around the broad theme of the dynamics of the changing forms of consumer culture. Design, fancy lifestyles, good looks and advertisements have been pervasively influential. It could, however, be argued that these have already existed since colonial times. However, conspicuous consumption was restricted to the upper elites, which emulated in lifestyle either the British colonizer or their counterparts, the French, with their civilizing mission ideology. Many well-bred Egyptians were more royalist than the king in priding themselves on their ability to recite Corneille and Lafontaine in perfect French. The culture of the *"Aubusson* salon" was widespread in the Levant and Egypt. Old elites are still proud to state that they were among the first to be accepted at the Gezira Club, to rub shoulders with the British officers. So what is new today about emulating imported lifestyles? It is the change in taste with the decline of empires and cosmopolitanism being replaced by "globalization" that interests us here. If the ideals were England and France in colonial times, today one observes increasing American influences in every small detail. "Whenever, I enter a house of the new rich classes and fail to recognize the style of the décor, I am later informed that this is American style. This has occurred in a systematic way," said Menha al-Batrawi, a freelance writer for *al-Bayt* Magazine. The American way of life, fast food, Hollywood films, pop stars and rap music seems to be more

than ever pervading Egypt. English
has become the second most spo-
ken language. It is certainly taking
over the long tradition of "francophonie" in Egypt and evidently
affecting Arabic. It is as if those who
equated globalization with Americanization proved to be finally right.

In this chapter, I am basically
interested in how emerging forms
of consumerism have affected notions of beauty, fashion and lifestyles
amongst expanding middle-class
Cairenes during the past two decades
and how this is sharpening class distinctions. While consumer culture
has pervaded all aspects of social

Fig. 44. Ad Wonderland.

life, in a developing country like Egypt, class and social inequality
still remain dominant factors in defining everyday social interaction.

Cairo's thirty shopping malls and centres, all constructed in the
last ten years, are a symbol of this change.[1] Shopping malls have
reached the most remote villages of the Egyptian Delta. Cairo's
supermarkets have everything one can imagine. ATM cards, non-
existent some ten years ago, are becoming popular. Who would have
thought that Egyptians, who have such mistrust for anything related
to the government and by extension its banking system, would con-
vert to this plastic card? There are now more than 900 ATM's in
Egypt most of which are Master Card, Dinner's Club and Visa. The
number of ATM's is expected to reach around 10, 000 in the next
ten years.[2]

"Every Wednesday, 1200 cards are shipped to Cairo, individually
packed under strict security measures delivered to customers: cus-
tomized report provided to bank . . . all within 24 hours". This is the
advertisement of Aramex Banking Team in Cairo's magazine *Business
Today*. ABC Bank (Arab Banking Corporation) provides credit cards

---

[1] This is the most recent number of malls and shopping centres provided by
Noha El Hennawy, "Window Shop until you Drop", *Egypt Today*, April, 2005, pp.
102–107.

[2] Joseph Vess, "Paper or Plastic", *Business Today*, May 2005, p. 83.

for people with a salary of at least 2000 L.E. and a time deposit of no less than L.E. 5000.

Mobinil, the largest mobile phones company in Egypt has reached in September 2005 the impressive number of 6 million subscribers.[3] The number of thefts of mobile phones is also on the increase. This of course goes hand in hand with the flourishing trade in second-hand mobiles in popular quarters. Would mobile phones have a democratizing effect? The relatively reasonable price of the device means that "everybody" can carry a mobile. From domestic servants, to housekeepers, to drivers, to children, mobile phones became popular and

Fig. 45. Ads for condominiums in gated communities in magazines.

available. Those who resist it are today stigmatized as "odd". It is no longer a status symbol, as many Cairenes would vehemently argue. Yet, not so long ago it was difficult to acquire a telephone line. This has changed but the installation of a land-line is still much more expensive than a mobile. In fact, the less well off classes have been until recently deprived from this means of communication.

Internet cafés are everywhere. Youngsters now have many alternative ways of spending their time at various prices. Leisure time can be spent in bowling centres, playing computer games, in cinemas and air-conditioned fast food chains, all available in either shopping malls or as independent spaces. Discotheques and nightclubs are widely available but only to cater to the richer strata. The Far East has become an exotic tourist destination for the Egyptian rich who discover Thailand, Malaysia and Singapore; international music is available everywhere, Arabic music video-clips are becoming increasingly hybridized. The Far East is often shown on satellite channels as a "mixing" of for instance Indian, Thai dances and landscapes, as well as international tastes and music. Professional belly dancing

---

[3] See "About Orascom" http://www.Orascomtelecom.com/about. (2005).

has been globalised in Cairo, where a large foreign contingent of around 5000 Russian, Argentine, Scottish and American dancers ply their trade. It seems that the Russian nationals have the lions share in this profession today. As a result the government has imposed severe restrictions on non-Egyptian belly dancers in order to protect the local professionals.[4] Russian, Moroccan, Tunisian, Algerian and Western European prostitutes compete with the local courtesans. Tourism, first in Cairo, Luxor, Aswan and then all along the Red Sea has certainly changed local norms of male sexuality. Male fantasies have changed among young rural men in this sector who, for the first time in their lives, experience sexual encounters with Western women. Many believe that satellite channels will make us happy; we no longer need to travel abroad. On the other hand, around eleven million people are living in unplanned housing, put simply, living in slums in Egypt without sewage and running water. But is all this new? Modern Cairo-the Western, grid down town city with its double (the Islamic city) always consisted of split worlds. Cairene and Alexandrian cosmopolitan life existed centuries before the concept of globalization.

The Cappuccino Egyptianized

The culture of coffee shops has become very successful in Egypt. However, it would be erroneous to believe that these have emerged only in the last decade. What we see today is a different coffee culture, which caters to younger sections of the society, who can afford to pay for a cappuccino. The "ancient regime" elites emulated the colonizers and long ago adopted the café culture. According to Artemis Cooper, in her impressions of Cairo between 1941–1942, the Groppi Garden in 'Adly Street, because of its privacy attracted both British officers and Pashas with their Levantine mistresses. The officers envied the Pashas as there was a dearth of respectable available females.[5] Downtown, Groppi in Soliman Pasha square,[6] Lapas,

---

[4] Issandr El-Amrani, "Government announces Intention to nationalize Belly Dancing", *Business Monthly*, September 2003, (32–34), 33.

[5] Artemis Cooper, *Cairo in the War 1939–1945*, (first published by Hamish Hamilton. 1989) Penguin, 1995, p. 121.

[6] Groppi was created by a Swiss named Giacomo Groppi. It became one of the most celebrated coffee houses by the elite and the royalty for its exquisite choco-

the Indian Tea House (frequented mainly by elderly men), were all coffee houses, which survived, less glamorously, into the sixties. Simond's in Zamalek, an Italian inspired coffee shop, was also popular in the sixties. The Cairene elite in the sixties enjoyed during summers the garden of Groppi in Adly Pasha Street. Groppi was famous for exquisite deserts and ice creams. These spaces were typical *beau monde* places for parading and showing off. The two Groppis have become run down, but Simond's continues to cater to the older generation of Zamalek residents.

The new coffee houses, and there are plenty, offer places for the younger generation of yuppies, students and school children who can afford to pay for a drink, a croissant or a sandwich. It is considered as an affordable outing with friends. Middle class Egyptians have in recent years been exposed to the culture of the breakfast croissant, espresso and cappuccinos. They have also learned to eat Japanese sushi, Italian, Thai, Indian, Iranian, and Lebanese food. In such coffee houses, the English *Cairo Times* (ceased to appear) and *Community Times*, are available. While they sip their coffee, customers can listen to the Buena Vista Social Club, Cuban music and to the most recent hits, all the while exchanging flirtatious looks with their partners. Also worth noting is the English language *Al-Ahram Weekly's* restaurant review, often written in slightly pretentious language, which is certainly diffusing a new taste for the Egyptian palette The *Weekly* is attempting to promote an image of cosmopolitan Cairo. There is even a Café Gevara which has been labelled by the *Weekly* columnist Youssef Rakha as being one of the most successful "radical hip" restaurants.

Fancy coffee houses and restaurants are multiplying with names such as: La Bodega, Le Morocco, Le Peking, The Cellar, Justine, Villa Rosa, Cortigiani, Le Bistro Provençale, Shahenshah, La Creperie des Arts, SS Nile Peking, Cairo Jazz Club, Le Tabasco, Mermaid, Villa D'Este, Sangria, Blues, Casablanca, La Gourmandise, Flux, Bam-bu, Ruffino, Rithmo, Le Grill, etc. And for the special occasion of Ramadan, international hotels, like the Ramses Hilton compete

---

late. According to Samir Ra'afat, by 1900, it was already a prosperous enterprise and it exported large quantities of eggs to the United Kingdom. Groppi's was also known to be the first *chocolatier* in Egypt to employ women' (Ra'afat p. 23). For further information about the history of Groppi, see Samir Ra'afat, *Cairo, The Glory Years*, Harpocrates, 2003, pp. 22–25.

to offering the best *fitars* (the breaking of the fasting) and traditional Ramadan evenings with whirling *dervishes*. Special tents are set for the occasion, such as Abu Ali at the Nile Hilton, Ayam Zaman at Cairo Capital Club, Cairo Marriot and Cairo Sheraton, Le Pasha. Sahar al-Layali, Sahrana at Intercontinental Pyramids, Sidi Mansur, Sonesta Hotel and the First Mall. Some stylish cafes provide *shishas* (the water pipes). Smoking *shishas* has become a popular pastime among the adolescents and the sight of women smoking them in public areas has become common.

Walter Ambrust has watched television programs during Ramadan, in particular the riddle (the *Fawazir*), to argue that the ritual has undergone a sort of Christmas-tization in relationship to mass culture and materialism. During Christmas the family takes a dominant role in the commercialization of the event.[7] Without doubt, in Egypt an increasing commercialization of the religious event of Ramadan is taking place, but this is not necessarily leading towards enhancing family values. For example, twenty years ago hardly any middle- and upper-class Egyptians broke the fast in international hotels. It was a family event. Spending the late night after breaking the fasting in international hotels such as the garden of the Marriot, and the Hilton only became very popular in recent years, which means that Egyptians increasingly go to public places associated with international tourism. My impression however, is that family gatherings and reciprocating invitations during the month of Ramadan seem to have decreased due to financial hardship. Many complain that it has become extremely difficult to maintain an open and hospitable house as their parents did. However, in relation to coffee houses, something would be missing if we ignore the continuing pervasive role of the *Baladi Qahwas* and how these have been integrated in such modern spaces as the mall.

Baladi Qahwas *(Popular Coffee Houses) in Malls*

Only one Cairo institution is more common than the mosque: the *qahwa* or coffeehouse. Statistics are less accurate now than when

---

[7] Walter Ambrust stated that he borrowed his concept from Daniel Miller's edited work, *Unwrapping Christmas*, Clarendon Press, 1993. See Walter Armbrust, "The Riddle of Ramadan: Media, Consumer Culture and Christmas-ization of a Muslim Holiday". http://nmit.georgetown.edu/papers/warmbrust.htm

Napoleon's army counted 1,350 coffee houses in the city of a Thousand Minarets, but the ratio of 200 citizens per café has not declined much. By this reckoning the cafés of modern Cairo must number well over 30,000.[8] Max Rodenbeck's observation reminds us how crucial the coffee house has been as a traditional institution for socializing, gossiping, playing backgammon and grouping people according to profession. But it has also been a crucial front-stage space in popular quarters where people sat commenting upon passers-by and where the news of the quarter was exchanged. The coffee house has been for many years exclusively a male space. The coffee house as a locus for commenting upon the physique of passing women is a repeated theme in novels and Egyptian films.

Lovers of the city of Cairo also boast about the special cultural milieu of downtown intellectuals, painters, writers and essayists, which has seen a revival during the 1990s. They meet in the same places (coffeehouses and bars) nearly every night to drink, joke, exchange news, ideas and information, gossip about politics, art or the latest scandal. The most famous landmarks of this scene were: the *qahwat al-Bustan*, also called the *qahwat al-muthaqafin wal fananin* (the coffee house of intellectuals and artists), the Greek Club, which is located above Groppi's coffee house, the Grillon and the Odeon bars, the Estoril restaurant, the bar of the Windsor hotel and the famous Café Riche which recently re-opened. Café Riche catered to leftist intellectuals in the sixties. Every Friday, intellectuals, journalists, and lawyers met for breakfast with the owner and spend hours in discussions and exchange of news, politics and jokes.

Can one conclude that coffee houses in today's malls are becoming the cultural counterpart of the long-standing downtown bars? Are these bars and local downtown coffee houses hangouts for a new counter-culture counter posed to the aggressive consumer culture in shopping malls? It is most unlikely that one will replace the other. But these observations need further reflection and elaboration. For students of consumerism, it is extraordinary to observe the incorporation of modernized Egyptian coffee houses within the space of shopping malls. Currently, many malls like the Ramses annex and the Yamamah Centre have created an Egyptian *qahwah* where one can smoke water pipes in the air-conditioned space of the mall. Quite

[8] Max Rodenbeck, *Cairo, The City Victorious*, AUC Press, 1998, (1999), p. 263.

often, a typical Egyptian street-seller's cart sits nearby with popular (*sha'bi*) food like *ful* (beans), chickpeas and oriental salads. Some coffeehouses have artistic ambitions, such as the coffeehouse on the ground floor of the Yamamah Centre in Zamalek, which incorporates a gallery. This coffee house has become a meeting place for young writers and painters. This is where young boys and girls meet to flirt. It has become a place where one can smoke the *shisha* (water pipe), discuss art and exhibit paintings for sale. There is a noticeable folklorization of culture through the flourishing of tourism in such public places, like baking popular *baladi* bread in the Marriott and Sheraton hotels, and the installation of tents with belly dancers and popular singers, a kitschy mimicry of Bedouin life. In the malls, the smoking of water pipes, display of ambulant food carts, selling *ful* and *ta'miyyah* (vegetarian rissoles) – originally the diet of the poor and the lower classes – has become fashionable with the revival, celebration and purification of popular traditions. The Geneina Mall in Nasr City offered some three years, in a tent restaurant inside the mall, pastries (*fitir*) and *kushari*, a popular dish, which consists of rice and noodles topped with a rich tomato sauce with onions. The Tiba Mall attracts youth from the popular quarter of Manshiyyat Nasser City, which is considered today as a squatter area. The Grand mall of Ma'adi is a fascinating place to study the various nationalities. On weekends, female maids from the Philippines gather at the bowling centre to play and chat. Besides Americans, the members of the Korean, Japanese and Southeast Asian communities frequent this centre because they can purchase Asian goods now available in Egypt.

Resorts

Leisure resorts, secondary residences, walled or gated communities such as Qattamiyya Heights and Beverley Hills, have multiplied. Advertisements sell a simulated dream of grandiose villas, incorporated in a larger condominium unit that would include a swimming pool, a fitness centre, and ultimately a golf course. In other words, everything is catered towards the notion of leading a healthy, luxurious and unpolluted life on the fringe of the desert. An "Idyll" is being sold as a counter image to the rotting, polluted old Cairo. Topless women and Western visitors give the feeling that this is a different Egypt.

Most fascinating is the hybridization in design and architecture in such new-gated communities and beach resorts. The beloved word for architectural innovation in the advertisements is "the blending" of tastes, where West meets East. Al-Gouna resort on the Red Sea is one of those spaces, which can hardly compare with any other place in Egypt. Constructed by the Orascom group, one of the most powerful financial groups in Egypt, al-Gouna lagoon consists of conglomerates of fancy stylish villas. Al-Gouna's advertisements show off the sophisticated interior decoration of these villas. Interior decorations range from the exotic India,

Fig. 46. El-Gouna Ad in *Egypt Today*, September 2004.

Indonesia and Thailand to Western styles. Certainly architecture in Egypt is being influenced by outside taste, but this is not a new phenomenon at all considering that Downtown was in its entirety constructed by European architects at the end of the nineteenth and early twentieth century. Again at al-Gouna, one is given a variety of choices from pseudo Italian Tuscan villas, designed by Alfredo Freda, on the Hill to a re-invented Arabic-Islamic architecture by the internationally acclaimed Princeton architect Michael Graves, or entirely different Greek style villas. The White Villas, for example, designed by the famed Egyptian architect Shehab Mazhar, demonstrate a Mediterranean flair.[9] Is this emulation or blending of styles?

Fig. 47. White Villas. Courtesy of El-Gouna Real Estate. www.elgouna.com.

---

[9] See *El-Gouna Real Estate*. www.redsea-realestate.com.

The irony here is that the style
of late Egyptian architect Hassan
Fathi, has often been adopted in
these resorts. The new rich class
has, today adopted Fathi's concept of searching for authentic
traditional styles and "popular"
materials such as mud brick. "Constructing for the poor",[10] which
was Fathi's philosophy in reviving vernacular architecture and
traditional craftsmanship is carried out by his disciple Rami al-

Fig. 48. Courtesy of El Gouna Real
Estate. www.elgouna.com.

Dahhan and adopted by the new Egyptian leisure class. Fathi, the
romantic idealist who dreamt of reconstituting the paradise lost of
the Egyptian village, spent many years studying Nubian art and
architecture, which tremendously inspired his work. Domes, arches
and vaults which were central to Fathi's brilliant revival of tradition,
are consciously re-popularized in the resorts and five stars hotels as
part and parcel of the "folklorization of culture".[11] The idea of the
"village" is then reproduced in a sanitized and soporific manner in
such beach resorts, but of course for the gated happy few. Fathi's

Fig. 49. El Golf Villas. Courtesy of El
Gouna Real Estate. www.elgouna.com.

disciple, Ahmad Hamid considers
that, sadly, Fathi's second generation disciples "have all got stuck
with the form, in reproducing
vaults arches and domes to build
discotheques, resorts and restaurants or anything . . . the conti-
nuum should be in the evolution
of thought, like what happened
with the disciple of the Bau-
huas . . . they continued to think
in solving practical solutions",
which did not occur in the case

---

[10] See Hassan Fathy, *Gourna a Tale of Two Village* translated into French as *Construire
pour le peuple*, Sindbad, Paris, 1970.
[11] See also the section on fashion in the next chapter, specifically Shahira Mehrez,
also a Fathi disciple who revived traditional dresses, which have been equally appropriated by the bourgeoisie.

of Fathi. For Hamid, many have failed to understand Fathi's theories whose theoretical contribution is as important as Le Corbusier's. To reduce Fathi simply to the vernacular is a mistake. Fathi was in fact a modernist who searched for practical solutions deriving from the local environment and tradition. In other words, by appropriating Fathi, his followers have separated him from his ideas. They made out of his work "a collage of a whole life cycle . . . a pastiche (a commodity) . . . very much like the computer button used by architects called 'stretch'. It is comparable to Lycra stockings, one can stretch buildings and designs . . . and this is where meaning, proportions and semiotics get lost . . . very much like the context is lost".[12]

With the recession of the early years of the new century, and the recent deflation of the Egyptian pound, Sharm al-Sheikh and al-Gouna resorts are experiencing a real transformation. Large numbers of Russian new comers are the new wealthy, able to buy real estate all along the coast. Another example of selling "deluxe" lifestyles is "Star Living", the newly constructed residential component of Nasr City's mega project Citystars. Star Living is offering model apartments which sell for 1500–2000 $ per square meter with an average size of 317 square meters. The two level 1.250 square meters pent houses sell for $2.5 million.[13]

One cannot speak of Gouna without mentioning the main investors behind such gigantic projects. Namely, the influential role of Orascom in fostering contractor ship, which will evidently have a remarkable effect on the urban landscape.

Orascom

I would like to emphasize the role of Orascom group that constructed the newly finished Nile Towers. The transformation of the quarter of Bulaq is closely related to Orascom. The emergence of such a concentration of wealth in the hands of few families is in fact the logical continuation of the open-door policy, which was introduced by Sadat. The Egyptian World Trade Centre was considered until a few years ago a success story, symbolizing the triumph of the new class of tycoons in Egypt. First founded in New Orleans in 1968

---

[12] Interview with Ahmad Hamed, 15 May 2005.
[13] *Business Today*, June 2003, p. 67.

to encourage the expansion of world trade through the World Trade
Centre concept, the WTC Association has grown to become a net-
work of over 220 member WTCs in over 190 cities worldwide. The
World Trade Centre in Cairo was founded in 1990, as a joint ven-
ture supervised by the architects Owings and Merril Skidmore from
Chicago and Ali Nour el Din from Egypt. Orascom completed the
second phase in Bulaq by constructing the Conrad Hotel and the
Nile Towers.

The Sawiris family, which founded Orascom, emerged during the
Mubarak regime. As Mitchell pointed out, such family capitalism
brings to mind American families like the Rockefellers or the Fords.
Samir Ra'afat drew an analogy between the earlier merchant entrepreneurs of Jewish origin, the Suares Brothers, Felix, Joseph and
Raphael who prospered in Egypt at the end of the nineteenth century and who created, at the beginning of the twentieth century the
Credit Foncier Egyptien and were the launchers of a modern trans-
port system, and the local Egyptian Sawiris patriarch, Onsi, with his
three sons, Samih, Nassif and Naguib. There was a similarity in
terms of the clannish aspect of family capitalism and in closeness to
the centre of political power. Raphael Suares was the advisor of
Khedive Abbas Hilmi II and the Sawiris' close connections are with
the Mubarak regime.[14]

Inflated stories of the Sawiris family and their origins are fed by
rumours that they accumulated wealth through having obtained loans
from the World Bank and US aid. Onsi Sawiris, the father founded
his company in 1950. Today, it includes Orascom Construction
Industries, Orascom Projects Touristic Development and Orascom
Technologies. Onsi Sawiris made his fortune in Libya where he went
in 1961. His company constructed the US Embassy in Cairo, which
was evidently one of the main sources of having access to US loans.[15]
Orascom is a holding company which controls eleven subsidiaries[16]
"including Egypt's largest private construction, cement making and
natural gas supply companies, the country's largest tourism developments (funded in part by the World Bank), an arms trading company and exclusive local rights in cell phones, Microsoft, McDonald's

---

[14] Samir Ra'afat, "From Suares to Sawiris", *Cairo Times*, December 24, 1998.
http://www.egy.com/people/98-12-24.shtml.
[15] Personal communication with John Sfakianakis, March 20, 2005.
[16] Mitchell, 1999, p. 31.

and much more".[17] The Egyptian cement company (ECC) belonging to Orascom is the third largest cement plant in the world, producing 7.5 million tons in 2004. ECC is the largest exporter of cement in Egypt.[18]

Orascom construction industries (OCI) functions as a contractor and has undertaken numerous projects, including the world's largest swing bridge over the Suez Canal, and the Conrad International and Le Meridien hotels. It has formed alliances with Bechtel, Consolidated Contractors Besix, Morrison-Knudsen, Krupp and various others investment companies in strategic infrastructure projects. Orascom's first touristic project was El Gouna in the Red sea. El Gouna is spread over 9.5 million square meters. It consists of six hotels, 315 villas and apartments, a Nubian style village, a local airport, a shopping arcade, and many restaurants. Orascom's second project is the Taba Heights, which consists of 8 million square meters south of Taba including six hotels, 200 villas and apartments, and other facilities. Orascom has another tourist resorts projects in Sahel Hashish, and a further one is planned in al-Rouboue in Fayyoum.[19] Orascom Telecom, the Cairo based mobile phone and Internet Company, managed to make a net profit of $ 178 million in 2002. Mobinil subscribers are increasing 23 percent up year on year. "Mobinil and the other Egyptian operator, Vodafone Egypt, are negotiating a deal whereby the state owned Telecom Egypt would postpone for five years plans to launch a third mobile phone system".[20] Orascom Telecom has expanded in the last few years to Bangladesh, Algeria, Tunisia, and most recently to Iraq (Iraqna). Their subscribers have reached 9 million worldwide, with profits rocketing by 743 percent to L.E. 1.155 billion (about $ 185 million).[21]

---

[17] Ibid. However, John Sfakianakis denies that Orascom has an arms trading company. Personal Communication with John Sfakianakis.

[18] Orascom construction Industrial, Cementing our Presence in an EmergingWorld. Annual Report, 2004. http://www.orascomci.com/filestore/oc12004.pdf.

[19] http://www.orascom.com/organiz/htm.

[20] "Global News Analysis. Egypt: Orascom Telecom's Dramatic Turnaround". http://www.ebusinessforum.com/index.asp 21 May 2003.

[21] "Telecoms & It. OT moves into Bangladesh", *Business Today*, March, 2005. http://www.businesstodayegypt.com/article.aspx?ArticleID=2399.

Fig. 50. McDonald's in Ramses Hilton.

Eating Out (McDonald's in Cairo)

George Ritzer's (McDonaldization) thesis, with the world undergoing a transformation through the new means of consumption exemplified in fast food restaurants, credit cards, shopping malls, mega-malls and superstores will lead to a form homogenization and "banalisation" of the world. Ritzer discussed at length Max Weber's rationalization thesis and its impact upon a globalized work organization. These ideas have been picked up, criticized and extended by Asian and South East Asian social scientists.[22] However, Southeast Asian scholars have developed a much more sophisticated understanding of the interactive process of consumerism. Take for instance, Chua Beng Huat's study on McDonald's in Asia, in which he challenges Ritzer's argument about the McDonaldization of world as the trope of a

---

[22] J.L. Watson (eds.) *Golden East: McDonald's in East Asia*, Stanford University Press, 1997.

world wide form of rationalization, by demonstrating in the case of Singapore that in order to conquer the market McDonald's had to be Asianized. The food offered was indigenized. For instance, chicken Nuggets is offered with curry or sweet-and-sour sauce.[23] A careful reading of Ritzer's thesis tells us that "going local" is part of the global market strategy of McDonald's. Everywhere in the world McDonald's adopts hybrid local tastes in their menu. Looking at the German McDonald's advertisement, you see a young, slim and "healthy looking" couple eating McDonald's salads. The ad says "Ich habe mir fest vorgenomen, mehr auf meine Ernaehrung zu achten" (I have taken the firm decision to take increasing care over my nutrition).[24] The effect of the culture of the Green movement in Germany has evidently played an influential role in such advertising.

It is possible to argue that fast food is not an American invention. Cairene streets have always been colourful, with stalls and street carts selling *ful* and *ta'miyya* sandwiches, *kushari* (a mix of rice, beans and noodles in tomato sauce), salads, and grilled meat *kofta*, sausages or liver. These stalls are practical, cheap and quick stand-by eating alternatives. They are far from vanishing with the introduction of McDonald's. These two markets provide for different publics, which seem to coexist quite well. But the menus in Cairo's McDonald's are carbon copies of American ones, although the service might not be as efficient, nor would the newly imposed work ethic stimulate any form of rationalization. The press has even hinted at the dubious hygienic condition in the kitchens. However, the regular customers of Cairo McDonald's quickly notice that this chain has "Egyptianised" by deteriorating into a slow and sometimes inefficient service, without catering to the Egyptian palette.

McDonald's did make a modest attempt to sell the popular vegetarian snacks, called *ta'miyyas* or *falafel*. These are considered to be the diet of the poor, and are sold at every street corner from ambulant carts. One risks exposure to dubious hygienic conditions by eating from these. Thus, when McDonald's launched McFalafel as a vegetarian alternative, during the period when Egyptians became concerned about mad cow disease a couple of years ago, enthusiastic voices about "localising" McDonald's were to be heard. *McFalafel*

---

[23] Beng Huat, Chua, "Singaporeans Ingesting McDonald's" in: *Consuming Asians*, pp. 183–202, p. 195.
[24] Auf zu McDonald's!, *Der Spiegel* Nr. 4/19.1.04.

was squeezed in McDonald's buns instead of the thin Egyptian *bal-adi* bread. The *McFalafel* campaign was launched by the popular singer Sha'ban 'Abdel Rehim, a former "ironer", who gained fame with his song "I hate Israel". The result of this was a serious diplomatic crisis and protest from international Jewish organizations about his alleged anti-semitism. McDonald's then had to withdraw the ads. But it later declared a pro-Palestinian political stand in order not to loose its credibility with the local public it caters to. Sha'ban 'Abdel Rehim is a typical mass culture phenomenon worth reflecting upon. He is an illiterate, who is proud of originating from a *bi'a* milieu. 'Abdel Rehim appears in the media wearing bright, flagrant shirts, gold necklaces, and straightened curly hair that looks as if its been done at a cheap hair salon. All his songs are sung with the same rhythm and the topics are highly political and class sensitive. He first became known through the "I hate Israel" song. His other popular songs also expressed strong anti-American feelings after the invasion of Iraq, or the mad soaring price of the dollar. His popularity is due to the fact that he truly expresses the resentments and sorrows of the silent majority. Thus, the idea of selling *ta'miyya* sandwiches at McDonald's was aborted. Some say that McDonald's prices were perhaps too expensive in comparison to popular restaurants. They have been labelled by *al-Ahram Weekly* as "Aristocratic falafel" for their unaffordable price.[25] Since then, McDonald's has introduced a *McArabia* Chicken sandwich. What gives it a supposed "oriental" flavour is that the chicken pieces are wrapped in thin oriental bread instead of the standard McDonald's buns and offered with chilli sauce.

In relation to the topic of boycott, McDonald's seems to have suffered during the last few years from the worldwide reaction against American politics in the Middle East. According to some sources, McDonald's witnessed the worst losses since its founding 45 years ago; these amounted to 343.8 million dollars in 2003.[26] The Arab boycott of American and Israeli goods was launched after the Israeli attack and politics in the occupied territories during the second

---

[25] Tarek Atia, "Good Night Mr Hamburger", *Al-Ahram Weekly*. http://weekly.ahram.org.eg/2001/540/li1.htm 28 June–4 July 2001.

[26] Mustafa Abdel Halim, "Muslims Rally Against U.S. Products, Big Mac fells Backlash", IslamOnline. http://www.islamonline.net/English/News/2003–02/08/article03.shtml.

intifadah. In year 2000, the boycott was supported by the then Grand Mufti Nasr Farid Wasel.[27] During the Iraq war, Cairo University students signed petition for the boycott. Mohammed Sayyed Tantawi and Sheikh Youssef al-Qaradawi equally issued similar *fatwas* urging for the boycott.[28]

McDonald's started to function in Egypt in 1994. Huge companies such as the Mansour-Orascom group, names repeatedly appearing on many gigantic projects, were major participants in its creation in Cairo.[29] The special attention in catering to the Egyptian taste is translated through selling a children friendly image. McDonald's proposes new spaces for children's games such as "Play Lands" and "Play Place", "Ronald's Room" and "Ronald's Corner". The McDonald's at the Hilton Ramses became quite popular because of the fancy children's playground. McDonald's also caters to children's birthday parties and offers three different price packages. Here again, Egyptians are experiencing the novel habit of celebrating birthdays by renting public places. In some cases, music and a DJ are brought in while each invitee pays his own entrance fee.

As Egypt is a Third World country, burdened with economic problems, one aspect of McDonald's local strategy is adopting a charity, "assisting the poor and destitute", as an initiative to embellish its image. The McDonald's website boasts about its charity work with the Association of the Friends of the National Cancer Institute, with a contribution of 2,000,000 L.E. It also works with other charity institutions, such as Caritas Egypt, SETI, Love and Care, the Egyptian Red Crescent, Awladi, and Association Dar al-Hanan.[30] However, while fast food in the US offers cheap and quick meals for people who could not otherwise afford to eat out, in Third World countries such as Egypt, it obviously caters to the middle and upper well to do classes. Going to McDonald's is meant to be an outing on a Friday, feast days or holidays.

---

[27] Asma Waghih, "Local Chain Exploits, 'American' niche", "American Chamber of Commerce in Egypt". http://www.amcham.org.eg/publications/BusinesssMonthly/July%2002/reports8monthlythrives).asp.

[28] Mustafa Abdel Halim, "Muslims Rally Against U.S. Products, Big Mac fells Backlash", IslamOnline.

[29] http://www.*cyberegypt.com/mcdonalds's/*ehist1.htm, McDonald's Egypt History.

[30] http//www.mcdonalds.com/countries/Egypt/Egypt.html Welcome to McDonald's in Egypt. Egypt-owned, operated and proud to serve you.

Also worth noting is the emergence of Egyptian fast food chains
as serious competitors to the
American chains. The local food
chain Mo'men (meaning believer)
profited most from the Arab boycott of American and Israeli
goods. Several sources draw a
direct association between the
losses of the American food chains
with the rise and success of its
Egyptian counterpart. The Egyp-

Fig. 51. Mo'men advertisement
in *Al-Ahram*.

tian fast food company Mo'men was founded in 1988 with one large
site in Heliopolis. The chain expanded to twelve franchised branches
in Egypt and one branch in Kuwait. It employs 1300 workers and
it is considered to be a "market leader" in the Egyptian fast food
industry. According to its promotional material, Mo'men is "is the
only domestic company among the top four fast food chains operating in Egypt, and the only Egyptian firm competing effectively,
professionally and ethically with the leading international fast food
giants".[31]

Ironically, Mo'men is relying on American technology and machinery to produce bread and bakery products.[32] Mo'men runs a 34 L.E.
million high-tech mass-production factory with a full range of pro-
cessing, quality control and storage.[33] Mo'men offers sandwiches ranging from shish kofta, shawerma, tawook, Kiev, the Mexican, to potato,
chicken and seafood salads. Recently (in March 2005) *Mo'men* started
to advertise in *al-Ahram*, hamburger sandwiches that look identical
to McDonald's but are cheaper. But would these alternative Egyptian
fast foods be able to compete with the over 50 McDonald's chains
all over the country? Cairo alone has thirteen McDonald's restaurants. Some argue that the identical Mo'men hamburgers are a suit-

---

[31] Wael Kortam, *Mo'men*, Partners for a Competitive Egypt-MDI Phase 2, Strategic
Objective 17 Skills for Competitiveness Developed September 2004, USAID/
EGYPT/HDD P. 3, http://www.pfcegypt.com/M&E/General%20Reports/Case%20
Study-Mo'men.pdf
[32] Asma Waghih, "Local Chain Exploits, 'American' niche", "American Chamber
of Commerce in Egypt".
[33] Wael Kortam, p. 7.

able alternative for those who go along with the growing boycott of American products in Egypt. In fact, Mo'men's success is attributed partly to his Islamic political orientation, which seems to attract increasingly the pro-boycott, anti-American public.

This brings us to the phenomenon of the expansion of other international fast food chains in Egypt, which witnessed a boom in recent years. The number of fast food chains quadrupled in the late nineties. It seems that the Egyptian Company for International Tourist Products (Americana) holds the monopoly for the franchise of several companies such as Wimpy's, KFC, Pizza Hut, Subway, TGI Friday, and Baskin-Robbins.[34] According to the market assessment, food is one of the few industries, which seems to be doing well. Perhaps this would explain why food business in general and fast food in particular never failed in Egypt. However, the secret of the success of the food industry is due to the introduction of home delivery service, which began in the eighties. Today many can indulge in the laziness of running an entire household through the telephone. This is the cardinal privilege of living in Cairo as many would say.

One thing is evident, eating habits are changing among urbanites. According to a study undertaken by the Nutrition Institute, the number of meals eaten outside the home has increased from 20 percent in 1981 to 46 percent in 1998. Annual meat consumption has risen from 17 Kg per capita to 21 Kg over the last ten years. Similar increases have been recorded for oil and sugar. But the reverse side of "the plenty" is revealed in the fact that 20 percent of the well-off Cairenes suffer from diabetes.[35] It is also estimated that 65 percent of Egyptians are suffering from obesity.[36] It is estimated that 56 percent of Cairo's female population is overweight. Yet, at the same time, the widening gap between the well-off Cairenes and the poor means that stunting among children, which was on decline in the 1980's, increased in the nineties, along with the decline in overall average per capita calorie consumption.[37]

---

[34] http://strategis.ic.gc.ca/ssg/dd73614e.html, Egypt-Fast food Franchising – Market Assessment – ISA 981201, U.S Department of Commerce, 1999–02–02.
[35] *Egypt Almanac* 2002, p. 117.
[36] Manal El Jesri, "Fast Food Nation", *Egypt Today* August 2003, pp. 72–81.
[37] This is according to the World Bank. See *Egypt Almanac*, 2002, p. 117.

Differing Notions of Beauty and Consumer Culture

> "*Tastes in food also depend on the idea each class has of the body and of the effects of food on the body, that is, on the strength, health and beauty, and on the categories it uses to evaluate these effects, some of which the different classes may rank in very different ways. Thus, whereas the working classes are more attentive to the strength of the (male) body than its shape, and tend to go for products that are both cheap and nutritious, the professions prefer products that are tasty, health-giving, light and not fattening*".

Pierre Bourdieu, *Distinction*, 1984, p. 90.

The body as a site of consumption, the body's relationship to health and illness, the body and the "medicalization" and "feminization" of dieting as culturally and socially defined, have developed in recent years as fascinating fields of study. This concern developed when feminists embraced the Foucauldian notion of the "body politic" and pushed it in the direction of gender concerns.[38] Global consumer culture, has promoted idealized norms of beauty praising slimness and eternal youth. Thus change led feminists to rethink women's self-identity and sexuality, which, they argued, have submitted for centuries to the male gaze and the docile posture of being the eternally pleasing "sexy" objects of male desire. The contemporary globalized notions of beauty have been clearly pervaded by a consumer industry that has in recent years sold an aggressive image of the "perfect body", an achievement possible for the common mortal, one which requires constant effort and financial outlay The image promoted is that one has to work for one's body and beauty through exercise, dieting, modification and through maintaining an ascetic life style, a stand which had its origins in religious world views.[39] This has led to a rich variety of literature on the subject.[40] One study[41] on the female clientele frequenting Cairene diet clinics found

---

[38] Iman Farid Basyouny, *Just a Gaze: Female Clientele of Diet Clinics in Cairo: An Ethnomedical Study*, Cairo Papers in Social Science, Volume 20, Number 4. Winter 1997.

[39] Bryan S. Turner, *The Body and Society*, Basil Blackwell, 1984, p. 17.

[40] To cite some examples, Mike Featherstone, Mike Hepworth and Bryan Turner Editors, *The Body*, Sage publications, 1991. Chris Shillings, *The Body and Social Theory*, Sage publications, 1993, second edition 2003 and *Body Modification* ed. by Mike Featherstone, Sage, 2000.

[41] Iman Farid Basyouny, *Just a Gaze: Female Clientele of Diet Clinics in Cairo: An Ethnomedical Study*, Cairo Papers in Social Science, Volume 20, Number 4. Winter 1997.

that the concern with "overweight" and "fatness", which became treated as an "illness", has already pervaded the Egyptian middle-class imagination. The advent of globalized media images of skinny American stars (Dallas and Denver Clan), Hollywood and Western consumer value are, one main reason for such transformations in these six clinics, all located in the middle-upper class area of Mohandessin. The study informs us that middle-class Egyptian women seem to be trapped by Western notions of beauty and slimness, which contradict traditional forms of plump beauty. That food is still one of the main elements of seduction in traditional Egyptian culture as expressed in the proverb: "the way to a man's heart is through his stomach",[42] explains the growing tensions faced by these women. Furthermore, the study reveals how women perceive their bodies through the gaze of their husbands. Let me now return to child-hood memories and evoke the painful and yet ironical sufferings involved in becoming a socially accepted "beauty".

One of the "universals" of adolescence may be the unease asso-ciated with a sexually maturing body. I certainly did not feel at ease with my growing body. I recall that my mother urged me constantly to have my hair firmly tied back. My curly and untamed hair was a source of trouble and shame. When we had a wedding or a for-mal feast, all the female members had to pay a visit to the "coiffeur" (hairdresser) and emerge with straightened hair. The "coiffeur" lit-erally "ironed" our hair (wikwi al sha'r) with hot, long iron scissors. The burning iron was heated and repeatedly stretched on the squeezed hair. We all had African, abundant and curly hair, like millions of Egyptian women, but it was a source of anger. We all wanted to look like the Hollywood stars, a mission impossible, especially dur-ing summers in Alexandria where invincible humidity attacked every-thing in a few hours. Hair always betrayed origins.

Older female cousins applied powder to whiten their face. They never sun tanned like the "crazy" foreigners who liked to look like toasted Africans. The fairer one looked, the sexier one was regarded. Even today, many Egyptians still boast of their Turkish ancestry with a slight tendency to look down on the "pure", "dark", and there-fore "ugly" Egyptians. I guess what is imagined as "pure" stock is the peasants and perhaps the Copts since they were the original

---

[42] Ibid., p. 104.

dwellers of Egypt, a stereotype that evidently implies discriminatory judgments.

My cousins' value in the marriage market was believed to rise with their success in attempting to look blonder and blonder. One of my aunts started dying her daughter's hair when she was twelve years old, insisting that her daughter is the fairest of us all. The "mèches" was a fashion that dissimulated darkness. Is not our national movie star and sex symbol of the fifties and sixties, Hind Rustum, an artificially tinted blonde?[43] On the other hand, Laila 'Alwi, a quite plump contemporary actress, owes her success in the cinema as a personification of the ideal beauty for middle-class Egyptians. Although clearly overweight, she is yet fair and has blue eyes. In short, she represents the oriental blonde beauty. *Ya-ishta, ya-malban* (fresh cream and jelly like Turkish delight), are the flirtatious words, which men utter in appreciation when women walk in public. Taken differently, it is a form of harassment clearly stating that the ideal beauty is fairness, and generous plumpness, crowned with green or blue eyes.

Older unfortunate female cousins who happened to have a darker skin were stigmatized. All sorts of jokes about dark skin and curly hair fill the vocabulary of Egyptians. "*Heya karta was soda*" (her hair is like a pot cleaner and she is black). Dramas resulted from such a punishment of nature. In one and the same family dark skinned sisters envied the fairer other. Maria Golia describes Cairenes as expressing a tremendous urge to imitate foreigners.[44] The *khawaga* complex is identified "as a post-colonial trauma". She too mentions the adulation Egyptians have for Caucasians, including Circacian Mamluks and Turks, which is expressed in the love of fairness. But she also remarks that on the popular level there is praise for the beauty of the dark lady expressed in popular songs. If popular songs reflect an admiration for blackness, Gamal Nkrumah, a journalist at *al-Ahram Weekly* remarks that "this fondness for darkness in popular songs is not reflected on the streets of Cairo".[45]

By observing students at the American University in Cairo, who are definitively representative of a minority elite, I could see genera-

---

[43] In the popular imagination she was identified as a sex bomb in her early movies when she stared in Youssef Shahin's by now classic, *Bab al Hadid*.

[44] Maria Golia, *Cairo City of Sand*, AUC Press 2004, p. 128.

[45] Cited from Maria Golia, p. 130.

tional transformations related to emerging notions of beauty. The Afro or ethnic look has become acceptable and even fashionable among young students. The Afro look, I would say, became acceptable via the black Americans rather than any conscious African awareness. AUC hosts a large number of second generation Arab-Americans. This is where ideas, fashions and looks are coming from. Henna body decoration, considered in the sixties as old fashioned and perhaps too "peasant" like, returned as a folkloric fashion thanks to the growing Sudanese and Nubian communities in Cairo. Upper class Westernized women and foreigners emulate it. However, all classes do not share the Afro look. Creams and powders to whiten the skin seem to be popular, and are still sold in pharmacies and beauty shops. Women who almost all have hair straightened portray the high society in the press.

More and more bodies freshly shaped by gyms and aerobic exercises can be noticed on campus. Slim and trim young females, on the edge of looking anorexic, are filling the campus, very much like any Western campus. Yet, these girls are rubbing shoulders with many obese girls. This seems to be the other side of the same coin, since as mentioned before obesity is a growing problem among Cairene women. At least the culture of the body as a commercialized icon and as a consequence gym centres are today filling larger spaces in ads, magazines and satellite programs, especially as promoted by very young pop singers. These spaces are not only created for the search for the perfect body, but also as found in a study on interaction in fitness gyms in Florence, they are sites with their own rules and "where a vast array of meanings and identities are negotiated".[46] The organization of gyms also revealed how time and space are managed in relation to oneself and one's own body. The study undertaken in Florence is useful and it could well be applied to the Egyptian context. Advertisements of fitness centres and slimming clinics are increasing every day.

Plastic surgery among the Cairene middle classes will become routine. However, it may result in unfortunate incidents for those frequenting cheaper clinics. These were labelled by the press as "bogus centres", when two women died in 2002 during liposuction operations.

---

[46] Roberta Sassatelli, "Interaction Order and Beyond: A Field Analysis of Body Culture within Fitness Gyms" in: *Body Modification*. Ed. Mike Featherstone, Sage Publications, 2000, pp. 228–248.

As a result, the Ministry of Health declared that it closed over 1,000 unlicensed private clinics. A specialist in the field commented that these became popular, as they are so cheap when one consults the real costs of conducting such operations safely. Even though some of these centres were shut down, they managed to reopen again.[47] A report released from the Egyptian Ministry Health states that in 2004, a total of 120,000 women had plastic surgery, in contrast to the number of 55,000 in the previous year.[48] *Horus*, the *Egyptair* inflight magazine,[49] advertises thirteen private clinics and hospitals offering hair implants and hair removal, plastic and bone surgery, skin cares, teeth

Fig. 52. Ad for a beauty salon for *muhaggabat* from *shopping Magazine*.

beautification and slimming. They have exotic names such as Venus Plastic Surgery Centre, Amman Plastic hospital, Golf hospital and London Laser Beauty Centre. Even the *muhaggabat* are very well catered for in specially segregated beauty salons, which offer among other services henna body painting.

Supplements for bodybuilding seem to be popular among young males and are widespread in clubs. Indeed body modification,[50] be it in piercing, plastic surgery, teeth and hair implant, stomach tightening operations, and laser eye operations are gaining popularity in Egypt for one main reason, the costs are definitively cheaper than in Europe or the US.

---

[47] Dena Rashed, "Looks that Kill" *al-Ahram Weekly*, 18–24 September 2003 (issue No. 656) http://weekly.ahram.org.eg/2003/656/fel/htm.

[48] Daily Star Staff, "Racy Music Videos Banned in Egypt", Wednesday, June 22, 2005, p. 3.

[49] *Horus*, the *Egyptair* in-flight magazine, July/September 2004.

[50] Concerning this topic see Mike Featherstone (editor), *Body Modification*, Sage, London, 2000.

Fashion Today

Social forms, apparel, aesthetic judg-
ment, the whole style of human expres-
sion, are constantly transformed by
fashion, in such a way, however, that
fashion – i.e., the latest fashion – in
all these things affects only the upper
classes. Just as soon as the lower
classes begin to copy their style, thereby
crossing the line of demarcation the
upper classes have drawn and destroy-
ing the uniformity of their coherence,
the upper classes turn away from this
style and adopt a new one, which in
turn differentiates them from the masses;
and thus the game goes merrily on.

Georg Simmel[51]

Fig. 53. Beauty Salon Ad. Geneina Mall.

The topic of fashion has attracted the attention of several sociologists in recent years thanks mainly to Pierre Bourdieu who reminded
us of the paradoxical status of fashion as being on the one hand a
prestigious topic for study, but equally perceived as frivolous.[52] Georg
Simmel's work on fashion, which he wrote a century ago (1904) still
remains one of the most inspiring and contemporary works on the
issue. Thanks to these two sociologists a new scholarship on fashion
has emerged.[53] Simmel saw that fashion entailed a paradox, a tension between two opposing poles. Tensions between heredity and
variation and between imitation, uniformity and inactive similarity
compared to differentiation. Imitation gives the individual a feeling
of belonging to the group and it is productive. Fashion as imitation,
or rather as a "charming imitation" fulfils the role of social adaptation. But it also provides a feeling of differentiation and dissimi-
larity. It provides, according to Simmel "... the desire for change
and contrast, on the one hand by a constant change of contents,

---

[51] Georg Simmel, "On Individuality and Social Forms", *Selected Writings*, see the
chapter on Fashion, edited and with an Introduction by Donald N. Levine, The
University of Chicago Press, 1971, p. 229.

[52] Pierre Bourdieu,"Haute couture et haute culture" in: *Questions de Sociologie*, Paris:
Editions de Minuit, 1980, (pp. 196–206), p. 196.

[53] One can cite here the journals *Theory, Culture and Society* and *Fashion Theory* as
two good examples promoting stimulating fashion theory.

which gives to the fashion of today an individual stamp as opposed
to that of yesterday and to-morrow, on the other hand because fashions differ for different classes . . .".[54] Also, according to Simmel,
imported fashion occupies a higher value within a group because it
comes from somewhere else and is therefore a rare good. Simmel's
observations are still valid for today's Egypt. Imported clothes have
always been clear-cut status markers. This dates back to early as the
beginning of the twentieth century owing to the large number of
foreign women who "played a key role in fashion transmission providing journals, patterns and stores".[55] We are informed by the travel
guides written during the first two decades of the last century, that
Cairo competed admirably in the realm of fashion with any European
capital.[56] Thus, needless to say, social distinction, through Chanel,
Dior, Cardin and the "griffe" (branded) items, has existed since
grandmother's generation and continued to delineate classes today.
Egyptian upper classes were for years -and are still- obsessed by
branded items. One main aspect of conspicuous consumption was
boasting of travel every year, if not twice, to Paris, Milan or Rome
specifically to purchase the last fashions. This is still the practice
among the rich. But classes meanwhile changed and with it also
fashion. For the sake of comparison, today the phenomenon of women
travellers in the Asia/Pacific region has impressively increased to
draw the attention of specialists in the field. It was noticed that the
ratio of women travellers, (especially middle ages women in their
forties) increased noticeably in the last few years in Singapore, Japan
and Korea. Travel, for many Asian women has turned out to be a
way of life. The specificity of the Asian Pacific female travellers is
related to the fact that they are "dedicated shoppers" and that shopping has become one of the main reasons for travel. The fact that
Asian cities witnessed a boom in shopping malls and advertise an
image of an exquisite shopping experience explains this trend.[57]

  Pierre Bourdieu looked at fashion from the perspective of the "sociology of intellectual production". Bourdieu equated fetishism and

---

[54] Ibid., p. 296.
[55] Nancy Mickelwright, cited from Mona L. Russell, *Creating The New Woman . . .*,
p. 30.
[56] Ibid.
[57] Sharon Siddique and Sree Kumar, "Women Travellers of Asia/Pacific A New
Powerhouse", *Insights, MasterCard International*, First Quarter 2003. And "Benefiting
from the Synergy between Travel and Retail: Hong Kong, Singapore, Bangkok and
Seoul as Tourist Destinations", *Insights, MasterCard International*, Second Quarter, 2004.

magic in earlier anthropological works with today's fashion. He looked at the competing forces in the structure of the "field of production" in the French "haute couture". For Bourdieu a field is the space of game, a field of objective relations between individuals or institutions struggling for an identical share. In such a field, the dominant actors are the ones who have the power to constitute the so called "scarce" and rare objects by the procedure of the "griffe". While the newcomers in the field, defined by Bourdieu as latecomers or perhaps also as parvenus, do not possess a specific capital,[58] the old players would then defend the strategies of conservation which they acquired through an accumulated capital in time. The new players respond by strategies of subversion. It is the tension and competition between various actors within one and the same field, which fascinated Bourdieu. He explained this by analyzing the discourse of the designer Courreges, who made a revolution by promoting a modern image and style of the woman as free, sportive, and spontaneous, in contrast to more classical designers like Chanel. Bourdieu here reminds us that what is at stake is the dialectics of pretentiousness and social distinction, as the principles in the transformation of the field of production, in the space of consumption.[59] I think that Bourdieu's analysis is extremely enlightening and very applicable to Egypt, as it pertains to the ascending competing agents, which aspire to promote differing, and counter-current trends in fashion.

The variety of fashions multiplied, and the public space hosts a large variety of fashions, especially among the youth. Some would interpret that as a dissonance of tastes; others would see it as "everything goes". Clothes range from the sexy, fashionable *muhaggabat* (with the veil as fashion accessory), wearing fancy colourful clothes, or tight jeans, lipstick and makeup, to short and tight skirts, (to the nun type who is fully dressed in black without makeup) to the *munaqabat* (total veil, covering the face). Islamic attire has taken on layers and layers of meanings and it is worn very differently. Some women cover the head while wearing tight jeans, others insist on wide long and ample dresses. Some wear very fashionable outfits such as colourful trousers, jackets or skirts below the knee, and still cover the hair. Many don't cover up and wear jeans or the latest Western imported

[58] Pierre Bourdieu, *Questions de Sociologie*, Les Editions de Minuit", 1980, pp. 197–198.

[59] Ibid., p. 201.

fashion. Some American University in Cairo (AUC) female students are proud to show naked bellies, below short shirts. Mini-skirts and, tiny see-through T-shirts and very tight trousers are not unusual on campus. Some students adopt the cool loose trousers, sports shoes and reverse baseball cap. Branded clothes such Gucci, Versace, and others are more than ever a sign of distinction and worn by the well-to-do students. The variety of dress, if not to say the "cacophony", is very revealing of fragmented lifestyles.

The cacophony of tastes is to be observed on display in downtown shop windows where, again, everything goes. One often encounters in shopping malls the chains of *malabes al-muhaggabat* shops (Islamic dress shops) next to sexy underwear shops that convey more than a hint of pornography. But this juxtaposition does not seem to bother anyone. Next to these two shops would be three or four shoe shops. Cairo's downtown astonishes any newcomer by the abundance of its shoe shops. Do all these shops make a profit or would some of these be a cover for money laundering? A "culturalist" answer would be that Egyptians have been used to purchasing new shoes for the all members of the family for the *ʿid* feasts,[60] but this seems to be a simplistic explanation for the exaggerated profusion of shoe shops.

It is possible to see two main new trends in Cairene fashion today. For those interested in the sociology of the body, Cairo is a fascinating laboratory in which the variety of outfits represents obvious statements and markers.[61] There is a flagrant contrast between what the Egyptian press called "the madness of the new look" in fashion and the totally black covered up *munaqqaba*. But these styles seem to coexist peacefully; the question is for how long? Some observers have pointed to the growing public visibility of the Islamic attire in the street in the last three decades. On the other hand, *Al-Ahram al-Taʿlimi* (a supplement of the official *al-Ahram* newspaper) published an article recently[62] warning that the country is facing a major calamity because youth are following disgusting expensive and shameful fashions. These consist of extremely tight t-shirts, revealing the

---

[60] This interpretation was given to me by one of the malls managers who wishes to be kept anonymous.

[61] For an interesting collection of articles on the recent discussions on the body and social theory see Mike Featherstone, Mike Hepworth, Bryan Turner, *The Body, Social Process and Cultural Theory*, Sage, London, 1991.

[62] Nevine Shehata, "gunun al-new look" (The madness of the new Look), *al-ahram al-ta ʿlimi*, 12 November, 2004, pp. 4–5.

navel. The article, published in the semi-official newspaper, conveyed a warning that youth have lost their reason, and are becoming delinquent by following imported Western fashion. The moralizing tone goes together with the official discourse, which infantilises and belittles youth constantly for lax sexual norms and loose morality in public. As a consequence, state interference is requested to restore order and public morality.

But the total veil is also abhorred in official circles since it is the icon of extremism and possibly violence and terrorism. The official press and government circles, it seems, are trying to promote an image of a "respectable" middle-class *muhaggaba*. For example, almost all female state employees, with the exception of the female Copts have adopted the headcover as an official dress code.

Affandiyas *versus* Galabeyyas

Since fashion owes a lot to imitation, distinction and distancing, intellectuals have often raised the question of apparel in relation to identity. When Egypt is compared to other Third World cultures in relation to identity construction vis-à-vis Western hegemony, why is it that Egyptians failed to preserve or even create a national dress? Indian women pride themselves on their saris, the Malays their *Baju Kurung*, the Indonesians their sarongs. The art of batik making has become a major tourist attraction in Indonesia. The rich ethnic differences in Indonesia produced a wide assortment of "indigenous" aesthetically appealing outfits that are worn at weddings, national days and feasts. Whether these styles have been re-invented with globalization is yet again another issue. Singapore is a fascinating case in point, where the streets are so colourful with Malay, Indian and Chinese, as well as modern outfits. Clothes have been adopted as national markers, as statements to the "right of difference" in a globalized homogenized world.

Compared to Egypt, it seems that in India the issue of adopting the western dress during the nineteenth century entailed a wider interactive complexity in perceptions between the British and the Indians. Emma Tarlo's work on dress and identity in India wonderfully describes the intricate ambiguity of the British towards the Indian educated elite, which was considered a threat to their hegemony. The British colonial administrators feared the perfect mimicking by

the Indians. If they wanted to spread civilization, they did not necessarily encourage the Indians to be dressed like British gentlemen.
Tarlo discusses the various Indian attitudes to European clothes that
ranged from polluting and demonizing Western garments, or amal-
gamating both Indian with European dress, to Westernzing the Indian
dress and changing clothes according to the occasion and thus possibly creating a duality.[63]

Gandhi for example, brought forth the issue of clothes as a priority for national identity construction against British rule. His politics of rejecting English clothes and adopting the simple loincloth
in solidarity with the poor was meant to expose colonial exploitation.
This became the subject of research among scholars who were interested in the politics of semiotics.[64] Gandhi stressed the importance
of weaving in order to counter act English products. His demonis-
ing of Western clothes and the popular image he enjoyed as a religious ascetic meant that the politics of clothing were crucial in the
national liberation. The way Gandhi was perceived by the British
rulers, led to various readings of his moral significance of clothes.[65]
Garments continued to be crucial nationalist symbols in India when
later Nehru became famed for the "Nehru jacket" as an alternative
non-Western dress. Even when Rajiv Gandhi went to politics he
"threw aside his European dress and aviator's uniform in favour of
khadi".[66] This was hardly the case with Egypt's nationalist movement
launched by the young officer Nasser who appeared at earlier times
in military garments. In fact, the rejection of Western clothes never
really played a role in Egypt. The *tarboush* or (fez) was abolished
because it was the symbol of Ottoman rule and feudalism, but western clothes remained fashionable and solicited as discussed in Chapter
3. The fashionable male consumer represented in the twenties ads
by the Egyptian Clothing Company was "a large sketch of a man,
clad in a European suit, wing-tip shoes, fancy ties, *tarbush*, and sometimes carrying a walking stick and/or cigarette".[67] However, critiques

---

[63] Emma Tarlo, *Clothing Matters, Dress and Identity in India*, The University of
Chicago Press, 1996. See her chapter Searching for a Solution in the Nineteenth
Century.

[64] Emma Tarlo, *Clothing Matters*. See her chapter on Gandhi and the recreation
of Indian Dress.

[65] Winston Churchill described Gandhi as "posing as a half-naked fakir" quoted
from Emma tarlo, p. 79.

[66] Emma Tarlo, p. 123.

[67] Mona L. Russell, *Creating The New Egyptian Woman . . .*, p. 62.

of the danger of adopting Western fashion and cosmetics were evoked in the Egyptian press at the turn of the last century. These critiques were expressed in the nationalist, scientific, popular and women's press, which were not entirely against the new patterns of consumption, but advocated a more careful selection of what to adopt; "but rather that Easterners should adopt only that which is in harmony with their morals and disposition".[68]

Indian friends have told me that no Indian male would feel ashamed to walk into a Ministry in India with Punjabi clothes. While in Egypt, the *galabeyya*-I mean here the peasant *galabeyya*-is clearly a stigma and those wearing it are immediately subject to discrimination by state employees. This discrimination against the *galabeyya* is probably due to the nature of Nasserite modernization, which was directed towards enhancing and enlarging a culture of middle class employees of the *mowathaffin* and *affandiyyah*, which was by nature antagonistic to peasant culture. Even though the official rhetoric was in praise of peasants, clearly peasant culture was not a model for the new regime. For example, the first images we have in our minds of Nasser, his ministers and their families are associated with modern Western outfits. *Al-Ahram Weekly's* photographs archive of Gamal Abdel Nasser, provided by his daughter Hoda 'Abdel Nasser, tells much about Nasser's family and lifestyle.[69] The pictures reveal that he was in his youth dressed as a military. He switched later to Western clothes. Nasser always wore a tie for official occasions. Nasser's daughters in the family's villa were posing in sleeveless, short dresses and fashionable hairstyles of the time, identical to European women.

I cannot recall Nasser wearing a *galabeyya*, in contrast to Sadat who wore the *galabeyya* out of a political desire to identify in an exaggerated way with "peasants", with a grain of megalomania. It is ironic that Sadat who opened up the country to Westernisation is the president who appeared most in peasant *galabeyyas*. Clearly, his image of the village life and the peasants was over-romanticized.

The official ceremonies of the fifties and sixties saw few women in *galabeyyas*. In fact, on official occasions one hardly saw any woman with a head cover. The fifties and sixties films show actresses wearing *décolleté*, bikinis and tiny skirts. Modernizing meant adopting a

---

[68] Ibid., . . ., p. 39.
[69] See *Al-Ahram Weekly*/Photo Gallery/Gamal Abdel Nasser. http//weekly.ahram.org.eg/gallery/Nasser/index.htm, site visited 13.09.2005.

Western look. As for the working class, it was portrayed in the media in a socialist format. "Happy" looking male and female workers, in their working clothes, looked identical to those in socialist countries. By today's standards these simple ultimately Western "uniforms" are seen as decadent compared to the Islamic dress.

Fifty years ago, in Egypt as elsewhere, it was much easier to identify a person's class by their clothes than it is today. In Egypt, a person could be identified through, first the *galabeyya* which was worn by both men and women and, second, through the absence of shoes.[70] As a child a member of my family told me, before the revolution no barefoot person was allowed to enter the modern downtown, thus excluding all peasants. The head kerchief could also distinguish lower-class women. It is possible to argue that the *galabeyya* and the head kerchief are still the dress, which designates *baladi* and peasant classes. But by now they no longer go barefoot. Today, one can observe that the new generation of sons and daughters of peasants in the countryside who had schooling adopt either shirts and trousers and even jeans for males, while the females wear the urban Islamic attire and *higab* even when they are in the village. Most if not all girls who went to high school wear mainly Islamic attire when they are out of the village. The *higab* replaced the peasant head kerchief.[71] I presume that it gives these youngsters a feeling of elevation mingled with a feeling of superiority towards their parents' culture. One can also read the female "Islamic attire" as a statement of being urban and educated. It is equally possible to notice that there has been a change in peasant *galabeyyas*. The long black female "velour" *galabeyya* has disappeared, to be replaced with black synthetic material that is much cheaper. The style of the male *galabeyya* changed mainly in the form of collar. A Western shirt collar was introduced to the newly named *galabeyya afranggi*, and a Saudi type collar was introduced instead of the round cut. The white transparent Saudi Arabian *galabeyya* has been introduced into Egypt in the last fifteen years, due to the massive migration of rural workers to Saudi Arabia. More Pakistani types and long *abayyas* for both women and men have

---

[70] Galal Amin, *Whatever Else Happened to the Egyptians*, AUC Press, 2004, p. 72. See the entire chapter on dress.

[71] These are my personal observations of my family village in Dakahliyyah that I have been visiting frequently for the last twenty-five years.

replaced the traditional *galabeyya* with the *sufra* (The Europe style, of Napoleonic origin).

Salwa Mesbahi, a Moroccan designer resident in Cairo, was intrigued by this dilemma. Mesbahi, after having studied design in Casablanca was for many years was interested in creating a new style, the elegant Moroccan *caftan*. Egypt, in contrast to Morocco, has not managed to maintain a "national" traditional dress. Until today according to her, Moroccan women are proud of their *cafetan marocain* and the *galabeyya* that is worn like a mantle on top of other clothes and is very practical in everyday life. According to Mesbahi, it would be unthinkable for well to do Moroccan women to dress in a Western "robe soirée", like Egyptian women do. The dresses for partying and weddings have to be Moroccan style; otherwise women would be ridiculed and even ostracized. Mesbahi was among the first designers to have modernized the traditional style, by respecting the elaborate work of embroidery and the main lines. She varies the colours, the depth of the cut and the materials. Mesbahi worked in Cairo for the *Atlas* boutique, in the Khan al-Khalili Bazaar. She developed a hybrid style by introducing Moroccan embroidery in the Egyptian *galabeyya*. *Atlas* amalgamated Western outfits such as trousers jackets, and shorter *'abbayas* with embroidery. Mesbahi's long experience in Egypt has led her to conclude that one of the reasons why Egyptians have failed to develop marketable Egyptian stylish embroidery is because such a meticulous handwork is badly remunerated and not respected. Moroccan craftsmen, in comparison, were highly praised and in constant demand. Besides that with the advent of migration to the oil producing countries, the whole community of textile craftsmen was dismantled and the long generations of accumulated and transmitted knowledge withered away.[72]

The wide ample long robes, which are designated as the female Islamic dress, appeared in Egypt only during the last three decades. Would these be, then, considered as the national dress of today's Egypt? There is no definite style to these long robes. These are copied from various Islamic fashion magazines and they can be found in Egypt, Saudi Arabia, Pakistan or Indonesia. They do not carry any specific national trait. Nevertheless, the "absence" of an Egyptian national dress needs further reflection. Even when some traditions

---

[72] Personal communication with Salwa Mesbahi, 23 September 2004, Zamalek.

are invented, for example the *galabeyya* which underwent various alterations with the introduction of the upper *sufra*, with the influence of the Napoleonic conquest of Egypt,[73] is worthy of note as an indicator of how cross cultural encounters affect tradition.

Rulers of foreign origin ruled Egypt for centuries so at least two different cultures always coexisted. That for the ruling classes the perceived "high" and refined culture was the European had certainly repercussions on the Egyptian life styles and manners. The Mamluks, the Turks and the descendents of Mohammed Ali of Albanian origin, had little to do with Egyptian culture or the Arabic language. Instead, the ruling classes turned to Europe. The two centuries of pervasive Westernization could explain why middle class Egyptians found the question of searching for authentic Egyptian dress irrelevant.

Islamic and Ethnic Chic

I borrow the term "Islamic chic" from the specialists who studied the recent growing Islamic movement in Turkey and observed new tendencies towards gentrification. Jenny White uses the term "Islamic chic" to argue that in recent years the Islamic movement underwent tremendous change and witnessed political and economic success.[74] In fact, success became associated with being Islamic. The appearance of expensive Islamic fashions and lifestyles began to designate "the new urban conservatism".[75] It is possible to see similar trends in Egypt and apply this term in the Egyptian context. The trend toward Islamic attire began under Sadat, who in the early seventies encouraged its adoption among the expanding population of university students. It was promoted as a practical solution to poverty and many students of rural origin found it a comfortable way to escape the acute class differences on campus. Sadat's main aim was, however, to counteract communist and secularist forces by using the state apparatus to enhance the Islamic trend, which was antagonistic to both the Nasserites and communists. Meanwhile, more than three decades have elapsed and the symbol of veil has undergone a significant "gentrification". It has evolved from being identified with the

---

[73] See Max Rodenbeck, Cairo, *The City Victorious*, AUC Press, 1998, p. 154.
[74] Jenny B. White, "Islamic Chic" in: *Istanbul, between the Global and the Local*, edited by Caglar Keyder, Rowman and Littlefield Publishers, Lonham, Boulder, 1999.
[75] Ibid., p. 80.

underground, harsh looking *jamaʿat* anti-establishment, and pro-Iranian revolution movement, to being associated with a better-off looking, Saudified and petro-islamized ideology. What made the difference was the massive Egyptian migration to the Gulf countries and remittances back to the home country.

If the fashion industry is now blossoming in Egypt, it is in both in the domain of the Islamic dress and the local private companies selling locally produced modern Western clothes. *The Ultimate Guide to Shopping* 2004 (issue 2) advertises circa 133 fashion shops, some of which are franchised brands. The

Fig. 54. Shopping Magazine in Arabic.

Maʿadi Grand Mall has plenty of fancy shops specialized in Islamic attire with Western names like *Suzanna* and *Pour Elle*. To make it appealing to younger females, the Islamic attire is advertised as *al-ʿabbaya al-shababiya* (the youngish *ʿabbaya*), *ʿabbaya*-jeans and the hippy veil. The appealing colours of the long dresses and trousers are well matched with the head covers, which can be bright red, blue or purple. The Islamic dress like the *ʿabayyas and the hijab*, advertised as *écharpe*, have now become fashionable. There are several chains of *malabes al-muhaggabat* in various malls and shops. Some *ʿabbayas* can be very expensive, and the price range depends on the fabric. In summer, Cairo is filled with Gulf visitors who overpopulate the malls and who are the main clientele for expensive "chic" *ʿabayyas* and *galabeyyas*, which could reach the price of L.E. 1500 to 2000.

Tour Egypt Monthly[76] is an online magazine, which advertises clothes in Cairo, and has highly praised the growing industry. It states: "Beside the usual souvenir shops and bazaars of all kinds, the whole of Cairo is a large shopping centre for modern, Western style clothes, too. Well done, I would say to my friends, nice shirts or trousers do not get dusty, bulky and boring at home – like water pipes and

---

[76] *Tour Egypt Monthly. Buying Clothes in Cairo. June 1st, 2001. http://www.touregypt.net/magazine/mag.*

leather camels". The rest of the article provides an extensive list of addresses of shops and shopping malls where one can buy branded clothes ranging from Versace, Bvlgari, and Aigner in the First Mall, to Benetton, Adidas, and Ted Lapidus in Horriya mall.

It is possible to observe a burgeoning of certain professionalism in the local design industry. During a design conference in February 2005, designers expressed a strong wish to acquire the competence of their Turkish colleagues who managed to conquer European markets. They felt that Egypt has still a long way to

Fig. 55. Shopping Magazine in Arabic, September 2004.

go in the road of export, but their ideal is definitively Turkey. They wanted to capitalize on Egyptian cotton that has been famed for its high quality, which led to the flourishing of local retail chains.

The last decade has witnessed the blossoming of a greater variety of local fashion companies. Some of these became very successful and managed to export clothes to Europe. One can mention here *Safari*, which is very successful in promoting leisure and travel clothes made with local fabrics. *Concrete, Mix and Match, Mobaco, Sahara, Wild, 69, Daily Dress, Marie Louis*, and many other businesses have promoted the idea of local "chic". Some of these brands have several branches in shopping malls, in international hotels and in boutiques. They vary in size from small workshops to big companies and they have revived Egyptian linen and cotton in fashion, as well as using synthetic fabric. These companies are truly producing highly competitive fashionable products, with excellent finishing, at quite affordable prices compared to imported clothes. One can conclude that the younger generations have more choice. From this perspective one can see a possible "democratization" in taste, in that Egyptian fashion, although not particularly cheap, now offers an alternative to a wider middle class. In fact, class disguise through dress has become subtler than it was some twenty years ago.

Fashion shows seem to have increased. Information about the *haute couture* Dior collections show in Cairo can be found in the *Ahram Weekly*. In Spring 2004, The Goethe Institute in Cairo organized a fashion show under the direction of the German designer Suzanne Kuempel. The show was reported in the German magazine *Der Spiegel*, which entitled it: "Veiled Girls Make a Much (whole) Unveiled Fashion".[77] The article stressed the fact that these middle-class students from the faculty of Design at Helwan University – being proud of their head-scarf are precisely the most gifted and creative in fashion design. Paradoxically, they are the ones who make sexy designs, while they are proud to wear the *hijab (heggab)*. The theme of the show was called "Insideout" and, with few exceptions the designs were made for unveiled girls. Suzanne Kuempel explained that the majority of her students originate from middle class backgrounds and are not encouraged to be flexible and cosmopolitan. She adds. "When one lives in Cairo, one cannot understand fashion".

Suzanne Kuempel is herself an ethno-designer, who is working on a project financed by the *Zentrum fur International Migration und Entwicklung* (the Centre for International Migration and Development), which is titled "Apparel, Design, Management and Technology". She became interested in the local traditions of the Bedouins of South Sinai. She set up a project and together with her students and went to the Eastern desert to learn from the Bedouins embroidery and patterns. The outcome was modern and fashionable "ethnic" inspired appar-els. The "ethnic look", which I will expand on below takes an inter-esting turn path with a "foreign designer" working on a development project who says that her dream is to contribute with Egyptians to find an "identity" through clothing. But there are two points to be drawn from this example. First, in the conclusion of the article, Kuempel said that these young women would be the future design-ers who should be encouraged if Egyptian designing is to meet inter-national standards. It is thus one way of integrating the symbols of the middle class exemplified in the headscarf and normalizing it. Second, considering their social conditions, these girls aspire for recog-nition and integration. They are the trigger of the "Islamic chic

---

[77] Christian Meier, "Verschleierte Maedchen machen ganz unverschleierte Mode" *Spiegel* Online-10 Februar 2005, URL: http://www.spiegel.de/unispiegel/wunder-bar/0,1518, 336544,00html.

look". Rather it is possible to combine the Islamic attire with being attractive. Hence, integration in fashion is taking place, at the expense of perpetuating patriarchal and submissive norms.

Lebanese designers seem to be conquering the Egyptian scene. I would like to evoke here one of the fashion shows I attended at the Sheraton Giza hotel in Spring 2004 to point to some contradictory and competing images of women and fashion. The designers were all Lebanese and the models were Egyptian. Strikingly the audience consisted of families with women wearing headcovers and Islamic attire. The Sheraton Hotel is known for hosting a large numbers of Arab tourists from the oil producing countries. Meanwhile, the first floor hall, where beautiful looking female Russian musicians play wonderful classical music, is well known as a place for young Gulf men to pick up women. It was therefore expected that this fashion show would attract plenty of single males, mostly from the Gulf. There were also several designers and people from the media. The *défilé* took place with music. The audience could see the details of the models bodies through the magnified screens. The long, fancy and extravagant dresses were revealing sensitive parts, transparent cloth and very short skirts, with low *décolleté* revealing almost all the breasts. The young Egyptian women felt very insecure at first. This being said, the *défilé* did not differ from any fashion show in Europe. However, one photographer was thrown out at least five times after constantly sneaking in and zooming on the models. I suppose that security personnel considered him indecent. It is difficult for me to describe how most men looked while they were staring at the half-naked beautiful young Egyptian models. But most interesting was the fascination of the *muhaggabat* (headcovered) women and their gaze, which to my astonishment was full of admiration. Some were taking pictures with great wonder. The external observer can only be caught in such contradictions between the image of the respectable Muslim woman confined by public morality, and the double standards revealed by the proper, respectable, untouched veiled wife as opposed to the sexy, unveiled and thus possibly "prostitute" looking women. It was evident to me that norms were in conflict and men became uncontrollable.

Parallel to that trend, one can observe among the upper-middle strata a change in taste and fashion. The "ethnic" and so-called Egyptian inspired fashions have been introduced and became popular among the wealthy.[78] In the two Hiltons malls of Cairo, (especially the *Dukkan* shop in the Hilton Ramses Mall) and in the Marriot Hotel one can purchase such ethnic clothes like *galabeyyas*, silk jackets embroidered with oriental patterns, *kelims*, and Bedouin crafts, scarves, and silver jewellery, which are replicas of African (Tuareg), Yemeni and Indian designs. It is no coincidence that such clothes are to be found in international hotels. In fact, the revival of ethnic clothing goes hand in hand with the flourishing of tourism in Egypt and the role of the state in attempting to promote tourism. In both the Hilton and the newly opened Arkadia Mall, with around 500 shops,[79] it is possible to purchase fashionable expensive *galabeyyas*. In this context one could also mention the clothes of *Nagada*, which are inspired by traditional Egyptian textiles, designed in a refined "remake" of peasant and Bedouin culture. Nagada has popularized ample stylish cloaks or long robes, *'abayas, galabeyyas* (the long peasant robes) being inspired by the *milaya laff (the female black garbe)*, scarves, ethnic cloth and curtains for interior decoration which are all inspired from the colours of the desert and popular dresses. *Nagada* is proud that it is 100 percent Egyptian and it is inspired by tradition. The cloth is manufactured in *Nagada*, a village in Upper Egypt and the clothes are given a modern touch. *Nagada* seems to be doing very well today, perhaps because it mostly caters to the expatriate community who are not feeling the economic pressure of their Egyptian counterparts. Meanwhile, the designers have travelled extensively to India, Southeast Asia and China and have incorporated Indian and Batik designs with Egyptian cloth to create an interesting hybridization of tastes. One can purchase Indonesian *ikat*[80] hats and *ikat* cloth and made in a very special style that combines Egyptian *galabeyas* with Indonesian patterns. A Lebanese designer and a Swiss

---

[78] To be reminded, the ethno-look was first popularised by the known Western maisons de couture. In the early seventies Yves Saint Laurent invented the "gypsy" style. Zandra Rhodes and Thea Porter created the princesses' style of long ample robes, kaftans and perles inspired by Far Eastern motives. In the US, the ethnic look was expressed in reinventing native Indian American garments. See Tracy Tolkien *Schick und Schrill, Klassiker der Designermode*. Knesebeck, München 2001, English title *Vintage-The Art of Dressing up*. Pavilion Books Limited, p. 90.

[79] In Arkadia Mall, *H and H* is a shop run by a former American University graduate who has revived a new style *galabeyya*, quite different from Meherz's work. The prices are expensive and the *galabeyyas* are very stylish.

[80] An Indonesian style of weaving.

man, who lived for many years in the village of Tunis of Fayyoum, created *Nagada*. The Swiss man's wife produces remarkable pottery in Fayyoum, succeeding in reviving ancient Pharaonic and Islamic patterns in pottery. They also created a school in Tunis to teach youngsters the profession of pottery. Meanwhile, several students started selling their own products in their houses. Many foreigners who come specifically for pottery visit the village. A novelist constructed recently a hotel in the hope that in the near future tourism will pick up in that area.

Some Egyptian designers seem to believe that rich Egyptian women suffer strongly from the *khawaga* complex and therefore avoid anything Egyptian once they deal with fashion. One designer complained that the moment his client is informed that the material is Egyptian, she immediately leaves.[81] Probably the insecurity originates in the fear of being designated as *baladi*. Why would they want to blindly emulate Western fashion? How then to explain that so many Egyptian women die their hair blonde.[82]

Certainly, branded imported clothes are still regarded as the best, and they have always represented a clear status symbol, but Egyptian local fashion proposes a cool and modern look. As some of the locally made clothes are more affordable it could perhaps become a new way of disguising class and allowing more elasticity in self-representation in the public.

Shahira Mehrez's Search for Identity through the Galabeyya

A movement for rediscovering one's own culture and identity in lifestyle was launched by Shahira Mehrez, a specialist of Islamic art and architecture and a disciple of the late architect Hassan Fathi. Mehrez became known for popularizing the idea of wearing *galabeyyas* among the well to do classes and for rendering it chic and even fashionable for TV announcers. For Shahira Mehrez, the dress was a means for identity search: "Why should I wear other dresses that do not belong to my culture?"

---

[81] Lamia Gouda, "Fashion Victims", *La Revue d'Egypte*, April 2003, pp. 57–61.
[82] Ibid., p. 58. These were again the observations of one Tunisian designer living in Cairo.

Fig. 56. Shahira Mehrez Collection – Upper Egypt. Courtesy of Shahira Mehrez.

   Shahira Mehrez is the founder and owner of a gallery for the
promotion of traditional Egyptian crafts called Shahira Mehrez and
Companions. When Mehrez wanted to meet Hassan Fathi after the
1967 war, she knew that he would be playing a key role in her life.
She searched for him after having extensively read about his work
in various Western magazines. She was then introduced to him
through her best friend's mother. She had heard a great deal about
his work and his sensitivity in constructing buildings for the poor
adapting local materials and techniques. She knew that he was a
highly cultured aristocrat, a man at ease in both Western and Arab-
Islamic cultures who would help her in solving her "identity crisis".
Since she met him, she saw him on a daily basis until his death.
Mehrez is herself a hybrid product of French upper-class upbringing in Cairo; she spoke French better than Arabic. In fact, she hardly
learned Arabic at school; instead she had a private Arabic teacher
who was not the best person to introduce her to the Arabic language. The fact that she learned to read and write Arabic at the

left: peasant from the Delta
right: detail of headgear and
Nubian jewellery

Fig. 57. Shahira Mehrez Collection. Courtesy of Shahira Mehrez.

late age of eighteen, and that her brother had to read the TV programs to her from the newspaper, affected her tremendously because
she felt neither truly Egyptian nor French. It is no coincidence that
the interview conducted with Mehrez was mostly done in French,
the language in which she was most fluent. "For the French, I was
Egyptian and for the Egyptians I was French", she says. Like many
of her class and generation, she was afraid of being taxed during
the Nasser period as "the enemy of the people" when she went in
the streets of Cairo and spoke either Arabic or perfect, accent-free
French. This feeling of "être mal dans sa peau", of "ce mal de vivre"
was evidently the trigger for her identity search. When Mehrez told
Fathi about her "mal de vivre" because of her inability to speak
Arabic properly, Hassan Fathi took her to the Sultan Hassan mosque
and played her the violin to show how European classical music
fitted beautifully with Islamic architecture. "It is the meeting of the
genius of two cultures the Occidentals have the genius of music and
we have the genius of architecture", he told her.

Thanks to Hassan Fathi, her mentor and lifelong friend, her vision of the world was transformed through discovering the beauty and functionality of Islamic art and architecture. He made her realize the richness of being raised as a hybrid. He taught her to appreciate the fact that "it is the case of those who are not the common mortals". Hassan Fathi was concerned about one thing, how the liquidation of traditions and cultures in Egypt was taking place with such indiscrimination and brutality.

In a paper she wrote about Hassan Fathi, entitled *Fathi Citoyen du Monde* (Fathi, Citizen of the World), she described him as a vulnerable prince who had no place in the dominant, official discourse of Egypt. Shahira Mehrez recalled his romantic side in that he was generous with his time and refused to work for money. He tested people when they first visited him. If they liked classical music and had sensitivity for art, they could become his friend. He would design their house for free as a token of this friendship. In her article Mehrez describes Fathi as follows:

> In a world that is meant to be increasingly monolithic, in which the East and West are in confrontation. He [Fathi] was through his culture the meeting of civilizations ... the magnificat of Bach who received visitors in the courtyard of his Mamluk house.[83]

In another passage she says:

> ... Son of the rich, he defended the poor; ecologist before his time, he tried to warn us against industrial pollution, fearing for earth the effects of a uncontrolled technology, serving uniquely the powerful. ... Arab and Muslim, he was strongly impregnated by Judeo-Christian civilization, and Zen and Confucian philosophy.[84]

Shahira Mehrez became the disciple of Fathi, although she was never an architect. But this discipleship coincided with Mehrez's interest in clothing, which was developed through her earlier various travels all over Egypt's countryside. The fact that she belonged to an old feudal family, which had land in Kafr al-Zayyat, especially in the Ibyar area, meant that as a child, she often travelled there with her family. But Mehrez's family was well versed in Egyptian culture.

---

[83] Shahira Mehrez, "Hassan Fathi Citoyen du Monde", Unpublished paper, author's translation, p. 1.
[84] Ibid., Shahira Mehrez, p. 3.

As children, they visited Upper Egypt, the Pharaonic temples and through aunts they were shown mosques. The many children of the family were often taken to museums and they had the privilege of seeing the collection of Ali Pasha Ibrahim. When her brother went to an Oasis he brought her a Bedouin dress.

Since her childhood, she has been totally fascinated by peasant dress, which she started to collect in the villages. Little by little she started investigating old tailors and some *galabeyyas* she had seen elsewhere. She found out in the village that there were always more tailors who knew the old *galabeyya* designs, but who ceased making them when fashion changed. Later on, it was Fathi who introduced her to the craftsmen of Egypt. She travelled with him in the late sixties to discover the weavers and craftsmen of Kerdasa before it turned into a tourist attraction and later they visited Nagada, Garagus, Kafr al-Ballat in Upper Egypt and other places like Kharga and Dakhla in 1967, where she purchased plenty of costumes. Together they also went to museums and searched for various items all over Egypt.

At a later stage, Mehrez went to local village markets, such as the *suq* days in Kafr al-Zayyat, and Inshas. It was in these *suqs* that Mehrez found women from different villages wearing their distinctive local style of dress. She would then try to trace the tailors and ask what they used to make a long time ago. When I asked her if this would be a sort of reinvention of tradition, she immediately denied the idea and vehemently argued: "one rediscovers what has remained from tradition . . . there is no such thing as trying to revive tradition . . . one can preserve a know how, but one cannot preserve an apparel because there is a whole infrastructure . . . and techniques of weaving for instance that disappear".

By developing an interest in handcraft, over forty years ago, Mehrez started to collect Bedouin clothes. Today she owns a valuable collection of some 450 dresses from the countryside, deserts and oases, which she prefers to preserve in Italy. These *galabeyyas*, and accessories such as jewellery and *kelims* are exhibited from time to time in Western cultural centres and embassies in Cairo and all over Egypt.[85] Mehrez meanwhile has gained an international reputation

---

[85] I happened to experience one of her exhibits in the newly opened arts and craft centre (2003) of the old city of Fustat.

and organized several *défilés* of traditional Egyptian costumes in places such as the Caroussel du Louvre, in Castello di Sartirana in the province of Pavia, in Spain, and the US. Furthermore, in the 1980s, she became the manager of the El-Arish Needlework Program and a founding partner of the boutiques specialized in *galabeyyas* in El-Dukkan (Ramses Hilton Annex), Yamama Centre, as well as Mit Rihan furniture gallery in Zamalek, which sells ethnic style furniture.

Her marvellous and highly sophisticated flat in Dokki, designed by Fathi, included various Islamic artefacts such as mosaic fountains, large copper trays, carpets, fascinating wood work, built in platforms with cushions, built-in wooden cupboards and shelves, textiles, ceramics, rugs, various *Qur'an* calligraphies, glass painting, lamps, and *mashra-biyyas* given by Fathi and an authentic Turkish, marble bath. In the same building Mehrez has a fancy gallery, which sells sophisticated *galabeyyas* and *abbayas* for high prices.

Mehrez opened her shop in the late seventies. It started with some friends, then with exhibitions. She quickly became internationally known. She is credited for having pointed to the great regional variations in *galabeyya* styles, especially that between the waisted gown of Upper and the longer gown of Lower Egypt. These were also adopted by the well to do classes as a form of folklore. Expensive embroidered *galabeyyas* then became fashionable with "*galabeyya* parties" taking place in residential resorts like Agami and in private houses. But no state employee would today adopt a *galabeyya* to go to work.

Her clientele is definitively the well off who can afford to pay L.E 2,000 to 3,000 Egyptian pounds for a dress. Most Egyptians, according to Mehrez, still do not like to dress on daily basis *galabeyyas*; they are still infatuated with the Western dress. When they travel, they buy Mehrez's items as presents, being sure that their Western friends will appreciate these. But there are still some "égyptiens éclairés" who are interested in heritage and encourage her. Otherwise, her best buyers are the Arab customers from Jordan, Lebanon, Kuwait, and Bahrain. Gulf royal families come twice a year and buy huge quantities since they wear *galabeyyas* daily at home and to go out. They buy "en masse" fifteen, twenty or thirty costumes, and these people are indeed her real fans. It is possible to draw here a close similarity with India's ethnic chic, which was developed by the well to do elites. During the last phase, ethnic chic turned to be a trend "by which the elite educated minority has redefined its position and

taste to the Indian masses and to
the West."[86] Although Indian ethnic chic emulates popular tastes
and fashions, yet it differenciates
itself and has become a way of
distinction from the masses as well
as from the West by creating a
new Indian aesthetic that claims
superiority over Western fashion.[87]
A similar phenomenon could be
observed in Singapore in the early
1990's, whereby the Chinese female
attire, the *Cheongsam* was revived
after undergoing modifications.
It has been used as an identity
marker in public, formal occasions to be associated with power
circles and elite construction under
the recent Asianisation process
launched by the government.[88]

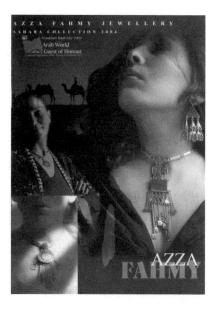

Fig. 58. Azza Fahmy Jewellery.
Advertised in Shopping Magazine.

Thus, be it in India, Singapore or Egypt, it is the classy aspect and
the elites' self-redefining, which asserts that there is a "kind" of
homogenization of tastes, nevertheless with variations that is taking
place with globalisation.

Jewellery

In the realm of jewellery, the silver work of 'Azza Fahmi was inspired
by the craftsmanship of the old *suqs* of Khan al-Khalili. Fahmi was
associated in a business with Mehrez at an earlier stage of her life.
Both 'Azza and her sister Randa Fahmi, who produces Oriental
lamps and artefacts, spent a long time in the Khan al Khalili Bazar
being trained by the disappearing craftsmen. It is interesting to see
at how the Egyptian magazine *Shopping* popularizes 'Azza Fahmi as

---

[86] Emma Tarlo, . . ., p. 324.
[87] Ibid., p. 325.
[88] Chua Beng Huat, *Life is Not Complete Without Shopping, Consumption Culture in Singapore*, National University of Singapore, 2003, p. 79.

the artist who became interested in "Arabic tradition". She is portrayed as having developed an interest in reviving the Emirates tradition *ihya' al-turath al-'arabi* through a "mixage" in the encounter
between civilizations. She is also the only Arab woman who was
representing the Middle East in international exhibitions of jewellery.
A careful look at the ads in *Shopping* tells me that Fahmi is now
involuntarily reproducing the same images of neo-orientalism. (see
figure 58) Her jewellery is exhibited by eroticized women dressed in
an "oriental traditional" way. The background is the desert, romantic moonlight and camels.

Suzan al-Masri is another fascinating jeweller. She has lived in
the US and France. Al-Masri highlights Egyptian stones and she has
successfully revived Pharaonic, Coptic, and Islamic designs, to come
up with extremely original jewellery. Her work is sold in a shop near
al-Azhar Mosque, Bayt Khatun. This shop is an excellent example
of the endeavour of younger artists who renovated a historical house
in the area of al-Azhar mosque and transformed it into a shop where
they sell designed handwork, cloth, leather, glass and wood work.
This endeavour is going hand in hand with a revival of craftsmanship in cloth, woodwork, and furniture fulfilling a tourist demand.
The "folklorization of culture" and the ethnic look have become
popular among Egyptians through the admiring eyes of the foreigners.[89] However, be it Nagada, Bayt Khatun or the pottery made
by the Swiss couple in Fayyoum, the audience these cater to, is basically the Westernized upper class well to do, Egyptian intellectuals
and the foreign expatriate community. Whether such trends will have
a significant impact on culture is hard to say, but they have at least
created new markets and tastes, which are now gaining international
ground through overseas exhibitions, and in the Gulf and Saudi
Arabian market.

---

[89] Very much like the ritual of the *Zar*, which is mainly performed to exorcise
jinns has been recently advertised in the magazine *Egypt Today*. By undertaking this,
it was folklorised, sanitized and emptied from its content. The *Zar* musicians have
been rediscovered by Dr. Ahmed al-Maghrabi a professor of Italian at Ain Shams
University who established the Egyptian Centre for Culture and Arts and who
toured them in Europe. *Zar* performances have today another powerful tourist attraction. See the front cover of *Egypt Today* on *Zar*, March 2005 and the article,
"Mazaher", pp. 56–59.

Arts and Crafts

'Izbat Tunis in Fayyum has to be mentioned in this context as a part of such a trend. Some twenty or thirty years ago a group of intellectuals who discovered the success and beauty of the residence of the Swiss potters in 'Izbat Tunis, and the cheap land prices, conquered the place and created a kind of resort village. These urbanite intellectuals (painters, journalists, foreign expatriates, AUC professors, writers, actors and architects) who obviously had an idealized vision of the architecture of Hassan Fathi, have created a ghost village, a dream about a retreat place which never materialized and which led to an interesting "imagined community". Most of the houses are constructed in mud brick with plenty of domes and vaults to give them an authentic; "back to the roots" look. Many built huge castles, inspired by Fathi's philosophy of constructing for the poor, but with lavish aspirations. The interior decoration ranged from the fancy, which is little different from any Cairene salon, to *kelims* and *tabliyyas* (low tables, used by peasants), mats and Bedouin style living rooms. Some included Arabesques, and *mastabas* (in built sitting space); others preferred entirely modern, simple furniture. Today, the visitor is struck by the observation that these intellectuals replicated the bourgeoisie in the sense that these houses remained secondary weekend residences. But still the two worlds, one consisting of the local (originally poor peasants/Bedouins) and on the other side the well to do intellectuals, do not really meet.[90] Evidently, most of those who decided to construct houses there, looked for an escape from polluted Cairo, and the price of land was then comparatively cheaper due to the remote location of the village on the lake of Qarun. Tunis is most revealing about the romanticized vision of these urbanites.

The Nadim Centre and the Egyptian Society for Folk Traditions are two institutions, created by Asaad Nadim, an applied folklorist, and his wife Nawal El Messiri, an anthropologist and graduate from the American University in Cairo. The idea was to revive traditional art and to create a new generation of trainees. The National Art Development Institute of Mashrabeya (NADIM) was established in

---

[90] Some of the intellectuals have started development projects and theatre plays with the local population.

1978 as a non-government organization. The furniture produced
is a fascinating blend of tradition
and modern. The emphasis is on
reviving *masharabeya*, the art of
interlocking turned wood pieces,
carpet weaving, and the restoration
of antique furniture. Here again
one can see an interactive global-
local dynamic enabling this NGO
to expand and flourish thanks to
external factors. NADIM seems
to have earned an international
reputation through catering to
hotels such as the Four Seasons,
Sheraton, Movenpick, Intercontinental, Oberoi, Le Meridien and
Shepheard's. Furthermore, the
NADIM Centre developed another interest in the art of *tally*

Fig. 59. Al-Nadim Centre Ad.
From Shopping Magazine.

(tinsel needle work) which is practiced by Upper Egyptian women.
The result is an interesting anthropological documentation undertaken by Nawal al-Messiri, published by *al-Majlis al-Qawmi lil mara'*
(National Council for Women) under the auspices of the Ministry
of Culture.[91] Since the Egyptian Society for Folk Traditions began
marketing *tally* dresses, scarves, shoes and bags, these have become
fashionable and the prices rocketed with the increasing tourist demand.

'Abdel Wahhab al-Messiri, a retired professor of English literature
at 'Ain Shams University, is another example of a certain intellectual trend which advocates a way of Islamizing life styles. He introduced in his concrete multi-storey house in Heliopolis, *masharabiyyas*
and woodwork as a personal statement for an alternative lifestyle.
Egyptian pottery and plants decorate the entrance of his house. Al-
Messiri's house has been recently featured in *al-Bayt* Magazine with
an emphasis on its fine mosaics and woodwork.[92]

---

[91] *Tally: A Folkloric Embroidery, Documenting the intuitive artistic creativity of rural Egyptian Women.* Under the auspices of Dr. Nawal al Messiri, National Council for Women.
[92] *Al-Bayt*, February 2005, no. 56.

Al-Messiri's article, "The interpretation of bias, or prejudice", "*fiqh al-tahayyuz*", represents an interesting reaction to the "Westernization" process, which the Muslim World has been undergoing in recent decades. Al-Messiri expressed severe resentment about the fact that he faced a serious prejudice in the US when he attempted to publish his Ph.D., which was refused by several publishers.[93] Every researcher faces prejudice, in the form of approval of norms and rejection of new different ideas, according to him, whether originating from the North or from the South. In particular, Third World intellectuals undergo the imposition of different civilizational and cultural models upon their instincts, thought, and society. Since the late eighteenth centure, due to the spread of the white man and imperialism, cultural invasion has occurred.[94]

What al-Messiri proposes as alternatives to this challenge is to alter dress and furniture. However, his claim for change could be contextualized in the broader trend among Egyptian intellectuals who in the last twenty years have been discussing the issue of heritage or tradition (*turath*), as having been usurped by the intrusion of an imported set of values and practices. I have elsewhere discussed the various positions pertaining to that discourse.[95] Suffice to say here, that the return to search for authenticity started after the 1967 defeat and strengthened with the open door policy. It is thus no coincidence that clothing, furniture, the living room and the whole Western imported project is more than ever challenged. Al-Messiri is then one among the many who raised various questions.

Al-Messiri passes harsh judgments on the middle class for their Westernised "salon", or living room, and the utilization of space (although it could be said that the gold chairs one often sees in middle class salons are a parody of the French Louis "something", it hardly has anything to do anymore with France). He considers the French style of furniture as a Western model, which should be replaced. However, this style has undergone so much mutation through imitation as to become, in my view, quite genuine Egyptianized

---

[93] 'Abd al-Wahhab al-Missiri, "The fiqh of Bias," in: (*The Problematic of Bias*) (Published by the IIIT in Cairo with the Syndicate of Engineers, 1996), (in Arabic), p. 9.

[94] Ibid., p. 9.

[95] See my *Debates of Islam and Knowledge Egypt and Malaysia: Shifting Worlds*, Kurzon-Routledge, 2002.

French furniture. After all, the imitation of Western-style salons in Egypt has existed now for more than a century.

Al-Messiri proposes as alternative aesthetic solutions that people make lower chairs, sit on the floor on carpets and *Kelims*. There are definitely no objections to the beauty of Bedouin and Egyptian carpets and *kelims*. Yet it is another aspect of the "folklorization" of culture. One could imagine that for the Egyptian middle classes, sitting on the floor and replacing the dinning table with carpets and the low table would imply the "Saudi Arabization" of manners, which the Islamists have adopted as a counter style. Peasants traditionally use the low table, the *tabliyyah*. In recent years, it has become a fashionable item in hotels, like the phenomenon of Westerners wearing *galabeyya*, or the baking of bread as a tourist attraction. Upper and wealthier classes have similarly in recent years have borrowed folklorized traits, which they reproduce in the rest houses, beach resorts and farms. However, when peasants "gentrify" after their return from oil-producing countries they would rather buy Western style furniture in order to look like the people of the city. Al-Messiri's idyllic, "imagined", oriental style is no doubt aesthetically appealing, but also symbolizes aspirations of "gentrification" and social ascent. These aspirations are no different from those of the older lower middle classes who adopted French armchairs. Al-Messiri, however, wants to construct identity with such artefacts and challenge the usage of chairs in the living room.[96]

To summarize, what unites al-Messiri, Fahmi, Nagada, Mehrez, and the NADIM centre is the fact that they all flirt with the rediscovery of "tradition" and the return to "authenticity" in tastes and lifestyles. Is it a coincidence that most of them started their projects in the late seventies at the height of the open door policy, when the country was opening up to global markets. This stand is not devoid of an exotic and idyllic imagination of the orient and traditions. Most of these protagonists are themselves hybrid in their training (Western educated), and the trajectories of many tells us that they have had a long interactive encounter with the West such as long sojourns in education. From that perspective, it is possible to argue that the "recycling" of authenticity and the rediscovery of the "local" beauty is still taking place via the Western gaze. It is no coincidence

---

[96] *Ibid.*, pp. 24–25.

that such new tastes are also celebrated and adapted for the tourist industry. In other words, the border between "ethnic chic" and "ethno-kitsch" is thin.

To borrow from Bourdieu's dialectic of the competing actors within one field, one could view both the ethnic look and the "Islamic chic" as the new agents advocating change. Both trends are newcomers in fashion and design compared to the Western imported *haute couture*, which has had a longer established tradition in Egypt. Both trends are promoting "distinction" and refined taste. Identity here could be seen as a forging element in shaping distinction. However, the merit of both the ethnic look and the Islamic chic is that it will raise the market for "local" tastes. In other words, a local "griffe" is in the making through providing the "local" with a higher social valuation. Clothes, and other items considered *baladi*, like *shishas* (water pipes), the tiny square Aluminium coffee tables in traditional coffee houses, *kelims*, tents, cushions and other items from the quarter of *Khayameyyah*, (the tent makers quarter) carpets, copper and brass items (round tables), traditional perfumes, fabrics, have become fashionable for the well to do. These traditional items have become "forefront" landmarks to be exposed prominently in international hotels and sold at the airport as "souvenirs". With tourism, popular items have been elevated to the status of high culture, or rather marketed as mass-culture. Henna painting on the body has again become a popular tourist attraction; much like massage techniques imported from South-East Asia are now found in many international hotels and tourist resorts in the Red Sea. Other ethnic items, such as Indian furniture, fabrics, and paintings, Indonesian "rattan" (Bamboo) furniture and Thai bibelots and furniture are sold through Egyptian importers. Such furniture shops are to be found in shopping malls as well as in separate boutiques in Zamalek and in Mohandessin.

Authenticity in Fashion and Folklorization

How would lifestyle shape identity construction? By adopting the Islamic style in dress and furniture, many Egyptians are certainly trying to re-invent an identity which they feel has been usurped by the sixties modernization. In some circles, Egyptians bring up the example of the Indian subcontinent. They argue that although both Egypt and India had the same colonizer, the Indians maintained distinct traditions of dressing, an exquisite cuisine, and a genuine artistic expression, which seems to have been lost in Egypt. Although one could view the ethnic look as a direct consequence of a global interaction, or rather a response to international tourist demand, it is an interesting endeavour, which is fostering local handicrafts and seems to be filtering through to reach Egyptian middle and upper classes, which are also consumers also of international hotels, and popular shopping malls.

The ethnic look is definitively catering to the well to do elites, but one can see certain parallelisms between the "chic Islamic attire" and the emerging ethnic look in that both are using fashion for social elevation and status markers. Most interesting is that the Islamic attire has itself undergone transformations from the austere style, symbolizing a resistance to Westernization and to anti-upper class dress when it appeared on Egyptian campuses in the mid seventies, to turn into a form of "embourgeoisement", implying aspirations for inclusion. Attractive, seductive, sexy looking, flirtatious, emancipated, *shisha* smoking *muhaggabat* – although perhaps a contradiction in terms – have become a daily spectacle in Cairene streets.

The Flowering of the Art Market

> The logic of what is sometimes called, in typically 'pedantic' language, the 'reading' of a work of art, offers an objective basis for this opposition. Consumption is, in this case, a stage in a process of communication, that is, an act of deciphering, decoding, which presupposes practical or explicit mastery of a cipher or code. In a sense, one can say that the capacity to see (voir) is a function of the knowledge (savoir), or concepts, that is, the words, that are available to name visible things, and which are, as it were, programmes for perception. A work of art has meaning and interest only for someone who possesses the cultural competence, that is, the code, into which it is encoded, p. 2.

"The 'eye' is the product of history reproduced by education", Pierre Bourdieu, *Distinction*, 1984, p. 3.

The market for Egyptian painting has expanded tremendously in the last twenty-five years. Egyptian art has been elevated and is finally taken seriously. The optimists see the expansion of galleries as creating a genuine private art market. Others believe that prices rocketed because of patronage of the rich clientele of collectors, a typical phenomenon no different from elsewhere. Cynics see the art market as still dependent on the will of the government, which can give or withhold approval of the production. In the 1990's the galleries witnessed a change in the clientele from foreigners and expatriates to Egyptian, mainly younger generation members of the nouveau riches, who acquired wealth in the seventies. They were the major benefactors of the flourishing private technology and real estate sector.[97] The new rich are able to purchase paintings of the former generation radical politicized painters like 'Abdel Hadi al-Gazzar (1925–65) who depicted brilliantly the popular, magical and *jinn* possessed world of the poor and simple people. These tycoons however, acquire such paintings without needing to adopt the political and social message of al-Gazzar's work. But do they really need to understand the politics behind any work of art? Certainly not, what counts is rocketing prices and the valuation of Egyptian art as clever investment. Still, the pessimists insist that the rich history of radical and revolutionary art, of concern about reviving popular and folk culture, of the significance of counter culture, and of the ideas behind "long live low art", and the movement of "Art and Freedom",[98] which existed before the 1952 revolution, seems to have vanished from the Egyptian discourse on art.

The expansion of the art market was preceded by an awareness of a national art and culture during the time of Nasser. *L'art contemporain d'Egypte*,[99] is an excellent example of this trend. This marvelously illustrated work brings together the most outstanding Egyptian painting, and producers of handcrafts, potters, jewellery, carpets, sculpture, Arabic calligraphy, as representing modern art in Egypt. The figural sculptures of Mahmud Mukhtar (1891–1934) and the paintings of Mahmud Sa'id (1897–1964) are described as the founding landmarks of modern Egyptian art. Mohammed Nagui (1888–1956) is portrayed as the poet, painter, thinker and free and well-travelled artist. He moved between Alexandria and Paris, and from Gourna, in Luxor, to Ethiopia where as a diplomat, he discovered his artistic talents. *l'Art Contemporain d'Egypte* also includes the architectural

---

[97] Jessica Winegar, "Governing Culture: Struggles for Sovereignty in the Globalization of Egyptian Art" Paper presented at *the Fifth Mediterranean Social and Political Research Meeting, Workshop IV*. 24–28 March 2004, Monte Catini Terme, p. 10.

[98] This is well explained by Liliane Karnouk, *Modern Egyptian Art, 1910–2003*, Cairo-New York, AUC Press, 2005.

[99] Publié par le *Ministère de la culture et de l'orientation nationale en collaboration avec la maison d'edition Jugoslavija'*, in 1964.

genius of Hassan Fathi's experience in Gourna. It identified three female painters, Sayeda Mesak, Taheya Halim (1919–2003) and Gazbieh Sirry (b. 1925), as well as Anwar 'Abdel Mawla (b. 1920), Mohe el Din al Taher (1928), Kamal Ibeid, Khamis Shehata, Sa'id al Sadr, Ehsan Khalil, Gayed Guirgis, Sa'ad Kamel, Ramses Younan, Gamal El Seguini, Ahmed Sabri and Hassan Soliman whose works are today exhibited at the museum of Egyptian Contemporary Art at the new Opera House in Zamalek. Thus one can argue that a greater awareness of an Egyptian national art emerged during the sixties. Since the appointment of Farouk Hosni (a painter by profession) as the Minister of Culture some twenty years ago, cultural institutions such as galleries, cultural palaces, museums, biennales and triennials, cultural funds and publication initiatives burgeoned. Symposiums, international exchange programs and awards for artists also flourished.[100]

During the late seventies Cairo experienced the emergence of private art galleries. The gallery-restaurant "Arabesque" downtown was considered to be among the first to open in the late seventies, under the direction of a former communist and free officer. The eighties and nineties experienced a real boom in both private and state sponsored exhibitions. This went hand in hand with the expansion of the private sector that made the art business lucrative. Recently, some galleries have done extremely well through providing hundreds of paintings to international hotels. The newly opened (2004) *Four Seasons* Hotel in Garden City, is a good case in point, where a painting of the Minister of Culture, Faruk Hosni is displayed in the lobby amongst many of other known Egyptian painters.

Painters known in the sixties such as 'Abdel Hadi al-Gazzar (1925–65)[101] and Kamal Khalifa (1926–1968) have been rediscovered

---

[100] *Al-Ahram Weekly* published recently an article listing Farouk Hosni's achievements since he was under attack after the incident of the Cultural Palace of Beni Sweif (5 September 2005) where 48 spectators were killed and many injured. One of the performers was carrying a candle causing a fire. The merit of this article is in providing a detailed list of the cultural and artistic institutions in Egypt. See Interview by Nevine El-Aref, "Farouk Hosni: Politics of Temperament", *Al-Ahram Weekly*, 22–28 September 2005, Issue No. 761, http://weekly.ahram.org.eg/2005/761/profile.htm.

[101] What contributed to the rediscovery of 'Abdel Hadi al-Gazzar (1925–1966) is the publication about his painting. Alain et Christine Roussillon (editors) *Abdel Hadi al-Gazzar, Une peinture egyptienne. An Egyptian Painter*, Dar al-Musaqbal al-'arabi, Cairo, 1990.

and their paintings have been circulating in the market mainly through the Safar Khan Gallery established in 1995. Sherwet Shafeʿi, the Safar Khan Gallery owner, says that her main clientele consists of the rising rich, young businessmen. The old bourgeoisie is her main provider of the first generation painters of the thirties and forties, like Mahmud Saʿid (1897–1964), Ragheb Ayyad (1892–1980), ʿEffat Nagui (1910–94), and Mohammed Nagui (1888–1956).[102] Tourism is not insignificant in the flowering of the local art market. Shafeʿi recognizes that American and European tourists liked the numerous paintings displayed in the recently opened Four Seasons Hotel and they contacted her via the hotel. Shafeʿi is optimistic about the art business in Egypt. "There are so many newly constructed houses on the Red Sea, all along the Mediterranean coast, the hundreds of new satellite cities, the Qattameya heights, the new hotels and restaurants . . . All these villas and condominiums need to be furnished. It is clear that the younger generation wants to furnish its salons with Egyptian painters . . . They are in great demand today".

Furthermore, the Saudi collector Saʿid al-Farsi, who purchased significant numbers of Egyptian works of arts in recent years, has contributed to promoting markets and raising prices. The late French President Mitterrand decorated Sherwet Shafeʿi, who also worked for years as the director of an art program for Egyptian television for promoting Egyptian culture and Francophonie.[103]

Forgery of Egyptian pioneer painters and the apparently wide circulation of copies seem to be a general complaint of both art dealers and painters. Forgeries of paintings by Ragheb ʿAyyad and Mohammed Nagui are known, especially of Mahmud Saʿid, whose paintings have sold for up to L.E. 500,000. This problem has been even referred to in the edited volume published by the Ministry of Culture on Mahmud Saʿid to celebrate the hundredth anniversary of his birth. It became an issue of concern when forgeries were found among some well-known collectors.[104] Ironically, Mahmud Saʿid never

---

[102] For the most detailed and comprehensive survey of contemporary modern art see, Liliane Karnouk, *Modern Egyptian Art, 1910–2003*, Cairo-New York, AUC Press, 2005.

[103] Safar Khan Gallery existed already before Sherwet Shafeʿi took it over from by Roxane Petridis. Safar Khan became prominent in the seventies for selling fine Arabesque furniture, paintings and antiques. Interview with Sherwet Shafeʿi, 6 June 2005. Safar Khan, Zamalek.

[104] Esmat Daoustashi, "hathal-kitab wal-thikra al-miʾawiyya limilad mahmud said" (*This book, A Hundred Year anniversary of Mahmud Said's Birth, Mahmud Said*), Ministry of Culture, Cairo, 1997.

sold any paintings during his lifetime because he was a well off judge. He was famed for donating his paintings as presents, and many entered the collections of close members of his family.[105]

The late Alexandrian painter Seif Wanly and Hamed Nada (1924–90) underwent the same fate. A scandal of forgery exploded recently during the summer of 2005 with two simultaneous events. First, seven of the priceless, heavy bronze sculptures of the well known sculptor Adam Henein were stolen from his garden in Harraniyya, near the Pyramids. Henein's famed sculptures are exhibited in Dolnick's Museum, for up to L.E. 500.000 per piece.[106] Rumours spread that his works might be appearing in the near future in Europe or in one of the oil producing countries where the rich developed an interest in Egyptian art and have evidently found illegal Egyptian providers. In fact, this was the second time that Henein's sculptures were stolen from his garden. It was clearly an art theft. Second, a court case was filed against some high society elderly lady and her associate for having sold several forged paintings to the new wealthy. This coincides with the discovery of another dealer who worked in a five stars hotel who flooded the market with fakes. The conclusion of the article in *Egypt Today* was that the market is "awash with fakes"[107] which could be purchased in downtown auctions for L.E. 2000.

Samir Gharib, an art historian and specialist who worked for years at the Ministry of Culture and is closely associated with the current Minister of Culture, observes that the way paintings are sold today to the new tycoons is similar to the *dallalat* system, the system of "women peddlers", with the art dealer knocking at the door of the tycoon's private house. Gharib confirms the rumour that a low level employee at the Ministry of Culture has been known for trading in fakes, "peddling" them around in the Qattameyya area where the rich live. Gharib argues that it is most unlikely that the registered galleries would sell forgeries. These would immediately loose their reputation and consequently their clientele. But the problem with

---

[105] Interviews with Sherwet Shafe'i. Zamalek.

[106] Manal el-Jesri, "Upon Closer Inspection", *Egypt Today*, July 2005, pp. 115–121, p. 115.

[107] Ibid., p. 120. For a counter argument in favour of the high society lady who has been accused of fraud and counterfeit, but for having being a victim of Cairene gossipmongers, see Hassan Elsawaf, "About Art Fraud and Witch Hunts", *Cairo Magazine*, Issue 17, 14–20 July 2005, p. 14.

the informal market is that there are no checks or controls and "any-thing goes".[108]

Galleries have multiplied in the last twenty years. In the down-town area, one can mention the following galleries: *Arabesque*, *Masharabiyya*, Karim Francis Gallery, Town House, Cairo-Berlin (but which closed after the death of its German owner some three years ago), the Atelier (which has a long and rich history), Atelier 5 × 5. The island of Zamalek has the following galleries: Safar Khan, the former Aisha Fahmy palace (state run), the former Mahmud Khalil Museum, Zamalek Art Gallery, Picasso, El-Sawy, the Saquia Gallery and theatre, Khan al-Maghrabi, the Botega restaurant, which both include a gallery and the coffee shop of the Yamama centre (a shop-ping mall which includes in a cafeteria). This is besides the various cultural centres, the German, Italian, French, Swiss and others, which are all extremely active in organizing visual performances, photog-raphy, theatre, painting and various others exhibitions. For young artists, Cairo has become a place where one's dreams are realized, in stark comparison to the impenetrable European market. Also many foreign artists are given the chance to exhibit in downtown galleries. Egyptian art seems to be doing well and is alive.

It would be misleading to concentrate on the private art galleries without pointing to the overwhelming role of the state in control-ling the art production. It was noted that because of the nature of the Egyptian central state, arts could not escape institutionalized dominance, which is hierarchical. For many artists, the access to the state as bureaucrats or state employees does provide a form of power and status to exercise control over the art production. Liliane Karnouk observes the following:

> As a matter of fact, the Minister of Culture, Farouk Hosni, is a painter, the Deputy Minister for the Fine Arts is still Ahmad Nawar, a print-maker. The Director of the National Art Centre is still the veteran artist Ahmad Fouad Selim, a painter. The Director of the Fine Arts program of the Bibliotheca Alexandrina is Moustafa al-Razaz, a painter.[109]

It is thus possible to speak of parallel markets, but in the final instance the role of the state in promoting, recognizing and hiring artists as holders of power is omnipotent in decision making. Moreover, the

---

[108] Personal communication with Samir Gharib, 26 July 2005. Zamalek.
[109] Liliane Karnouk, 2005, p. 5.

state has the upper hand in censoring works that are considered as an offence to "public morality".

The artists and intellectuals of *wist al-balad* (Downtown) are an interesting phenomenon worth mentioning. These rotate around the pubs and places of Downtown (the *Greek Club*, the *Grillon, the Qahwat al-Bustan*). Every Thursday, the *After Eight* pub brings a group of Jazz musicians called *wist al-balad*. The music performed is a captivating hybrid mix of Jazz with the classical Egyptian songs of Sayyed Darwish (an Azharite who revived Egyptian music at the turn of the century). The group consists of Egyptians and European musicians. The downtown artists and intellectuals have created friendship and work networks. They often collectively exhibit their work at Karim Francis gallery, or Town House Gallery. The interest in reviving the art of *wist al-balad* was best exemplified in the *Nitaq* festival, in January 2000, which included various exhibitions, concerts, plays and films of young artists.[110] The *Nitaq* festival was considered a success since it was visited by large numbers of people and the atmosphere of downtown during that period was even more lively than usual.

During the last three decades, *Wist al-Balad* witnessed a de-population, while offices and clinics and clinic survived. The European style buildings decayed and looked run down because they suffered from a lack of maintenance. However, it is noticeable that a few intellectuals and artists are reoccupying downtown today.

Mike Featherstone's notion of the "aestheticization" of everyday life, where good style and taste will pervade daily life, where new artistic cultural markets and the growing cultural intermediaries who expanded in Europe are also slowly happening in Egypt.[111] To be more precise this is still restricted to the metropolis of Cairo. The English speaking press witnessed a remarkable growth in the last decade,[112] the market for art and cultural and musical performances in Cairo is flowering, and architectural renovation has provided cultural centres, thanks to international funding. This is, in turn, creating intermediaries who are mostly "hybrid" in their training, outlook and life styles. The difference is perhaps that it is still a tiny

---

[110] See Jessica Winegar, "Governing Culture: Struggles for Sovereignty in the Globalization of Egyptian Art", *Paper presented at the Fifth Mediterranean Social and Political Research Meeting, Workshop IV*, 24–28 March 2004, Monte Catini Terme.

[111] I cite Featherstone from Steven Miles, p. 25.

[112] To mention a few, *al-Ahram Weekly, Cairo Times, Business Today, Cairo Today*, this is besides the French *al-Ahram Hebdo*.

minority, of the sixteen million people who live in Cairo, which in contrast to Europe does not constitute the broad middle classes.

Salons and Paintings

Today if one visits houses of well-off young couples, their "salon" might have a painting of the late Raouf 'Abdel Meguid, known for his vaults and calligraphy, or by Gazbiyya Serri, Hassan Sulaiman, or 'Abdel Wahhab Mursi. Hassan Sulaiman paints scenes from the countryside, peasant workingwomen, and scenes of popular life. It seems that to acquire a Hassan Sulaiman painting has become a "necessity", a social marker for the rising rich. He is much beloved because his paintings are realistic and easy to appreciate (abstract paintings are less appreciated). Perhaps also because it portrays flair of concern for "authenticity", with folkloric and rural landscapes contrasted with French or English style furniture. For the new wealthy, interior decorators are flown to Paris to purchase the furniture. The increasing demand for interior designers is perhaps an indicator that the new rich are extremely insecure about their taste.[113]

The reproductions of printings by David Roberts have become popular among the well-to-do middle class. They are cheaper that original paintings, but they make a statement about their owner's taste. The *masharabiyyas* and Islamic furniture, *Dikkahs*, (oriental large sofas), *mastabahs*, built in sofa, Ottoman furniture, carpets and cushions are back in fashion.

In this context, it should be mentioned that the so called "arabesque style" is a good example of the creation of orientalism. It happened through the process of local urban elites rediscovering their tradition through the Western gaze. It is through European designers and travellers who liked to take pictures in exotic oriental settings that the re-invention of the Arabesque style occurred. Arabesque became fashionable after Egypt, like many other Arab countries experienced the full-fledged Westernization by imposing Louis XV and Louis

---

[113] Menha al-Batrawi has observed during her various interviews, the extreme power which interior decorators are given. These are accorded a *carte blanche* and they are paid to fly to Europe to purchase the entire furniture. They decide on each single piece of furniture, while the owners are mostly deprived from any decision. Batrawi observed that these new rich villa owners live as if they are permanently in a hotel. Personal communication with Menha al-Batrawi.

XVI sofas, Queen Ann dining rooms and English silver tableware. Shahira Mehrez defines Arabesque as follows: "It consisted basically of western shaped furniture, tables, chairs, sofas, with "oriental" additions: mother of pearl and ivory inlay, incorporation of panels of interlocked star patterns, or of small fragments of the turned wood technique (by now inaccurately – called *masharabeyyas*)".[114] This confirms one thing, that invented traditions in lifestyles and what Appadurai has earlier defined as "tourist art" has existed for nearly two centuries and it has clearly affected the elites' own perceptions.

Let me shift to the past in an attempt at reconstructing a comparative perspective on present day upper middle class salons. When I visualize the residence of my grandmother, who was the daughter of a so-called "illustrious" politician in the early twenties, the furniture consisted of fancy heavy French and Italian chairs, sofas and Chinese tables. The house was full of what one would designate as "chinoiseries", blue China Lions, a paravan, which might have been Japanese. The house consisted of various salons; the walls were hung with *Gobelin*[115] tapestry and European paintings. It was a must to own an *Aubusson* sofa and chairs and a tapestry. It seems that France manufactured specific patterns for Egyptian consumers and a large traffic of *Aubussons* went on in the thirties and forties. Well-to-do Egyptians went to France to purchase these items or ordered them from the various shops in Cairo. The addresses of shops in France were circulated among friends and relatives. Before the 1952 revolution, groups of friends and relatives travelled together to shop for furniture and clothes.[116]

The salon was also decorated with massive China vases, and China statues, valuable tables, which we were told were the only replicas of Versailles. One corner of the salons had painted glass in the windows, made by an Italian glassmaker. This is where drinks were served before dinner. Nearly every evening, my grandfather had a gathering of friends who sat in the corner of the salon, which was

---

[114] Shahira Mehrez, "The Arab Interior, Between Orient, Orientalism and Globalization", paper presented at a Conference on the Arab Interior, Vitra Design Museum, Berlin, October, 2003, p. 5.

[115] The *gobelin* is similar to the Aubusson tapestry. Gobelin is the name of a family of dyers and clothesmakers who came from Reims and settled in Paris in the fifteenth century. During the seventeenth century Gobelin was transformed into a general upholstery manufactory. The tapestry was mainly used by royalty in France. See Gobelin, *Encyclopaedia Britannica*, Vol. 10, 1965, pp. 510–511.

[116] Personal communication with Mehri Foda, 15 May 1995.

two steps higher than the main salon.[117] The sofa was covered in red stripped silk, and opposite it there was another low copper table on which *mezzas* were served while the guests drank their whiskey. The "salons" were filled with various silver chandeliers, ashtrays, a piano, and plenty of stylish chairs. There were many statues and "bibelots", which gave the impression of overcrowding in this huge villa. The only four oriental items I could remember were two low round copper tables in the two salons and a carpet, which was said to have previously adorned the *Ka'ba*. The sacred carpet, a gift to my grandfather by the Saudi King hung up in the closed salon, which was rarely frequented. It was only used when my grandmother received her female friends. My grandmother performed her daily recitation of the *fatiha* (The opening *sura* of the *Qur'an*) in front of the sacred carpet while caressing it.[118] We had to emulate her on Fridays and on religious feasts. The fourth Egyptian item was an *'ud* (a musical instrument), because famous singers like Um Kalthoum, 'Abdel Wahhab, and 'Abdel Halim Hafez often came to these dinners, they sometimes sang.

Most if not all the paintings that hung on the wall were of European origin, landscapes and Italian renaissance paintings. We were constantly reminded that some of these huge canvases had a significant value because we were told the disciples of Michel Angelo painted them. There were Dutch paintings of flowers and nature's paintings. There were miniatures of European landscapes. There were also paintings of naked women and portraits of unknown people.

My grandmother boasted the great achievements of the sculptor Mahmud Mukhtar, one of the most important advocates of Neo-Pharaonism. She boasted his greatness only because he did a bronze bust of my great grandfather. But my grandmother never consid-

---

[117] My grand father's friends consisted of the old class feudalists, politicians and intellectuals as well as new regime free officers, ministers and lawyers. When I was older I learned that politics, collations, gossips and information about the next government moves were exchanged in these gatherings. Prominent singers and poets also figured among the invitees.

[118] My grandmother prayed five times a day, she measured *zakat* offerings in an astonishing precision and fasted during Ramadan. She refused to deposit her money in banks if it was based on interest. In contrast, my grandfather hardly ever prayed and was reputed for heavy drinking. The different lifestyles were a source of tension between the two. This brings me to the next observation: that religious observance varied extremely within the same family. Some members of my family were extremely religious, while others not at all.

ered purchasing any of his sculptures although she could have afforded to do so. Today when I try to make sense of this setting, I would say that it consisted of a mix of objects all imported from Europe, jammed statues, big chandeliers and so many chairs that hindered any movement remain as my last impression. It certainly displayed ostentatious wealth; it was bulky and totally unpractical.

Briefly said, there was hardly anything "typical" or purely Egyptian in the taste of my family. In retrospect, I would say that there were no paintings in my grandmother's salons by any Egyptian painter. Neither was the furniture Egyptian.

Until the early seventies, my mother possessed only a few European-style paintings, except for one Orientalist painting of the view of the Citadel by Hedayat, a Turkish painter residing in Cairo, whose works became popular among the Egyptian bourgeoisie during the thirties and forties.[119] I recall that there were some miniatures. In the mid-seventies my mother developed an interest in Egyptian painters through work in a gallery and started slowly developing her own collection of contemporary Egyptian painters.

The Mahmud Khalil Museum, a palace built in 1915 in Giza, became Sadat's private residence in the seventies and was inaugurated as a Museum in 1962 and reopened during the time of the current Minister of Culture, Farouk Hosni. The Khalil Museum is an excellent testimony to the pre-1952 tastes and life styles of the "ancient regime" Pashas. Senator Mohammed Mahmud Khalil was one of the founders of the society of "les amis de l'art" in 1921.[120] Mohammed Mahmud Khalil was a fine collector of contemporary European art, of "chinoiseries", sculptures, Gobelins, tapestry, Japanese style small boxes and ceramics. Khalil's vast art collection includes paintings by Camille Pissaro, Theodore-Auguste Rousseau, Paul Gauguin, Vincent Van Gogh, Claude Monet, Auguste Renoir, Alfred Sisley, Toulouse-Lautrec, sculptures of Rodin, wonderful miniatures and orientalist paintings. Khalil was a Francophile, whose French

---

[119] Sherwet Shafeʿi stated that the former royal family possessed many paintings of Hedayat and of Mahmud Saʿid. Saʿid never sold any of his paintings because he was a well off member of the royal family. Shafeʿi asserts that Saʿid mainly gave his work as presents to his friends and family members.

[120] The most important achievement of this society was the creation of the first Museum of Modern Art, which has been functioning since 1928. The Museum also included a permanent exhibition for Egyptian painters. Samir Raafat, Pre-WW 2 Cairo Art Scene, December 2004, http://7www.egy.com/cultural/04–12–16.shtml.

wife instigated in him the passion for art. Of the some 304 paintings, only thirty are painted by Egyptians. The Egyptian paintings
and sculptures are by Mahmud Sa'id, Mohammed Hassan, Youssef
Kamel, Taher al-'Amri, Saroukhan, Edmond Soussa, Georges Sabbagh
and 'Afifi. Of the some fifty sculptures, only two are by Egyptians;
these are Mohammed Hassan and Sa'id al-Sadr.[121] According to
Mohammed Sidqi Gabakhangi, rumors spread that Khalil despised
Egyptian artists. This was erroneous, but he definitely thought that
Egyptian art had still a long way to go to reach European standards. Although it is mainly thanks to Khalil and the society of "les
amis de l'art" that the large collection of Egyptian art was enlarged
to be included in the contemporary Egyptian Museum of Modern
Art in Gezira,[122] one can conclude from the Khalil Musem that
Egyptian painting in the thirties and forties was not taken seriously
by the bourgeoisie, whose ideals and criteria of judgment were based
upon European standards.

What a change of taste if we look at the well to do classes today.
The acquisition of cultural capital and tastes has evidently changed.
The salon can consist of Indonesian Rattan, Thai or Indian furniture and South and Southeast Asian decorative objects. It could well
be a modern, Bauhaus type of salon decorated with abstract paintings among the educated youngsters, as it is from time to time advertised in *al-Bayt* Magazine. But it could also consist of the most recent
Western designs and furniture (French, American, or English) that
go well with "Oriental" landscapes and Egyptian painting.

---

[121] Mohammed Sidqi Gabakhangi "muqtanayat mahmud khalil al-faniyyah"
Mahmud Khalil's Works of Art (Museum guide), Mahmud Khalil Museum, Ministry
of Culture, Cairo, 1995.

[122] The Museum of Modern Art was moved in 1986 by the Ministry of Culture
to the Gezira area inside the space of the newly constructed (1988) by the Japanese
Opera house. It displays more than 10,000 paintings and sculptures. See The Gezira
Center for Modern Art. http://www.touregypt.net/museums/gezira/gezira.htm.

CHAPTER SIX

CAIRO'S SHOPPING MALLS AND URBAN RESHAPING

An Introduction
You Can Suck or Shove
She wasn't a corpse yet.
Hind doesn't like wasting time because she's never been like other girls.
Place: Geneina Mall, the ladies' toilet.
Hind writes the mobile phone number on the insides of the doors of the toilets with a waterproof lipstick, then passes a Kleenex soaked in soda water over it, 'cos that way, cupcake, it can't be wiped off!
I told her to write it at the eye level of a person sitting on the toilet seat.
Above it two words: CALL ME
Why?
Because these things happen.

Fig. 60. Stars Centre – Young men and women.

The woman goes into the toilet to relieve herself.
The woman goes into the toilet to use something that emerges, from her handbag, to protect her.
Her sin, of which she is guiltless.
A naked fragile butterfly – and
Enter the terrible number.
The number gazes at her weakness.
The number permits itself to intervene instantaneously.
The number asks no permission and has no supernumeraries.
This is the number . . .
Zero-one-zero, six, forty, ninety, thirty.
CALL ME
010 6 40 90 30

Arkadia Mall:
CALL ME
010 6 40 90 30

Ramses Hilton Mall:
CALL ME
010 6 40 90 30

The World Trade Center:
Accept no imitations.
Zero-one-zero, six, forty, ninety, thirty.

CALL ME

There's a thing I like to get up to from time to time.
As though I was living like any other lunatic.
As though I was myself, with all the little stupidities I like to commit.
And with all the stupidities that have become – by now – part of my makeup, it was obvious I'd ask her to push it.
How far?
You guess.[1]

Ahmed Al-Aidi, opening page of *Being Abbas El Abd*

This is the opening page of *Being Abbas El Abd*, the much-celebrated short novel written by Ahmed Al-Aidi. The novel sold out its first publication run within three months after its appearance in Arabic in 2004. The writer, born in 1977 and barely in his late twenties, is representative of the younger generation of Egyptian writers. When

---

[1] Ahmed Alaidy. *Being Abbas El Abd*. Translated by Humphrey Davies. Cairo: The American University in Cairo Press, 2006.

reviewing the book, Yusif Rakha identified the work as defying any type of categorization, which was certainly accurate.[2] It is hard to follow the outline of the story. The technique is post-modern; there is in fact no consistent story, no beginning, no real end, and plenty of comical hallucinations and obsessions. What interests us in this emerging genre among the younger generation of Egyptian writers is that most of these incomprehensible human encounters happen in the public toilets of shopping malls. It is in the mall where the main character simultaneously dates two young women. Both young women are waiting for him there, but one waits in a café upstairs while he first meets the other woman downstairs. Both girls are named Hind, but one is a working-class prostitute who uses very common Arabic and the other is an upper-class American University in Cairo student who fills her speech with English words. Both are comical characters and the communication is Kafkaesque. He dates them instead of, or being mistaken for, his friend 'Abbas al-'Abd, his supposed alter ego, who is a working-class street fighter.

This style of writing has caught the attention of the critics through the amalgamation of multiple levels of language. Rakha says:

> Al-'Aidi is conscious of living in the electronic age and he invests the surface of his text with the omnipresent symbols of the internet and the mobile phone: clip art, English words like "cut" and "paste" and a constantly flickering visual plane of communication make an unusually disorienting . . . reading experience . . .[3]

The text is written in a hybrid language mixing colloquial street talk with different layers of classical Arabic. Rakha brilliantly summarizes the work by arguing that "al-'Aidi benefits from the irony inherent in a linguistic orientation that combines the latest Egyptian Arabic slang with standard Arabic, the traditional language of literary prose, and predominantly English expressions that, due to the spread of the implements of the electronic age, have been incorporated into everyday speech."[4]

Musika al Moll (Mall Music)[5] is another recently published novel (March 2005) by Mahmud al-Wardani. This is another surrealistic

---

[2] Youssef Rakha. "On Alternative Tracks" al-Ahram Weekly on Line, 18–24 December, http://weekly.ahram.org.eg/2003/669/bo21.htm.

[3] http://weekly.ahram.org.eg/2003/669/bo21.htm.

[4] Ibid.

[5] Mahmud al-Wardani, *Musika al-mol*, Cairo, Miret, 2005.

story where reality is constantly confused with fantasies and dreams. It is a story of a man who is transferred to another town on the coast, to escape his wife who turned mad after the loss of their first child. To kill time, he enters a mall for the first time, to end up being imprisoned with an Islamist and his completely veiled wife, a police officer who may be an imposter, since it is never clear whether he is lying or not, an American Orientalist fluent in Arabic, who must be either trafficking in antiquities or researching on the subject, and another young man who becomes his ally. They are all hostage of the mall, but no one really knows why and who are the ones behind their confinement. At the beginning of the story the narrator seems to be navigating in the fantasy world of a virtual consumer culture, sex shows, an unreal and imposing world of goods, and the constant returning ghost of his wife who he imagines to be one of the girls working in the nightclub. The events are interwoven with several passages of the *One Thousand and One Nights*, the book that the narrator is carrying around all through the novel. In the end the narrator finds a way out, after fires have devastated the town and police forces are all over the place. One is left unsure if this was a dream or a hallucination. Why chose the mall as the focal point of his novel? Al-Wardani answers by arguing:

> It wasn't until I went to Dubai a couple of years ago that I became interested in the idea of commercialism as it is embodied in the shopping mall – a disturbing thing, the shopping mania, the fake life it sustains. Realizing that the same principle held in Cairo, on however smaller a scale, I decided to explore malls, which turned out to be a meeting point for adolescents who look so alike you think they're mass produced . . .[6]

It is no coincidence that both al-ʿAidi and al-Wardani have a Kafkaesque, surrealistic inclination; both have something to say about the behaviour of youth, and sexual fantasies are vividly described. Al-ʿAidi's opening page alludes to a young woman who is possibly introducing into her body a contraceptive, leaving the reader to presume a forthcoming sexual intercourse in the mall. For both novelists, the morphology of the mall develops a life of its own, but perhaps for al-Wardani more than al-ʿAidi, the mall turns to be malefic and full of temptations. The starting points for my interest in the new

---

[6] Rania Khallaf, "My Favorite Mall", *Al-Ahram Weekly*, 5–11 May 2005, p. 18.

consumer culture in Egypt include questions about how alienation and meaninglessness is experienced by youth in these empires of consumption, and how the shopping mall has becomes the "locus" of alienated encounters. These two novels tell us a lot about the emerging lifestyles and the growing feeling of uprooted ness and alienation among the youth.

New Dating Patterns

The culture of "dating" and "rendezvous"[7] is a Western invention, which became popular by the end of the nineteenth century in America due to changing sexual morals. The practice grew with the increase of income amongst certain classes, the propagation of mass markets, and the creation of new public spaces where new forms of socialization could take place. Western critics note that the commoditisation of love occurred with the promotion of a new image of intimacy and sexuality through the leisure industry and leisure technologies such as the car and the cinema. Following the analysis of Eva Illouz this suggests a union between the modern popularization of romantic love in America with consumer culture and market expansion and how the institutionalization of romantic love has been codified and represented in clichéd symbols. These symbols were certainly associated with consumer culture exemplified in the "rendezvous", dinners, drinking champagne, honeymoon travels to far away exotic places, romantic pictures, and giving presents or diamonds and jewels. All these representations were promoting a luxurious lifestyle. Love developed cultural categories, which could be associated with the development of late capitalism and the individual economic conditions. In other words, love relationships, culture and economy were interwoven with each other. Thus, the practice of the "rendezvous" in nineteenth century America was closely related to leisure such as picnics and social meals, or religious functions. In contrast, in the countryside, in earlier times, free time and leisure was a communal activity.[8] Romantic interactions were later transposed

---

[7] Eva Illouz, *Der Konsum der Romantik, Liebe und die Kulturellen Widersprueche des Kapitalismus*, Campus Verlag, 1997. English version, *Consuming the Romantic Utopia*, The University of California Press, 1997.

[8] Eva Illouz, p. 52.

into a public form of experience, which took place in the anonymous public sphere of consumerism. The possibility of choosing partners developed in public consumer spaces where new borders between
private and public space were created. This is where an "island of
privacy" within the public space was created.[9]

Illouz then traced the historical evolution of dating and analyzed
the changing dating practices with the expansion of the car industry. For young middle class couples, dating became associated with
romantic rides, and the experiences of long distance travel. Dating
also meant inviting women to restaurants, movies and shows. A whole
etiquette, or rather, advice in magazines and manuals on how to
date, became fashionable. Importance was given to dress, and the
display of good manners, which were developed to help expanding
consumer culture and the market economy. Looking at dating through
the lenses of the political economy of romantic love. Dating created
further social distinctions between the upper classes and the working class who could not afford such activities. For the working class,
dating thus became very difficult because they were excluded from
such affluence.

Dating and the "rendezvous" culture and romantic love can be
seen as an alien import into indigenous Egyptian culture. In her
introduction, Mona El-Ghobashy, the translator of Ibrahim Aslan's
Nile Sparrows, a novel that presents a vivid picture of the rural-urban
relationship in the popular quarter of Warraq, clarified some Egyptian
customs for the Western reader. She informs us that in the first half
of the twentieth century, the practice of dating among the traditional
families was unfamiliar.[10] That women could have a say about the
choice of partners seems to be a recent phenomenon, emerging in
the 1950's. But it is possible to argue that, by the 1930's romantic
love was popularized through Egyptian movies and the press. Middle-
class Cairenes adopted engagement, *khutuba* in the sixties. Some families would not allow the engaged couples to go out without a
chaperon, which was most likely the younger brother or sister.

Steffen Strohmenger's[11] anthropological study of romantic love in
Cairo in the early nineties is extremely illuminating concerning the

---

[9] Ibid., p. 55.
[10] Ibrahim Aslan, *Nile Sparrows*, AUC Press, 2004, Translator's note, ix.
[11] Steffen Strohmenger, *Kairo: Gespräche über Liebe*, Edition Trickster im Peter
Hammer Verlag, Wuppertal, 1996.

cultural specificity of dating, flirting with the eyes and making one-self desired by becoming *tiqil* or by *tuql*, which literally means becoming "heavy", but implies being unavailable.[12] The rules of the game are that the young man has to take the initiative and never the other way around. But women learn to play tricks to attract men by pretending that they do not care about the attention given to them. Nevertheless, women have to wait endlessly until the right opportunity comes. But most of the interviewees said that such contacts were made behind the back of their families. The interviews revealed it is difficult to move from such contacts to real intimacy and many end up not knowing enough about the partners they marry.

Egyptian films of the late fifties and early sixties call to mind those unmarried middle-class couples who dated in the Zoo of Giza, the Japanese gardens of Helwan, the Fish (Grotto) Gardens in Zamalek, (these would be inexpensive public places), or in open air cafeterias on the Nile. Upper classes met in nightclubs, bars and restaurants. For those who could afford a car, dating could include a ride to the countryside, the Pyramids or Alexandria. Boats or "péniches" turned into nightclubs, which were mostly frequented by foreigners, but one presumes that a minority of Egyptians frequented such places. *Akhar Sa'ah* magazine reports about such nightclub-boats where the twist was danced until three o'clock in the morning.[13] Upper class youth met at clubs, like Guezira, Heliopolis, Ahli, the Shooting Club, which were ideal places for socializing, flirting and matchmaking for the better off classes. In the mid-sixties the middle class shifted to the duck pond in Merryland and the Guezira Tower. Flaneuring along the Nile was and still remains a typical lower classes pastime, always a cliché in Egyptian films.

As for today, it is possible to say that the shopping malls as semi-public spaces (which are camera monitored) have replaced the idyllic open-air gardens. In the mall are modern coffee houses, some of which are popular precisely for their dark and private atmosphere, ideal for flirting. The malls' bowling centres, cinemas, atriums and passages are also ideal for meeting and dating. The malls' discotheques and late movie shows are the best opportunity for flaneuring. As al-'Aidi's ironical short novel informs us, it is in these newly created

---

[12] See Steffen Strohmenger, p. 81.
[13] Tareq Foda, "hynama raqasu 'alal-twist" (When they Danced the Twist), *Akher Sa'ah*, 25 April 1962, no. 1435, pp. 44–45.

spaces of consumption that flirting, mixing, spending time, or simply gazing while standing on the terraces would be taking place.

Undoubtedly, not only dating habits are changing, but sexual norms too. At least this is the message conveyed by recent Egyptian films. Even though cinema could be a fantasy world, it tells us a lot about society's changing norms. In *muwatin, mukhbir, wa-harami* (A Citizen, an Informant and a Thief), a recent film directed by Daoud 'Abdel Sayyed, two couples have pre-marital sex. The two male protagonists, are a popular singer Sha'ban 'Abdel Rehim[14] and a young, upper-class Western educated, writer. They end up, in a way, swapping the women they sleep with. The director seems to deal with marital sex as a norm, yet the happy end is marriage for all. The wit of the story is that the former girl friend of the writer, an upper middle-class intellectual-type, marries the popular singer Sha'ban 'Abdel Rehim. He is a kind of good-hearted Robin Hood and the female intellectual is attracted to him because of his common sense and popular wisdom. While the writer's maid who was formerly engaged to Sha'ban 'Abdel Rehim, in a dubious way – perhaps in an *'urfi* marriage – ends up marrying the writer. Here, 'Abdel Sayyed reverses the code. He materializes the union between a "refined" intellectual who listens to operas and classical music, drinks wine and lives in a belle époque, decadent villa and yet falls madly in love with an illiterate peasant maid who stole small sums of money from him. After the informant, who is the third protagonist in the film, challenged his maid by torturing her, the writer develops a guilt feeling and discovers his deep love for her. The film conveys the message that women are no longer virgins (a concept very contrary to the Egyptian norm). The two couples then become very close friends, and experience wealth and fame. The writer's novels are successful, and Sha'ban 'Abdel Rehim's singing reflects the *sha'bi* (popular) culture. Both couples move into a "gated community" that could be in the Sixth of October satellite city. They share the same villa and at a certain point, couples are "again" swapped and adultery is committed, but no one seems to be harmed by it. In other words, it is not an issue in the story. The director passes on the message that such "casual" things can happen in society.

---

[14] Sha'ban 'Abdel Rehim has been previously mentioned in Chapter 3, in the section on eating out and for having made ads for McDonald's.

Sahar al-layali, (White Nights)[15] is a film that had a great success when it first appeared in 2003. It depicted the marital and sexual problems of several young, modern middle-class, well to do, and professional couples in a novel manner. The plot of the story revolves around the private and sexual life of four couples who are lifelong friends and who shared everything in their youth. One of the couples is having a sexual intercourse without being married. They do not hide it from society and one scene clearly conveys their enjoyment of a full sexual life. It is portrayed as a normal matter. Each lives in a separate flat, yet, as a "respectable" couple they go out in public without hiding their relationship. Both are professional and financially independent. It is interesting to note that their peers do not pass a negative moral judgment on their behaviour. The couple is well accepted in the group, which includes a *muhaggaba* (head covered) whose husband is constantly having affairs. In one scene, the birthday of the child of the *muhaggaba* couple is celebrated in a place that resembles a McDonald's. The birthday party is the opportunity for the parents and their friends to socialize and to celebrate in a semi-public space. Another woman of the group frequently visits a psychiatrist because she seems to suffer from the fact that she does not enjoy sexual intercourse with her husband. At a certain point, she narrates her daring sexual fantasies and dreams. I have not seen such an incident in an Arabic film before and it is quite revealing in its efforts to transmit a new message. One thing worth mentioning is that the couples seem to be communicating mainly through their mobile phones rather than seeing each other.

Inas al-Degheidi's *Dantella* is another film, which portrays a new image of daring women who are taking the initiative with men. The film shows two types of women: one is a shy, insecure, intellectual-type lawyer; the other, her cousin (the actress Youssra), is a daring, untamed sexy singer-dancer who works in an Alexandrian nightclub. Youssra is portrayed as flirtatious and quite aggressive towards men who stand in her way. Both women, lifelong dear friends, end up falling in love with the same man, a good-looking police officer. After a complicated three-way relationship, he marries both women and spends alternate nights with them. The film shows that both women are sexually demanding and open about their natural needs. Both

---

[15] The title is a famous song of the Lebanese singer Fairuz.

women end up doing "one thousand and one nights" tricks to seduce the husband. They develop nasty and jealous plots to spend more nights with the husband. Nevertheless, in the end the film takes on a feminist tone. The two women end up getting together after so much jealousy and fighting because they realize that their friendship is dearer than fighting over a man. They free themselves of the husband and both raise the lawyer's child.

Leaving aside cinema, I have noticed that compared to the midseventies, many youngsters have "loosened up" in their sexual behaviour in public spaces. One can observe in daily life in Cairo important changes in the body language of youth. In the darkened Abul Feda street, along the Nile bank in the island of Zamalek, the sight of *muhagabat* young women kissing young men and holding hands is quite frequent. Flirtatious, "emancipated", *muhaggabats* have become a common Cairene fact. But how far can this be a sign of emancipation when the issue of virginity and hymen restoration is still one of the most frequent operations among middle class Egyptian women? Are not Egyptian youth having to cope with very strong pressures stemming from, on the one hand, a glittering consumer culture selling luxury dreams, and of sexual freedom and, on the other hand, the nightmarish reality of inescapable family pressures and the scarcity of appropriate space in which to really get to know a future spouse. This is why the shopping mall becomes an ideal place for encounters and mixing.

Youth, Sexuality and New Spaces

One of the most revealing moments to be experienced in Cairene malls, is the first day of the *ʿid* (the feast after breaking the fasting). One ought to take a midnight stroll in the downtown Talʿat Harb Mall to experience the liveliness and density of the crowds in this mall. Thursdays and feast days are also marked by flocks of young men, mostly coming from slum areas and poor quarters, who walk in large groups through downtown. What strikes one is the visible and overwhelming male population. The Talʿat Harb Mall, which remains open until after midnight, becomes a huge place for hordes of youngsters who go up the seven spiral staircases and then walk down. Usually the mall is so full that security agents have to regulate pedestrians and watch that no one is pushed or harassed. Sexual

Fig. 61. Tal'at Harb Mall.

Fig. 62. Tal'at Harb Mall

Fig. 63. Tal'at Harb Mall: Stairs.

harassment on these packed nights is routine. With an average estimate of 25,000 people visiting the mall every day, the Tal'at Harb
Mall clearly deserves a study on its own.[16] Any observer can easily
notice that these people rarely buy any goods. A major past time
for the youngsters is window shopping or riding up and down the
escalators, seeing and being seen. What adds to the popularity of
this mall is the ground floor, which consists of many cheap coffee
shops and fast food restaurants. It always is crowded with people,
obviously from the most popular strata, until very late night and its
atrium has a mix of Kentucky Fired Chicken and *ful* and *falafel* from
the famed al-Tabe'i restaurant in addition to a series of other food
shops.

It is therefore possible to argue that these new public spaces, such
as the many emerging coffee houses and shopping malls, are becoming magnets for youth. These are clean spaces where youth can
socialize and simply move around. These young men and women
can still originate from the *'ashwa'iyyat* (slums, unplanned, scattered

---

[16] This estimate was given by its manager. Quoted from Noha El Hennawy,
"Window Shop until you Drop", *Egypt Today*, April 2005, p. 102. # 26 Iss 12.

areas) but once in these walled off, exclusive spaces, they are offered a simulation and an elevation (through dress), a feeling that they can participate in the better world, even if it is merely window shopping.

The issue of youth and the perceived "sexual perversities" of the younger generations seem to fill a significant space in the official discourse. Sexual perversion, we are told by officials and religious preachers, has spread in recent years through pornography, available now through satellite television. The invasion of "Western cultural" values, we are told again, is corrupting youth. This discourse goes hand in hand with an increasingly strict morality pertaining to public conduct. This is certainly related to the growing Islamization of the society, which has been taking place since the 1970's. The press is on a witch-hunt, infantilizing women and youth, who are thought to be easily perverted and therefore have to be constantly watched. Egyptians have acknowledged that they are facing a serious crisis concerning their sexual habits and the institution of marriage. The spread of *'urfî* (unregistered) marriage among students at the preparatory level, high schools and universities has become a preoccupation of the national papers.[17] Along with illicit unions, concerns over sexual harassment seem to take on a magnified importance in the press. The conduct of youth, especially with unbridled sexual behavior in public spaces, has become an obsession. Even if official discourse tends to express intolerance and witch-hunting, everyday practices of youth reveal that there is a "relaxation of norms" within the confines of the Islamization of society. Young lovers in Cairo find that the veil is no hindrance to kissing and holding hands as they walk along the riverbanks. The intermingling of mass culture and the reshaping of public space here becomes an interesting field for investigating a new hybridity in the behavior and culture of youth.

---

[17] Recent press coverage of what has been abusively coined as *'urfî* marriage seems to bear witness to evolving sexual norms in Egyptian society today. A customary matrimonial institution which has resisted the centralized registration policies of the modern nation-state by surviving alongside the Personal Status Law, *'urfî* marriage, which is acknowledged by Islamic law, requires two witnesses and a third party to oversee the contracting of marriage. Not exactly null and void from a legal standpoint as long as no problems arise, *'urfî* marriage generates social and legal problems the minute conflicts appear, since neither spouse can file a lawsuit to prove the marriage if the other denies the relationship, nor can women file for divorce or claim alimony or any of their marital rights. See Mona Abaza, "Perceptions of 'Urfi Marriage in the Egyptian Press", *ISIM Newsletter*, 7/ 01, March 2001, pp. 20–21.

However, the obsession of malls managers is constantly the uncontrolled sexual behaviour of youth. Indeed, it seems that the major concern of the security staff in all shopping malls in Cairo is how to gauge whether the young men and salesmen standing at the fringes of the malls are any danger.

The Official Discourse on 'Ashwa'iyyat (slums)

One cannot look into the government's conceptualization of the reshaping of the city of Cairo without looking into the dominant discourse on 'ashwaiyyat (unplanned construction, the squatters and slums). One could find other equivalents to the word such bidonville in French, and shantytown. 'Ashwa'iyyat simply means the slums. Under the category of 'ashwa'iyyat, 'ishash (sing. 'issha) and 'izbas are included as appellations of particular spaces. For example, slums include whole areas, which are called 'ishash al-turguman in Bulaq. Some argue that the word 'ishash is of Turkish origin and refers to huts constructed in the middle of swamps, or in a jungle. While 'izbas are conglomerations of peasant huts, originally made of mud brick.[18] 'Izbas and 'izba systems are also the old Egyptian "haciendas" which were owned by large landowners and which have been today dismantled after the successive agrarian reforms. 'Izba thus carries two meanings. One related to affluence, the owner of an 'izba, is a large owner who was in the past called a'yaan and thus did not really worked since he lived from his land. Today, it connotes utmost destitution, if one today lives in an 'izba in the region of Greater Cairo. Although the City of the Dead is not considered to be the worst in terms of shantytowns, it is the first image that comes to the many when visualizing Cairo. The phenomenon of massive squatting in cemeteries and the living creating dwellings on top of the dead has attracted the attention of many Western observers, photographers[19]

---

[18] Mohammed Riad, "al sakan al-'ashawa'i fi jumhuriyyat masr al-'arabiyya, anwa' al-'ashwaiyyat wa tawzi'aha al-gughrafi wa halat al-quahira al-kubra bishi' minal tafsil" (Slums in Egypt, Types of Slums, Geographical Distribution in the case of grand Cairo: Case Studies) in: al-'umran al-'ashwa'i fi misr (Unplanned Construction in Egypt) ed. Fathi Mohammad Musilhi, Cairo, al-majlis al-a'la lil-thaqafa, 2002, pp. 189–222, p. 189.
[19] The theme of the city of the dead has attracted the attention of many foreign travelers and artists. Various exhibitions and films have been made on this quarter.

Fig. 64. Car Repair Shops near the World Trade Centre, Bulaq.

Fig. 65. Talʿat Harb Mall: Atrium.

and urban planners. However, these are not the worse squatter areas, because many of these cemeteries consisted of beautiful bourgeois mausoleums with spacious gardens where the architecture is still on a much more humane scale. It is in fact aesthetically appealing compared to the kilometer long, ugly, tight, dark alleys, of five to seven floor red brick buildings with windowless sides, that occur in many poor areas in Cairo. El-Kadi on the other hand, rejects the idea of designating the unplanned, or informal quarters (Zones d'urbanisation spontanée) as slums or *bidonvilles*. She argues that there is nothing spontaneous about it since the development of such areas are the result of a tacit agreement between the state and local administrators through letting construction "going" informal. Most of the unplanned quarters were constructed on agricultural land where there is no violation of private property. It is rather a violation and transformation of its usage. Although al-Kadi notes the deterioration and the growing overpopulation in the popular quarters, the fact that the houses were constructed in red brick, that water, sewage and electricity were introduced, means that these cannot be designated as slums or "bidonvilles." These are rather to be considered as satellite "sous standard" i.e. (under standard) cities.[20]

The press has in recent years focused on the growing significance of the *'ashwaiyyat*. In official discourse, *'ashwaiyyat* became the equivalent of chaotic and "uncivilized" relations. The term has been used in different contexts, for example in relation to unregistered and therefore illicit forms of marriage such as *'urfi*. It is an attribute of the poor and has entered the official discourse of the state as a label for anything that is not "ordered". The government has often linked the expansion of the *'ashwaiyyat* with rampant crime and violence. The *'ashwa'iyyat* became synonymous with the violent acts of Islamist terrorists. Most of the Islamists originated from the quarters of Imbaba, Dar al-Salam, or Bulaq al-Dakrur. The two women involved in terrorist attacks in May 2005, as a revenge for the torture of some of their relatives in jails, originated from Shubra al-Kheima (one of the most densely populated and highly industrialized areas of greater Cairo). State discourse associated the rise of violent Islamist activities with the phenomenon of the uncontrolled growth of the *'ashawa'iyyat*.

---

[20] Galila El Kadi, *L'Urbanisation Spontanée au Caire*. Centre d'Études et des Recherches Urbama, Tours, 1987, p. 99.

Fig. 66. Car Repair Shops near the World Trade Centre, Bulaq.

The poor quarter of Dar al-Salam, a district of Greater Cairo, the most densely populated area in the Middle East, is an example of such poor areas.[21] There are around 400 areas or regions of unplanned housing in Egypt, with a population of seven million.[22] Some sociologists estimate that the population of these areas reached between ten or twelve million in 1995, which is twenty-five to thirty-five percent of the total population.[23] The magazine *Nisf al-Dunya* published an alarming report on the squatters in Cairo, accompanied by horrifying pictures depicting people living in inhuman conditions. Whole areas are being inundated by sewage and garbage, and basic sanitary conditions are lacking. The report stated that Egypt had 1172 areas classified as *'ashawa'iyyat*, which included 11.5 million people.[24]

---

[21] Official statistics state that the population of Dar al-Salam reached 96,844 in 1996. These numbers should in reality be doubled.

[22] Amani al-Hiddini, *al-muhammashun wal-siyasa fi-misr* (The Marginalised and Politics in Egypt), Cairo: *Centre for Political and Strategic Studies, al-Ahram* 1999.

[23] Saad Eddin Ibrahim, *Egypt, Islam and Democracy, Twelve Critical Essays*, Cairo: The American University Press, 1996, p. 87.

[24] Hanan Mufid, Sana' Madani, Amal Surur, Yasse Hamaya (The Forgotten on Earth *Nisf al-Dunia*), 25 June 2000.

Fig. 67. Wikala, Bulaq, behind World Trade Centre.

With regard to shopping malls, in what follows, I describe at length the transformations in two quarters, which have the largest conglomerations of commercial centres and malls, (Bulaq and Nasr City). It is important to stress that both quarters are adjacent to slums. Nasr City is located in the eastern part of Cairo. In spite of being a relatively new quarter, it includes at its fringes the following unplanned quarters: *'izbat al-'arab, 'izbat al-haggana, 'izbat nassar*, with a population around 200,000 by the early nineties. The slum quarter of Manshiat Nasser, another neighbour of Nasr City, includes 120,000 people and the total number of those living in slums in East Cairo amounts to 330,000.[25]

In Bulaq, on the banks of the Nile north of Cairo, the World Trade Centre, was constructed after the demolition of part of the popular quarter, which got rid of the *'ashwa'iyyat* surrounding it. The nearby Hilton Ramses Hotel and shopping complex has also eliminated part of the popular quarter. The land on which the World Trade Centre stands was sold cheaply by the state and bought up

---

[25] Mohammed Riad., p. 209.

Fig. 68. World Trade Centre, Bulaq.

by the new tycoons since it was located in a popular area. This process goes hand in hand with a massive restructuring of the whole of Cairo, in a process of "gentrification" similar to that in many European towns in earlier periods. The current Minister of Culture Faruq Husni launched a campaign to restore old monuments and gentrify popular quarters. Supporters see this as improving cleanliness and embellishing the city. Pessimists view it as an elitist move undertaken at the expense of hiding away and dislocating the poor who occupy such areas. Facades are painted in white but the antiquated sewage system remains and water shortages prevail. In short, nothing has changed inside these renovated areas. The old *warshas* (informal sector small shops) have been removed or renovated, and the economic activities related to them have withered away. Many see such an action as a way in which government can contain and control small-scale business, as in the case of the popular quarter of al-Darb al-Asfar, in the Bazaar area of old Cairo, in the centre of historic Cairo, designated to be a sanitized tourist area.

Bulaq

Much of the old quarter of Bulaq seems to have vanished, together
with its significant historical landmarks. Bulaq has been known since
the Ayyubids times (in the fourteenth Century) as important international port and centre of trade for large quantities of goods. The
quarter gained significance already in the fourteenth century. In 1983,
the Egyptian historian Nelly Hanna faithfully listed the remaining
historical monuments in Bulaq as a last cry and warning against the
massive destruction by land speculation projects that began in the
late seventies.[26] The project of urban reshaping covered the area of
south of Abul 'Ela bridge north to the area of the *dar al-kutub* (National
library). Already in the sixteenth century Bulaq incorporated residential quarters with commercial activities and a rich local aristocracy. Bulaq has been famed also as a residential centre and for the
remarkable architecture of palaces, mosques, *madrasa* (schools), *ham-
mams* (public baths) and *sabils* (public foutains) and for its *wikalas*,
funduqs and *khans*, which were spaces for wholesale trade, storing and
hosting merchants-travellers. The *wikalas* consisted of storerooms on
the lower floor with rooms for rent to travelling traders above them
and a courtyard. According to Nelly Hanna, sixty-five *wikalas* were
mentioned by the French experts in 1798.[27] These were mostly closely
grouped together and were located on the main commercial thor-
oughfare. Obviously all these *wikalas* are subject to erosion.

Bulaq had superb public baths, lively bazaars and markets.[28] In
1777, Savary said: "Boulak . . . was the port where all the goods from
Damietta and Alexandria were unloaded . . . it contains superb public baths and large okals". In 1784, Lusignan found it "very popu-
lous, having a continual bazaar or market for all sorts of commodities;
at this place all the rich merchandise are imported or exported to
and from different countries and in this town provisions of all kinds
are cheaper than in Cairo".[29] Bulaq's advantage was that it was a

---

[26] Nelly Hanna, "Boulaq-An Endangered Historic Area of Cairo", *Islamic Cairo*,
ed. M. Meinecke, London, 1980, pp. 19–29.

[27] P. 65.

[28] For an overview of the historical significance of Bulaq see the important work
of Nelly Hanna, "An Urban History of Bulaq in the Mamluk and Ottoman Periods"
Supplement aux Annales Islamologiques, Cahiers no. 3, Le Caire 1983, p. 32.

[29] Nelly Hanna. p. 32.

non-walled city in contrast to other cities like al-Fustat, al-Askar, al-Qata'i and Qahira.[30]

During the last century Bulaq turned into a refined bourgeois quarter. There are a few remaining magnificent European style buildings squeezed between high-rise buildings and smaller decaying houses. Today, it is one of the most densely populated areas of Cairo and is known for retail, textile and car-repair shops, and its second-hand markets in *wekalat al-balah*. Bulaq was also known for Egypt's first printing house, *al-mataba'a al-ammiriyya*, which has disappeared. Was it an incidental fire like so many fires, which became in the seventies and eighties a routine in many public sector companies? Sharia al-Mataba'a is today full of large shops selling cloth and textiles, both Egyptian and imported. Small shops belonging to Copts (the eastern Christian minority) sell second hand-material from the army such as tents, parachutes and army uniforms. A large number of these shops belong to Copts who display icons, mosaics and pictures of the Virgin Mary. These markers have gained significance with the growing Islamization and the confessional tensions that have affected Egyptian society between 1980 and 2000. In Sinnaniyyah Street, an old *hammam* (public bath) has survived not far from the beautiful Sinan mosque constructed by Sinan Pasha in 1571.[31] What a contrast – a few meters away from the imposing ultramodern mall, the Bulaq Friday market provides lively scenes of packed, with haggling and strong *baladi* women (dressed in long mostly black garb). The popular market is known for selling second-hand clothes in *suq al-kanto*. Not very far away, the stroller will end up at the famous large Sabtiyya market specializing in iron and second-hand metals.

The aggressive process of "cleaning up", and consequently modernizing the Bulaq area started during Sadat's time when the government decided to move five thousand working class families from Bulaq to be reallocated in the public housing area of al-Zawiya al-Hamra (1979–1981). Farha Ghannam analyses the state discourse in justifying its action by promoting an image of the civilized, modern and contemporary versus the criminals, and troublemakers and (riff-raff)

---

[30] P. 42.
[31] Andre Raymond, Editor, *The Glory of Cairo*, An Illustrated History, AUC Press, 2002, p. 314.

Fig. 69. Sinan Mosque, Bulaq.

Fig. 70. View of the World Trade Centre Towers from the Sinan Mosque.

Fig. 71. Conrad Hotel.

Fig. 72. Nile Cornishe, Bulaq. WTC and Conrad.

living in Bulaq.[32] Sadat was portrayed as the hero of construction and spiritual resources.[33]

In the last decade, in Bulaq and the area to the north, all along the Nile Corniche, a string of towers and skyscrapers hosting international hotels and empires of consumption have changed the landscape. North of the new Ministry of Foreign Affairs, the twin towers of the World Trade Centre, the Hilton, then the tower of the Conrad hotel.[34]

The WTC Cairo provided office space, housing apartments, retail centre and recreational areas. It offered its members and tenants a wide range of facilities and services, information services including computerized communication, extensive database and library facilities covering world markets, trade opportunities, government regulations, tariffs, business topics, trade research services, trade missions, meetings or conference facilities and exhibit space. The WTC is divided into three main areas: the residential and recreational area, the offices and the commercial complex.

A little further another two new gigantic, futuristic looking Nile City Towers have been erected, again by the Orascom enterprise. The Nile Towers are a $200 million project, which will include a 552 room international hotel, part of the Fairmont chain, which after its success in Dubai aspires to repeat the experience in Cairo. The Nile City complex is a 24 floor tower that includes 100, 000 square meters of office space and 11.000 square meters of retail space, restaurants and cinemas. Also a huge shopping mall is planned to open by 2005.[35]

Further north is the Arkadia Mall, which opened in 2000. It was constructed by the Sabbour family[36] who were shareholders with al-

---

[32] Farha Ghannam, *Remaking The Modern: Space Relocation and the Politics of Identity*, Berkeley, University of California Press, 2002, p. 2.

[33] Ibid., p. 35.

[34] The architects who designed the Conrad Hotel are Skidmore, Owen and Merill and it listed in the website under Orascom construction Industries. See http: //.orascomci.com/index.php?d=conrad1.

[35] Taqua Imam, "New Kid on the Block", *Business Today*, July 2004. http://www.businesstodayegypt.com/arttemplate.asp artID=23 issue No=6. July 2004.

[36] Sameh Sabbour is equally the executive Director of the Egyptian Capital Market Association which is related to the centre for International Private Enterprise that promotes "building Democratic Institutions through Market-Oriented Reform around the Globe". http://www.cipe.org/programs/global/partners/dispPartner.php?id=176. Sabbour Associates is a company founded in 1957 and it is registered with the World Bank, the African Development the Arab Bank for Economic

Fig. 73. Arcadia Mall. Cornishe al-Nil.

Ahli Bank.[37] The upper floors are luxurious privately-owned flats. Thus so far, the mall is considered to be a success, for combining fancy stylish shopping with leisure. Arkadia architects conceived levelled terraces with plants. Huge screens constantly playing shows and cartoon, as well as children's games, cafeterias and coffee shops have contributed to its success. Arkadia includes 500 shops, restaurants, and coffeeshops. Arkadia Mall is one of the few malls where 90 percent of its shops were sold to private owners. This poses a problem to the Sabbour owners because shop owners can escape paying maintenance and electricity fees. Electricity costs can reach up to L.E. 260,000 in the summer. The question is then will the owners be

Development in Africa, USAUD, ECC FAO GTZ and other companies. The Sabbour associates were involved in the following projects Yamama Centre, Arkadia, Tiba 2000 Commercial Centre, Sadat City Commercial Centre, Commercial/Apartment Hotel 10 Ramadan City, Darasa Multi-Storey Garage and Commerical Centre. See http://www.sabbpour-associates.com/proj/com/mltcom.htm.

[37] The Sabbour family are also administrators of the Tal'at Harb Mall (Downtown), which has been equally undertaken by the Ahli Bank after its first owner went bankrupt. The Ahli Bank has sequestrated three Malls the al-Aqad Mall (Nasr City), Tal'at Harb and al-Amir Mall in Shubra (This information was provided by several mall managers).

able to maintain the mall or be happy to give the mall to the Ahli
Bank in 2010 as was originally planned?[38]

Soon this new landscape will reach the nearby quarter of Shubra,
which is also one of the oldest popular quarters of Cairo. Shubra
has not been spared change, since al-Amir Mall consisting of five
floors (around 1200 square meters), started functioning in 2002. It
is striking to see the juxtaposition of these two different worlds and
markets, but the new Egyptian capitalist class is fast pushing away
the popular quarters. Traditional coffee shops and popular street life
have survived the change, but for how long? Nearby, on the same
riverbank, the Ramses Hilton has constructed another mall, which
is also expanding at the expense of the back street popular quarter.
The people of the quarter I spoke to expressed resentment and fear
of the government. Everybody knows that the days of the popular
quarter are numbered and eviction is soon to come. The population seems to be resigned to accepting the meagre sums given by
the government as compensation for dislocation. They are aware
that the WTC towers took the lion's share of water and electricity,
which contributes to shortages in the quarter.

Before its collapse, the World Trade Centre incorporated a new
conception of space for leisure containing (cinemas and discotheques,
shops, fitness centres, computer games with communication facilities
and apartments). A new way for the middle classes to occupy space
and spend time, seemed to be in the making. This huge complex,
with some hundreds of shops, restaurants and cafeterias, was meant
to integrate the residential with the recreational, business and commerce with *flâneur*-ing. The offices of international organizations such
as the United Nations, UNDP (United Nations Development Program),
UNIWFP (United Nations World Food Program), the International
Office for Migration, Thomas Cook, the African Export Import Bank
and many others were all located there. Mobinil, one of the largest
mobile phone companies, was based there. The Conrad and Hilton
residential towers sandwiching the WTC consist of twenty-six floors
each. Each tower has a large lobby and each floor consists of four
apartments of two to four bedrooms, which rented to US$1500 per
month for 200 square meters. The WTC customers kept changing
through the day: women, fashionably veiled or not; families wandering and window-shopping; groups of youth playing computer

---

[38] Interview with the general manager of Arkadia, 19 February 2005.

Fig. 74. City Centre. Nasr City. Mall-cum-flats.

Fig. 75. Facade Decorations during Ramadan, Geneina Mall.

games; young couples holding hands; hotel guests from the Gulf countries; Egyptian yuppies; regular customers of the night clubs and the billiard halls and expatriates working in international organizations. In summer, the visitors from the Gulf and Saudi Arabia who rented flats and studios from the Conrad and Hilton hotels, all seemed to frequent this space. Security measures were extremely tight photographs, for instance, were strictly forbidden. Designed symbolically in the form of an Islamic *wekala* (covered popular market), with wood carvings similar to *mashrabiyyas*, a so-called Pharaonic entrance and fashionable European tiles, the atrium is a central open space with public visibility; it gives the feeling that it could be any mall in Europe or Asia. According to a rumour, the space was originally intended to be used as a stock exchange, but the project never materialized. At Christmas, the Hilton provided the decorative atrium with Christmas trees. During the fasting month of Ramadan, large banquets were set in tents, located in the open space of the entrance. They bear a superficial similarity to the *mawa'ed al-rahman* (the public banquets for the needy). It would be ideal if the poor and the rich could fuse in the joy of banqueting, if only one could overlook the charge for the *fitar* (breaking of the fast) per head in the World Trade Centre. Surely, exclusiveness has become fashionable in Cairo, for such *fitars* are terribly expensive. The obsession of the rich of Cairo today is to push away the unwanted poor as far as possible. Here all these malls, the Yamamah Centre, the WTC or the Ramses Hilton annex mall, maintain strict security measures and video cameras monitor the public.

When I returned to the WTC Mall in November 2004, I discovered that it was completely dead; only three shops remained open. Many offices had closed down or moved elsewhere. The cafeteria was closed and there were practically no visitors. Is it the effect of economic recession? Or is it that the popular quarter life has triumphed against aggressive modernization? Is it dead because of the poor management? This was the argument of a successful stylish fabric shop owner who after the WTC collapse moved to the First Mall and her shop is doing very well today in the First Mall.[39] No one

---

[39] According to this shop owner who preferred to be kept anonymous, the WTC went down the drain after Tareq Nur, a successful businessman who owns a leading advertisement company, retreated from managing it. She insisted that the disadvantaged location of the WTC in the popular quarter of Bulaq was another reason that contributed to its collapse.

Fig. 76. Pegasus, Yamama Centre, a dying mall, 29 January.

Fig. 77. Pegasus, Yamama Centre.

knows, but the people of Bulaq feel a great pressure under the constant "strangling" from the government, which is putting increasing sanctions on vehicles entering the quarter, and are making it difficult to restore the crumbling buildings. In other words, the high officials would be happy to see the buildings of the popular area collapse so that they could grab the land.

The same happened to al-Amir Mall in Shubra, which was already dead in 2005. When it opened in 2002, the rent per square meter was L.E. 170 for higher floors and L.E. 300 in the first floor, which was considered extremely expensive. With the exception of the cinema most of the shops closed down and, as in many other malls, those who purchased shops lost a fortune. The shop owners went to court against the owners of the mall (it was partly owned and partly rented) and thus led to bank sequestration. Evidently, the mall shops could not compete with the kilometers long popular market and (small factory-sweatshops) located in the nearby street near the Catholic school the Bon Pasteur.[40] All those interviewed in the Amir Mall said that they loved to frequent the mall, but only for window shopping and passing time. It was out of the question to purchase anything there. Everything was twice the price of the goods for sale outside the mall.

Before it died, the al-Amir Mall was designated as a women's mall, "moll harimi". Since it is located in a popular quarter most of the women frequenting it are from the popular classes. It has a reputation for being *baladi* and complaints have been heard about constant sexual harassment. Many owners' shops see it as a failure, because it was poorly designed and too crowded with shops. Al-Bustan Mall in downtown also died and the official version was that bad reputed youngsters and drug addicts were frequenting the top floor Bowling Centre, which witnessed violent skirmishes. However, this does not explain why so many offices, clinics and shops closed down in such a strategically located area as downtown.

---

[40] Several shop owners had already gone to court in 2002 against the mall owner who, according to them cheated them by asking for high sums of down payment to be used for ads. Furthermore, they were given smaller spaces for the money paid and the mall construction was never finished.

Fig. 78. Shubra market, behind al-Amir Mall.

Fig. 79. Entrance, Yamama Centre, A dying mall.

Fig. 80. Poseidon, Yamama Centre.

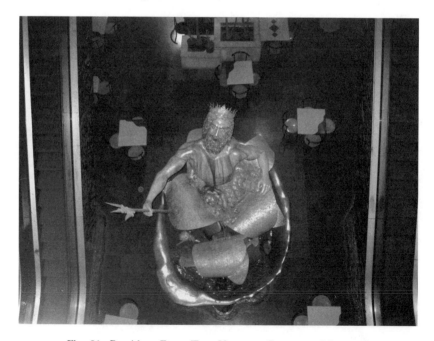

Fig. 81. Poseidon, From Top. Yamama Centre, a dying mall.

Madinat Nasr (Nasr City)

For those interested in consumerism in Egypt, the example of Madinat Nasr (Nasr City) raises many questions in relation to the sudden multiplication of shopping malls. However, the malls are successful, compared to those in other quarters. All these malls opened in the late nineties. Evidently, Nasr City has the largest number of these huge enterprises, seven malls, plus the Horreya Mall of Heliopolis. This is besides the recently opened huge City Stars Mall, mentioned in the introduction.

Nasr city was established in 1959, by a government decree. Three thousand feddans were allocated from the desert to construct the city. The project was strongly inspired by the nearby older satellite city of Heliopolis, which celebrated its centenary in 2005. The difference is that Heliopolis could be defined as an interesting example of a colonial imagination, while Nasr City was the pride of the revolution's achievement, an attempt to solve the growing overpopulation problem. The Heliopolis Oasis Company was founded by in 1905 by Baron Eduard Empain and Boghos Pasha who purchased 5,952 feddans in the desert. Baron Empain did not intend originally to construct a city but to sell the land after improving it. Instead he ended up constructing the core of the new city. In 1907, Baron Empain commissioned the French architect Alexandre Marcel to construct a Hindu palace, which became a remarkable architectural landmark, Marcel-inspired; we are told, by a well known Cambodian Khmer temple.[41] Today the palace has become the symbol of a vanished epoch. Heliopolis became known for its spacious squares and gardens, which were inspired by the European "garden city". Heliopolis also became known for its interesting hybrid architecture combining European with pseudo-Muslim and neo-Moorish styles, as well as Art Deco houses.[42]

---

[41] See the article of *al-Ahram Weekly* on the recuperation of the Ministry of Housing with the Ministry of Culture of the palace after long years of controversy. The palace was bought by two businessmen, one Saudi and another Egyptian. They finally obtained compensation from the government in exchange of giving back the palace. Gihan Shahine "Evicting the Bats" *al-Ahram Weekly*, 24–30 March 2005, p. 4.

[42] Andre Raymond, *Cairo*, Cambridge, Massachusetts, London, England, Harvard University Press, 2000, pp. 329–338.

Fig. 82. First Mall. Four Seasons. Façade.

Fig. 83. Four Seasons Cairo Mall. Courtesy of Mohamed Eid Soliman.

In 1963, Nasr city was advertised in *al-Mussawar* magazine as a progressive, revolutionary project, which demonstrated that Egypt was heading towards a renaissance and a new socialist society. The constructors of Nasr City were *al-mu'assassa al-masriyya lil-iskan wal-ta'mir*, which was supposed to build offices, government buildings and ministries, while the *mu'ssasat madinat nasr* built well off housing for the newly emerging middle classes. These houses consisted of cement matchboxes that remind many of the constructions in socialist countries. They looked like cheap Bauhaus buildings. The government intended to transfer, all the ministries from central Cairo to the newly constructed unpolluted city in which inhabitants will "need not resort to medicine or medical treatment". The Ministries of Industries, of Reserves and Treasury, of Social Affairs, of Youth, the Ministry of Planning, the Centre for Statistics, the House of Accountancy, the committee for Electricity, the Civil Aviation, the Petroleum Ministry, the Courts Complex, the Cairo Taxation Building, and the Civil Affairs were all expected to move there.[43]

This being said, today Nasr City has the largest concentration of military institutions and military subsidized housing in Egypt. Being located on the fringe of the desert, the quarter developed by incorporating sizeable military zones in the early seventies. Then, little by little the military sold these plots to civilians and Nasr City became the quarter it is today. The main road of Nasr City, which leads to the airport has a large complex of high rise buildings called *al-'ubur* (the bridging), which were constructed after the 1973 victory to house army officers. These flats were later sold to private owners. Today, Nasr City hosts the main central direction of the army (*al-qiyada al-markaziyya*), the Military Academy *al-fanniya al-'askariyya*, the Ministry of Defense, the various Officers' clubs (the Tanks and *madfa'iyya* artillery), the *mabaheth amn al-dawla* (Internal Security Apparatus) which moved recently from Lazoughli square and the Military Industries (*al-masane' al-harbiyya*). The Military Museum, a military hospital and various housing complexes for the military are also located in Nasr City. The military also owns a few hotels. The firm hold of the military on Nasr City explains why when I undertook field work with my assistants, a strong feeling of suspicion and resistance was expressed

---

[43] Ibrahim al-Ba'athi, "Qissat al-madina allati lan yahtag sukkanuha ila 'ilag", (The Story of the City, which inhabitants will need no medical treatment), *al-Mussawar*, 6 December 1963, no. 2043, pp. 50–59, pp. 56–57.

at various times. Several managers and retired army officers reported
that the "Israeli intelligence" has been using the shopping malls to
collect "spying" information. To undertake research on Cairo's "malls",
we were told, was an extremely politically sensitive issue. But the
question remains if there is there an indirect link between the army's
extended occupation of the space of Nasr City and consumer culture? Or is it sheer coincidence?

Many attribute the success of these commercial centres in Nasr
City to the simple and, if one dares to say boring grid architecture
of this comparatively newly constructed satellite city on the edge of
the desert. Nasr City could be easily described as consisting of shape-
less, geometrical, cement matchboxes, block buildings lining the longest
streets in Cairo, such as Mustafa al-Nahass, al-Tayaran and Mustafa
al-ʿAqad streets. These wide roundabouts intersect streets where streets
cross at right angles. Nasr City has expanded as new quarters one
after another have encroached on the desert. The heart, or rather
the centre of the city, seems to be missing but this seems to bother
no one. It is true that the streets are wider and the average size of
flats is larger than elsewhere. Real estate is definitely cheaper than
in the quarters of Mohandessin or Zamalek. Green spaces and parks,
like the international Garden (al-hadiqa al-dawliyya), have been included
and Nasr City gradually became known for its literally endless variety of shops, spaces for leisure, restaurants, coffee shops and cinemas. For many, the newness of the district and the lack of a definite
spatial structure symbolizes the tastes of the returning middle class
professionals who spent the last two decades if not more, as migrants
in the Gulf oil producing countries.

Madinat Nasr incorporated a large military zone to become later
one of the main residential areas for the army officers. Many view
Madinat Nasr as a suburb, which "smells" of new money. It symbolizes the Cairene nouveau riche suburban culture. But why are
the malls of Medinat Nasr more successful than others? Huge crowds
visit these on holidays and during hot summer nights. The coffee
shops, McDonald's, and atriums seem to be full until very late at
night. During Ramadan, Oriental desserts can usually be purchased
in the pastry shop at the Geneina Mall. The cinemas, and childrens'
games areas are full on Thursdays and Fridays. One interpretation
of the success of the mall culture in Madinat Nasr is that it is an
import from the Gulf and oil producing countries. It is a result of

Fig. 84. Geneina Façade during Ramadan.

the successful Saudi Arabization of Egyptian customs rather than an American import.[44] Countless Egyptians have experienced malls while working in Saudi Arabia and the Gulf. This appears evident in interviews with managers and the public, where Saudi Arabia and the Gulf, especially Dubai are constantly mentioned as having the best malls they have seen.

The returnees have continued a pattern of leisure time spending they know in closed, walled off, air conditioned spaces, built to escape the harsh weather of the Arabian Peninsula. The Egyptians are changing their leisure habits. Middle-class Cairene moviegoers today would either see films in one of the annexes of international hotels or in shopping malls. During summers these malls are also popular with Arabs from the oil producing countries.

---

[44] Of course the mall is an American invention, but it came through the interviews that the success in Madinat Nasr is due to the different public that has been defined as *nafti, naft* (petroleum) meaning that they are migrant returnees from the oil producing countries.

In Madinat Nasr, *ard al-ma'ared (the Fair complex)*, Snow City, was constructed in emulation of Saudi Arabian influence.[45] This is a direct import from the Gulf countries, as Gulf Arabs seem to be infatuated with spending their leisure in snow games and ice skating rinks in the middle of the burning desert. In the case of Cairo the customers in Snow City rent heavy winter clothes to ice skate and play among ice forms shaped like Tour Eiffel, the White House, the Kremlin, the Pyramids, Pharaohs, Abu Sembel temple, and the Sphinx.

The architecture and the facades of some of these malls definitely emulated those found elsewhere. In fact, the manager of the Ma'adi Grand Mall stated that its owners travelled to Southeast Asia and were inspired by the architecture there.[46] They even watched videotapes from the Far East showing indoor fountains. The architecture of Wonderland Mall in Nasr City easily evokes an invented Hollywood style Orient. The manager and salesmen describe Wonderland's kitschy style as *tiraz al-sindibad*, the Sinbad style. The mall was originally meant to be an Egyptianized Disneyland or amusement park, *moll tarfihi, malahi*. Some facades like the Geneina mall's transparent glass elevators, remind me of Southeast Asian malls in Kuala Lumpur, Singapore and Jakarta. Their success could be explained because this is a relatively new area.

If the birth of the mall in America was closely related to a suburban lifestyle that depended on the spread of the car industry, and what follows as the drive-in culture, Nasr City would be the best example of such a concept. In fact, Nasr City is a suburb par excellence. The big Nasr City malls such as Geneina, Tiba, and al-Serag, have large parking garages and lots, which many see as a great advantage. Even for Mohandessin residents, from the opposite side of the city, it is easier to shop in Nasr City than drive to downtown where parking is an ordeal. The Nasr City shops, in particular the newly opened City Stars, offer a wider variety of both affordable as well as very expensive, high quality imported and Egyptian goods. From the architectural point of the view, the malls of Madinat Nasr are the largest and most spacious in town. In fact, many of the

---

[45] When I visited the Snow city, it was closing down, because the owners did not seem to cope with the costs of maintaining it. The pictures were taken when the place was closed.

[46] The Ma'adi Grand Mall consists of six floors, with 410 shops and around 140 or 150 employees without including technicians.

Fig. 85. Al-Seraq Mall, Nasr City. Three buildings interconnecting three atriums.

Fig. 86. Geneina Façade, January 2006.

downtown Malls would hardly qualify as malls. Shemla, an established old *grand magasin* for example, has been transformed into a
mall by ostracizing the main hall and by cramming shops in every
inch so that there is practically no space for sitting. The same has
happened in the old Omar Effendi *grand magasin* in Abdel Aziz street
near 'Abdin square.

The Malls' vicinity to each other in Nasr City is what makes them
intriguing. Most of the directors of these malls maintained that they
do not compete with each other because of the wide variety of customers, which each mall can attract and also the difference in goods
and prices. There are goods for all prices. Tiba Mall, for instance,
caters to large families. According to the managers and salespersons,
Tiba is "a family mall", whereas Geneina Mall, with its huge skate
rink, bowling, billiard centre and computer games, attracts the younger
generation. Wonderland Mall is a pick-up place and has a "bad reputation", but it serves that purpose and caters to flirtatious youngsters who frequent the discotheque until late night. The Geneina
Mall consists of 12,000 square meters, integrating a huge ice-rink
and parking space for 800 cars. Also the Serag like the Geneina
Mall and several other malls have incorporated housing areas or flats
or on top of the shopping area. The Serag Mall in Nasr City with
14 thousand square meters competes through its size with the second largest mall in Nasr city, the Geneina Mall.[47] The Serag Mall
is designed as three complexes, joined together with passages so that
each complex has its own relatively small atrium.

Nasr City: The Army and Malls

*We are at the point where consumption is laying hold of the whole life, where all
activities are sequenced in the same combinatorial mode, where the course of satisfaction is outlined in advance, hour by hour, where the 'environment' is total –
fully air – conditioned, organized culturalized.*

Jean Baudrillard, *The Consumer Society*, Sage Publications, 2002, p. 29.

---

[47] This is according to the manager of the Serag Mall who insists that it is the
largest mall in Cairo, next is the Geneina Mall, with 8600 square meters, then the
World Trade Centre, 5200 square meters, next is the Hilton, 5000 square meters
then the Arkadia, 3200 square meters (Interview with the manager Amru Kamal
December 2003). Once again, according to him there are around one million people living in Madinat Nasr. If divided between six malls, this would mean that there
are around 20 thousand people visiting each mall.

Fig. 87. Arcadia Mall.

Fig. 88. Geneina Mall during Ramadan.

Fig. 89. Geneina Mall, January 2006.

Fig. 90. Veteran military, monitoring Talʿat Harb Mall.

In recent years, much has been said about the privatization of the army, or rather the army "going civil". Since Egypt signed the Camp David peace treaty, many predicted that the military role of the army would be shrinking. In the early eighties, the war was ended and many retired army officer were recruited to work in the "Food Security projects" launched by the government. Today, many retired army officers have turned into successful businessmen. Egypt, a "military society" was the title of the prominent work by Anouar Abdel Malek who brilliantly explored the continuity and the swelling of the army in civil and cultural life, and public sector companies after the revolution.[48] One can see a certain continuity and validity of this argument because the presence of the army is to be felt in the administration and governmental life. For example, since 1952, the army has controlled the administrative framework of the city of Cairo. Cairo and Giza governorates have had three governors who were retired high-ranking army officials.[49]

In looking at the phenomenon of malls, the public visibility of the "retired army" staff is to be felt everywhere. Take, for example, the emerging phenomenon of the retired army officers who opened private security companies to offer services in private protection. Today, these security companies monitor practically all the malls. One can often see retired army officers and generals sitting in atriums observing passers by. They control the younger security guards who are spread all over the mall. This is logical since these retired army functionaries would be the best candidates to enforce law and order. Some see the business of private security company as yet another American import into Egyptian society.

Some malls are owned or managed by retired army officers. A retired army officer manages Tiba Mall. Another retired general manages Cairo Centre, another fancy mall, even though its owners are civilian businessmen, entrepreneurs and engineers. Al-Amir Mall was run by a retired police officer, formerly the Director of prisons. He had established a "quasi" police station in the mall to control sexual harassment. These private security companies recruit the

---

[48] Anouar Abdel Malek, *Ägypten: Militärgesellschaft. Das Armeeregime, die Linke und der Soziale Wandel unter Nasser*. Suhrkamp Verlag, 1971.
[49] Eric Denys, "al-takhtit al-hadari wal-numuw fil-qahira" (Urban Planning and Cairo's Growth) in: *al-qahira fi-lahzat tahawul (Cairo in a Moment of Transformation)* ed: Mustafa Kamel al-Sayyed and Asef Bayat. Centre for the Study of Developing Countries, Cairo University, Cairo 1998.

Fig. 91. Maʿadi Grand Mall.

Fig. 92. Maʿadi Grand Mall, Islamic Boutique.

guards. Usually a mall like al-ʿAquad in Nasr City requires around 150 security guards, Arkadia requires 125 guards in three shifts. The guards' salary ranges from 250 to 300 Egyptian pounds, but in other malls salaries can only be 150 L.E.[50] Arkadia Mall offers a daily free meal to all guards.

In Tiba Mall most of the security guards originate from Upper Egypt and they sleep in the garage of the mall. They return only once a month to their village. However, other guards are young university degree holders who were desperate to find jobs. The guards have the main task of controlling sexual harassment, a routine complaint in all malls, and shoplifting. Even with all the cameras, control and retired army officers monitoring space, shoplifting is an unresolved problem, which many salesmen and women have complained of. However, this is not a novel phenomenon. Shoplifting became a concern during the nineteenth century with the emergence of department stores and the irresistible attraction of the massive display of goods. Women were the most exposed to kleptomania. This led to a prolific literature about the psychic and neurotic effects of kleptomania and shoplifting on women and eventually it provided plenty of work for doctors and psychiatrists.[51]

Al-ʿAquad Mall in Nasr City, which opened in 1999, is a good example of how the army has managed to go civil. This mall was constructed by the cooperative of the officers of the Republican Guards, who sold it later to a group of individuals. The land purchased for the mall also included a complex of six buildings consisting of numerous flats. The families of the Republican Guards also occupy the flats. The space of al-ʿAqad Mall consists of 30,000 square meters, includes 250 shops ranging in size from fifteen square meters to 220 squares meters. It was constructed after Tiba Mall. The manager made it a point that the owners consciously did not want to include billiards room, games shops, cinemas or restaurants. The mall has no space for flaneuring. The planners of this mall, we are told, were mainly targeting families, which would mainly come for shopping. 66,6 percent of the shops are rented and 33.3 percent are owned. At first the shops were offered for sale but prices rose so

---

[50] In al-Bustan Mall for example, an advertisement read: Wanted security guards to be paid L.E. 120 per month.

[51] On the subject see Maurice Bontemps, *Du vol, les grands magasins et du vol a l'étalage, etude medico-légale*, Thèse, a la faculté de médecine et de pharmacie de Lyon, 1894. Francis Ambriere, *La vie secrète des Grands magasins*, Flammarion, Paris 1932.

much that there were no purchasers. There are several managers, and technicians for fixing and repairing the escalators and electrical installations. The mall has around 200 employees, 150 security guards and around 200 cleaners, 32 cameras and regular videotaping is taking place. The cassette is saved for one week and the video is reused.

How To Spend Time in Polluted Cairo

"The mall is much cleaner than the street . . . to a certain extent the client is finer than the one of the street."
Director of a shop in al-'Aquad Mall.
"The client likes imported items, even if good quality Egyptian items are available, the client prefers imported ones."
Shopkeeper (Silvie) City Centre.
"The mall is controlled. . . . But the street is not. . . . You find *harag wa marag* (noisy and frenetic, chaotic behaviour in the street) . . ."
Shopkeeper, al-'Aquad Mall.
"The street is always busy . . . it takes a lot of time to enter any shop . . . while here in the malls it is an agglomeration of varied shops. . . ."
A 42-year-old engineer interviewed in al-'Aquad Mall.
"Outside the mall there are very popular shops and it is *zahma* (packed with people) . . . but the mall is better and more secure than outside . . . the place is more refined . . . the people here have 'style' . . . they are guaranteed clients."
Shopkeeper, al-'Aquad Mall.
"The mall is a good thing . . . it is a great place for youngsters . . . it is ordered . . ."
Ahmed 'Ali, 19 years old, Student of Medicine from Tanta. (A frequent visitor of Cairene Malls, Cairo Mall Giza).
"The mall is secure . . . it offers work opportunities for young people . . . it is better than the street . . ."
('Ali al-Sayyed, engineer, Cairo mall)
". . . the mall is more refined and cleaner than the street (*arqa wa andaf*), even though the prices might be higher . . ."
Mohammed 'Abdallah, a shopkeeper, Gregor, Cairo Mall Giza"

Most of the public's views about visiting and shopping at malls were astonishingly optimistic and positive. Many of those interviewed expressed satisfaction with their tight security measures. In fact, security guards were appreciated and very few people worried that these low paid workers might be restricting their freedom or controlling them. Cairo is however, a safe town and it makes no difference –

security wise – if one walks in the streets or in a mall. But, nobody seems to be bothered by the fact that in some malls cameras were monitoring the public for 24 hours a day.

The malls are popular, according to my informants, because they are more pleasant and cleaner than the chaotic street. The mall provides a feeling of "elevation," of being modern and protected from the outside world. For example, the Geneina Mall has become a tourist attraction for rural Egyptians. I was told that buses filled with visitors from the countryside often tour the mall and if one lives in Tanta, it is possible to spend the day touring the malls and return in the evening (Ahmed 'Ali, 19 years old, Cairo Mall).[52] Every year, Al-'Aquad Mall makes fashion shows which are much appreciated. Films and *musalsalat* T.V. serials are often screened in this mall as if this is the best place to be in town.

However, a paradox emerges. On the one hand, almost all those interviewed seemed to repeat identical sentiments: that the mall is cleaner and offers protection from crowds in the street, that it provides order and security, and that it is definitely more pleasant, although expensive. But they did not want riff-raff and *baladi* people there. On the other hand, many of those interviewed said: "the mall incorporates all levels and classes" (Islam 'Adel and Ahmed 'Adel, both 17-years-old, Cairo Mall, Giza). The mall includes everything and is less exclusive and certainly cheaper than the club. Thus, it is perceived as a restricted space, where even if one comes from a popular background, a disguise is desired. The malls are less restrictive than private clubs, which makes them attractive to many youngsters, but once so called "riff-raff" are spotted, they are in trouble.

When I started my research in 1999 some malls such the World Trade Centre and the Horreya Mall put restrictions on those wearing *galabeyyas* (the long robes), which are mostly worn by peasants and lower "popular" classes. I believe that this restriction was later lifted because of the strong influx of the Gulf visitors who also wear white traditional *galabeyyas*.[53] The General manager of Arkadia Mall

---

[52] Ahmed Ali comes very frequently to Cairo from Tanta for just shopping and wandering around. He revealed to have a wide knowledge about price differences between the various Cairene malls. It is his favorite past time.

[53] In spite of the fact that both Gulf customers like *baladi* people wear long robes *galabeyyas*, no security would stop gulf customers from entering a mall. The class origin of the poorer is on the other hand immediately spotted.

(2005) stated that he gave instructions to security at the doors to "filter the public through appearance (*bil shakl*)".[54] *Galabeyyas*, flip-flops and popular looking attires were good enough reasons to stop what he thought to be the "invading" public from the popular neighbourhood of Sabtiyyah,[55] which was seen as causing serious problems for the mall maintenance. It is this sort of public, according to the manager, which often steals electricity bulbs and water mixers from the public toilets. They are "the undesired 'class D', while the mall only wants to attract classes A and B".[56] He also stated that undesirables from Sabtiyyah and Bulaq have no manners whatsoever, and use the public toilets to have baths. They use the liquid soap to wash their hair. This is why Arkadia Mall is in constant struggle with its outer surrounding.

The interviews conducted with salesmen and women in shopping malls were most revealing in that although many of these shops are not doing well financially because of the high rent and the economic recession, many still insist that it is better to work in a mall than elsewhere. In spite of the frequency with which mall shops close down, the atmosphere in malls is preferable to that in the street. The street is "vulgar", people are bad mannered, the air is polluted and people are constantly pushing around. It was clear for many, both sales people and customers that the prices in malls are much higher than in other shops, but still it is more civilized and pleasant to be in a mall. What has to be taken into consideration is that the salaries of the salesgirls and salesmen in these malls start at L.E. 150[57] and reach a maximum L.E. 450, which is certainly not even half of what a foreign domestic servant would get. Although some of the salesgirls and salesmen manage to obtain commissions that can reach L.E. 750, their salaries would not be higher if they were to work in shops outside of malls. Nevertheless, salesmen and women seem to prefer working in the malls, despite their relatively modest wages, because they are cleaner than the street and more protected. They argue the people are better behaved since cameras are watch-

---

[54] Interview with the general manager of Arkadia, 19 February 2005. Note that he used the English word "filter" in the interview.

[55] Sabtiyyah is known for being one of the largest secondhand iron and metals retail markets of Cairo. It has large depots for old fences, ironwork, and gates; anything one can think of in metal.

[56] Interview with the general manager of Arkadia Mall, 19 February 2005.

[57] One dollar equals approximately L.E. 6.

ing and security is strict, while the street is "vulgar," the air is polluted and people are constantly pushing around and have bad manners. It was clear for many that the higher prices in malls did not stop people from shopping, or at least browsing, since it was still a more "civilized" and pleasant place than the street.

For many, Cairo's pollution, traffic chaos and crowded streets have become a major hindrance to window-shopping and strolling the streets.[58] One salesman said: "The weather in Egypt has become very hot and humid and there is dust in the air". Thus, the financial success of a mall has much to do with the fact that many customers today prefer to shop in an air conditioned area, especially in the hot summers. To a European or an American, it seems odd to discover that the malls' peak hours begin around 10 p.m. and shops do not typically close before one or two o'clock in the morning. Coffee houses are indeed full long after midnight. Especially in summer, Egyptians turn into night owls. In most of the malls, with a few exceptions like the Tiba Mall, *shishas* (water pipes) in cafes are very common and malls don't even open until late in the morning, around 11 a.m. No one is astonished that beauty salons and hairdressers work until midnight in Geneina Mall.

The most fascinating point in the interviews, which were conducted in Arabic, is the overpowering intrusion of English language mixing with Arabic dialect to describe the malls. Whether managers, the public, or shopkeepers, many answered our questions in Arabic but used English words. This may have been done to impress the interviewer, but it also reflects a pattern found in many films and television serials, and talk shows, which constantly insert English words. First of all, the word "mall" has been Arabicized to be called *al-moll*, plural *al-mollat*. The shops selling casual clothes are called as *mahallat kazual* (casual shops), and are the most popular among youngsters. In fact the word casual or *kazual*, is used in Egyptian Arabic to mean informal dress or an informal situation. For example, one shopkeeper in Cairo Mall describes the set of shops on his floor as specializing in *kazual* dresses. Shopping, internet cafes, coffee shops, bowling, billiards (*billiardo*), disco, the underground, sound system, décor, modern, are all words which have intruded into the Egyptian dialect. The English term "all in one" was used to include leisure,

---

[58] But the sheer size of masses one sees downtoun at night, especially on Thursdays, reveals that the street will always be full.

shopping, walking, cinemas and children's games by one manager in Nasr City when he was asked to describe what the concept of the mall means. Some informants often used the word "style" in their descriptions of malls, which has been also Arabized. Others speak of *estyle gidid*, new style, and *hay kelass*, high class, to describe the wealthier public frequenting malls compared to the street "riff-raff." The names of shops are also frequently Westernized, sometimes with incorrect spelling. While one can still find many Arabic names in malls, and franchised brands like Lapudis, Adidas, or Movenpick, one also finds foreign names like Bellini (men's wear), Dandy (men's wear), Wild (casual dresses), Sky Class (women's clothes), Fablos (women's clothes), La Reine (patisserie), Twiti Shoes, Diamond Canary (children's wear), Dream Cafe (coffee house), Lisa House (women's shoes and hand bags), New Brand, (casual clothes), Crazy House, Ted Lamond, Mix, Haidy, Fantasia, Frutti, Chance, Cadre (for frames), Western, Baby World (maternity clothes), Champion Women's clothes, and Chico (children's toys). The public was divided on the choice of Western or Arabic names. Some said that the name of the shop did not really matter, although there was a tendency among younger men to think that Western names are "cool" and would attract more customers. *Al-asma' al riwsha'*, derived from *riwish*, is a newly introduced word in Arabic used, to define cool looking, fashionable youngsters. Thus, foreign names are associated with such a definition.

It is not new to argue that the usage of foreign languages is certainly a clear class marker. Increasingly, we find that English words are becoming part of Arabic Cairene dialect. The Human Resources Report of 2004 mentioned that the Arabic language as it is badly taught in schools. Also because of the incorporation of many foreign words, especially from English, Arabic is facing a serious threat.[59] Moreover, foreign private schools concentrate on teaching foreign

---

[59] The Arab Human Development Report of 2003 mentioned that Arabic language is facing a serious crisis due to its mediocre pedagogy in the schools. Classical Arabic is facing a serious threat since many give priority to foreign private schools that concentrate on teaching foreign languages at the expense of Arabic. The result is that many young students end up with a very low level of Arabic, which seems to be no longer in demand in the modern sector of the economy like banking, advertising, management and business. The report also mentions that there are few published works translated from English into Arabic (*taqrir al-tanmiyya al-insaniyya al-'arabiyya li'am, 2003*, UNDP Report 2003, pp. 120–125).

languages at the expense of Arabic. In addition, Arabic is no longer needed in the modern sector of the economy, in banking, advertising, management and business. One can see how this *'uqdat al-khawaga* (the foreigner complex) has filtered through and the intermingling of foreign words with Arabic is affecting everyone. This is now part of the new culture related to malls. It is not new to argue that the usage of foreign languages is certainly a clear class marker. The intermingling of foreign words with Arabic is now extending to reach wider classes.

Popular versus "Chic" Malls

In just a few weeks, Fifi had taught her all she had to do: she had to take care of her appearance, paint her fingernails and her toe nails, open the neck of her dress a little, and take her dresses in a bit at the waist to show off her backside. It was her job to open the store in the morning and mop it out along with her colleagues, then set her clothes straight and stand at the door (a way of attracting customers familiar to all the clothing stores). When she had a customer, she had to talk to him nicely, comply with his requests, and persuade him to buy as much as possible (she got a half of one percent of the value of all sales). Naturally, she had to put up with the customers' flirting, however obnoxious.

'Alaa al-Aswani, *The Yacoubian Building*, The American University Press, 2004, p. 44.

The various Cairo malls attract very different customers. If the World Trade Centre during its hay days catered mainly for middle-class housewives, students and emerging Egyptian yuppies parading their mobile phones, the Bustan Centre, which was meant to be mainly a parking place for downtown, and also turned into a shopping centre, hosted mainly lower-middle-class youth. The mall has a variety of Egyptian-style coffee houses, with loud Egyptian music and with dark corners for secret lovers' encounters. Groups of young boys and girls regularly hang out in such malls. Cheap, popular coffee shops, Internet coffee shops and large bowling or billiard centres have become available for the lower-middle-class youth, who wander about in the afternoons and evenings. It is no coincidence that most of these "malls" have been constructed near a popular market, as is the case of the Bustan Centre, which is adjacent to the Bab al-Luq traditional vegetable market, whereas the World Trade Centre is close to the popular Bulaq market. Khan 'Azzam is a new shopping mall that has been planted in the heart of the traditional Bazaar of Khan al-Khalili. The effect of such an intrusion into the market place in the centuries-old Muslim part of Cairo is disturbing. Inside it resembles a Parisian *grand magasin*, and this contrast is indeed offensive in relation to the streets of the popular *suq* (market) lying a few meters away. Many wonder if Khan 'Azzam Mall will be a success in view of the current economic crisis. Constructed in the style of a Western covered market, with wooden *mashrabiyyah* (Islamic style wooden carved windows) and Islamic style columns, it again displays the fashionable hybrid taste.

Can one speak of a possible interaction between these two different markets? Could there be a dialogue between modern and traditional sectors or spaces? It seems that two different populations are simply being juxtaposed and that what is being represented is rather the non-exchange or divorce between, say, the traditional market networks of cloth and second-hand goods and the modern joint-venture commodities sold at the WTC. However, it is possible to speak of a certain cultural specificity in the conception of what is understood among Cairenes as a shopping mall. Certainly any European would have doubts as to whether the Bustan Centre should be considered a mall or just an annex to the largest parking place for downtown.

The Yamamah Centre in the quarter of Zamalek, owned by Prince Bandar, a close relative of the Saudi Royal family, is an entirely different type of mall. Erected in 1989, it was the first mall ever constructed in Cairo and is the symbol of the Saudi financial presence. It was constructed by the Sabbour company, that later built Arkadia Mall.[60] The centre consists of nine floors with escalators and covers an area of 4000 square meters (it is run by Egyptian managers). Its location in Zamalek is ideal for the students of the various faculties of applied arts and music, which are located nearby. A few years ago there was a coffee house in the passage between the Yamamah Centre and the next building. It was closed down when it became a meeting place for students who, after classes, gathered to smoke water pipes and, reportedly, hashish. During the winter, the hall usually becomes a busy meeting place for the students between noon and four o'clock. Because the mall belongs to a Saudi busi-

---

[60] Several managers mentioned that some contracting firms such as the Sabbours and the Orascom have the monopoly of building malls.

nessman from the royal family, it is much frequented by Saudis and seems to be well known in certain circles for its jewellery shops and glittery shoes.

As in all the malls of Cairo, there are tight security measures. Secret cameras are everywhere and security guards are to be found on each floor. The major problems, according to the manager, are petty thefts, shop-lifting and sexual harassment, which increase in summer with the flow of Saudi Arabian visitors to Cairo. Sexual harassment seems to be the major concern, in which Saudi women are targeted. The manager stated that this might lead to serious trouble with the Saudi owner. In winter, visitors to the mall are mainly window shoppers, and the dangers of petty theft become the obsession of the administrators of this space. A few years ago, during the month of Ramadan performances of Arabic music took place in the hall and attracted a large audience. During this fasting month, Cairenes spend long nights in the streets and in public places and such malls are packed until late at night. The Yamamah Centre provides for specific tastes like high-heeled shoes, glittering clothes and children's games, attracting mainly Saudis. The quality of the products seems to cater to the needs of Gulf visitors who enjoy Cairene summers. In other words, the standards of taste are what upper class Zamalek residents would qualify as *baladi* or *bi'a* taste (popular, with the connotation of vulgarity). The most striking observation is that the mall attracts Egyptian women dressed and veiled in the Saudi style. Also, as can be detected from their accents, many of these women seem to be Egyptians who have been married to Saudis or men from the Gulf as part of the traffic of Egyptian poor women who are often "sold" as cheap brides by their families. Each of these malls attracts customers differing in terms of class and in their consumer demands.

But if the Bustan and Yamamah malls are regarded as catering for common and "vulgar" masses, labelled as *bi'a*, (with the exception of the expensive membership for the Gym in Yamama), the First Mall in the district of Giza, in one of the most expensive and lavish buildings of Cairo, illustrates how classy ones do their best to keep the masses away by tightening their security and introducing expensive restaurants and coffee shops that will exclude the poor. The First Mall is located within the complex of the Four Seasons Hotel. In the same complex, one of the most expensive apartment buildings of Cairo has been erected. Rumors spread that these deluxe flats sell at more than one million US dollars. Well-known multi-millionaires, belly dancers and singers have purchased flats in this building. The Four Seasons hosts important politicians, such as German Chancellor Shroeder when he visited Cairo.

Most, if not all, rent the space for individual shops. The rent differs from one mall to another, because there are differences between *baladi* and chic malls. The rent varies between L.E. 150 to 200 per square meter. Some shops can reach a rent of L.E. 6000. The rents vary from one mall to another, as they vary and decrease through time. For example, the Yamama Mall rents at L.E. 120 per square meter, Geneina L.E. 180, Ramses and Tahrir Hilton Malls L.E. 120–150, the First Mall started with L.E. 600 and went down to L.E. 160, while Carrefour has reached the highest rent L.E. 320 per square meter.[61] One example is the World Trade Centre, which has died and is a ghost mall today, whereas the First Mall which is annexed to the Four Seasons complex is today one of the most posh centres in town. It attracts clients by bringing in a pianist for the morning brunch. This is where one can purchase the best French baguette and gateaux thanks to French expertise in the matter.

The Tal'at Harb Mall is an interesting case study. It would seem that its original owner could not pay the bank loan, similar to several other owners of shopping malls erected recently.[62] The Tal'at Harb Mall was then sequestrated by the Bank al-Ahli. Rumors are that it has picked up recently and the rents have gone up to L.E. 240 per square meter. With economic recession, it is clear that the purchasing power has been extensively reduced. But people do not go to malls for shopping but rather windowshopping. These new spaces are basically a good way to stroll in cool air in hot summers, for walking up and down the escalators and going in rounds with groups of friends.

---

[61] These are the estimates of the managers of Yamama Centre. Interview with the Managers of Yamama Mall Ashraf Abu 'Aref and Ahmed al-Sukkary, 14 March 2005.

[62] In spite of the short lifespan of the shopping malls in Cairo, these continue to flourish, which explains the fact that these enterprises might be simply a way for money laundering or taking bank loans. However, another explanation is the bad management of malls and the economic recession.

Fig. 93. Tal'at Harb Mall Stairs.

Economic Recession and the Future of Consumerism

The flotation of the Egyptian pound during the month of January 2003 caused a generalized trauma among Egyptians. Rumours spread that by the end of 2003 the dollar would reach ten pounds. In 2003–4 it had already climbed to L.E. 6,50 and all prices of basic goods soared.[63] The economic depression has led to thousands of job cuts in various sectors of the economy. Depression has not only hit the working class, but also the managerial level and the banking sector. In such a gloomy atmosphere, one wonders how the opening of the Carrefour some two year ago (December 2002, and a second branch in Alexandria in January 2003) with a flamboyant celebration, and the masses of cars, packed in the parking lot can still operate, considering that two other branches will be opened next year in Cairo.[64] Will the expected outcome of depression be increasing pauperization? Are we going to experience a second Argentina?

---

[63] Meanwhile, the dollar fell down in September 2005 to 5.80 piasters.
[64] "Carrefour in Egypt", In Tour Egypt. http: //touregypt.net/teblog/fixer/?p=2

Fig. 94. Tal'at Harb Mall.

Many believe that the Sudanese crisis, which resulted in the collapse of the currency, will be the fate of Egypt. In such circumstances, can one still speak of the rising consumerist appetites among Egyptians?

According to observers, the Indonesian case teaches us that since the acute Indonesian economic crisis of 1997, Indonesians have changed their habits of spending time. Contrary to one's beliefs, frugality means that one spends increasing time in shopping malls in window-shopping. We are told that in Jakarta the number of visitors to malls and centres has increased by 10–20 percent since the crisis.[65] Shopping malls have become easier to visit, and much more comfortable on the weekends, a cheaper and more enjoyable alternative to spend in long hours in traffic jams escaping Jakarta. "Although temporarily 'unconscious' since the economic crisis hit. By 1997, the total area of shopping centres in Jakarta reached 1.519.932 square meters. This figure remained the same after the monetary crisis, or 'Krismon', was at its worst in 1997 and 1998.

---

[65] Dian N Sulaiman, "Shopping Centres, Alternative Tourism Destinations", *TEMPO*, Jakarta, June 17, 2002, p. 37.

However, today, it is estimated that the area covers two million square meters".[66] Therefore, the economic crisis did not hamper the multiplication of malls. On the contrary, they will continue to increase.

Is it possible to argue that recession in both Cairo and Jakarta did not stop the flowering of ambitious mega projects? It seems that in Egypt, as in Indonesia, private capitalists and the government are both increasingly obsessed by grandiose hyper-commercial spaces. Among business circles many believe that constructing shopping malls is the other side of the same coin of money laundering. Malls and mega projects have been used for a while to obtain huge bank loans, which were smuggled out of the country. This resulted into a series of scandals and arrests of businessmen. This might explain why in spite of the short lifespan of malls, these will continue to multiply. But how would such gargantuan projects survive with the frightening recession? Certainly no one can answer this question.

---

[66] Ibid.

CONCLUSION

In time, one is only what one is: what one has always been. In space, one can be another person. Benjamin's poor sense of direction and inability to read a street map become his love of travel and his mastery of the art of straying.

Susan Sontag, *Under the Sign of Saturn*, pp. 116–117.

I

Egyptian society seems to evidence a paradoxical phenomenon in the relationship between religion and market. Observers argue that the growing Islamization of the whole society was first instigated by the Sadat government to counteract the secular and communist tendencies. Later, when the Islamic movement expanded, the regime perpetuated a strategy of islamization from the top to counteract the underground Islamic protest movements. The reactions of the early Islamic opposition, (mainly young men and women) in the late seventies and early eighties were interpreted as a form of protest against the expanding world of consumerism and the Americanization of society as a consequence of the open door policy launched by Sadat. During the nineties, Islamization spread to various classes and the systematic association between protest and Islam became increasingly blurred with the proliferation of the Petro-Islam Saudi worldview. As argued earlier, the process of Americanization of the Egyptian society has been detoured through the "Saudi Arabization" and the impact of massive migration to the oil producing countries. The importation of hard-currency lifestyles, garments, and spending leisure time in malls has shaped the life-worlds of the Islamized middle classes. The marriage between religion and market proved so far quite successful. Islamic consumerism as demonstrated earlier seems to be doing well in the clothing industry and food chains such as the food chain Mo'men (rumours are that it is owned by an Islamic oriented capitalist) and several others.

The second paradox is that, despite an acute economic crisis, Cairo is witnessing a boom in the construction of shopping malls.

That shopping malls are dying does not contradict the fact that companies like Orascom and a few others are doing well financially and will thus continue to expand. The monopoly of wealth in the hands of the few has resulted in the construction of condominiums and swimming pools in newly reclaimed desert land. Beach resorts, and "gated communities", inspired by either the American or Asian model, or featuring an invented Islamic architecture, attracted the large savings of the middle classes. Developments with names such as Beverly Hills and Dreamland are the models for some of these "gated communities". However, if malls and gated communities in the West are associated with the spread of high incomes, the majority of the Middle Eastern countries are still characterized by low-income households.

While the pros and cons of the effects of consumer culture have been discussed earlier, this work remains ambiguous in relation to the "longue durée" effects of consumer culture in relationship to status and as an identity marker. It is clear that the urban remaking of the city of Cairo is taking place at the expense of visually excluding the mass of the unwanted poor. It is also clear that those goods as social markers are sharpening class distinctions, while the implementation of the neo-liberalist economy has mainly sharpened the power of the handful few families controlling the economy. When looking at shopping malls, although the managers' discourse is all about keeping them clean and wanting to attract the well to do, while excluding the riff-raff, malls paradoxically survive when the popular class appropriates them. They become available to masses by the mere fact that these are free spaces for window-shopping, hanging around and availability of cheap food. Shopping malls, like mobile phones and the growing Egyptian clothing industry have become available and affordable to wider and poorer classes. Cosmopolitan colonial culture, in comparison was restricted to the happy few, while consumerism under Nasser was restricted towards catering to the rising middle classes. Peasants, ironically, only participated in consumer culture during the *infitah* period and mainly through migration.

The optimists see in the flowering of the art market, the proliferation of local arts and crafts – even in a folkloric, tourist oriented style and the burgeoning of a local fashion industry – as welcoming signs of positive participation in the globalization process. The pessimists insist on the increasing class polarization. The art market evolves merely around decorative items for the salons of the rich.

The time of politically engaged, class conscious grass roots art projects seems to have vanished, very much like the social welfare discourse there has withered away leaving a free hand to wild capitalism. However, with the proliferation of both private and state art galleries, increasingly, young Egyptian artists from humble backgrounds have been given ever-growing opportunities to exhibit their work.

There has been a reshaping of the public space to merge shopping with leisure (movie houses, billiard rooms, discotheques, ice-skating rinks). These spaces often include modern offices housing a large stratum of professionals during the day. A new lifestyle in forms of dress, and the phenomenon of carrying mobile phones, has changed perceptions of public space. Architecture has noticeably transformed, and hybrid styles and fusions between, say, "oriental", "Islamic" or "Asian" and modern Western architecture have become fashionable. The cathedral-type mall incorporates many functions; its main advantage is being open and transparent to the public. Advertisements in both English and Arabic newspapers became more sophisticated, spreading the new lifestyles. One can find certain homogeneity in malls all over the globe. They look similar, whether they are in Singapore, Malaysia, Indonesia or Cairo. This holds true on the surface. However, the local variations between each individual case and the economic situation of each country provide a different setting.

The problem with these hyperspaces, especially in the Third World, is that the security measures are not always respected. Such was the case in the Horreya mall when it caught fire a few years ago, causing deaths and casualties. It was then discovered that the exits were not fitting to standards. These consumer areas have become in certain parts of the world the only islands against the outer violent world, as is the case of Brazil. In Asuncion, Paraguay on 1 August 2004, a fire took place due to a gas-cylinder explosion in one of the largest modern commercial centres. When the fire exploded, the director closed off all the doors fearing that the customs might run away without paying for the items. The son of the director was thought to be inside the centre and he was allowed to leave before the doors were closed. But 340 customers were cremated inside the commercial centre and another 300 were seriously injured. When the firemen arrived, armed private security guards shot one of them. The mall director has been convicted for voluntary homicide. The lesson to be learned is that even if the sanitized dream world of the mall is identical in Rio, Cairo, Beirut or New York, the Paraguay incident reminds us that when catastrophes happen, the price is evidently much higher in the Third World. Since many consider that there is an over supply of malls, these mega projects might turn into ghost towns much quicker than we imagined. It might be well that the archaeology of consumer culture has already begun as a field of study.

What worried me most in this field study was the uncritical and totally favourable attitude, which the majority of the public, shopkeepers and management staff have adopted towards malls in particular, and consumer culture in general. Another paradox is to be observed, as some argue that the Arab boycott to American goods has been on the rise. On the other hand, my personal observations reveal that the high popularity of McDonald's and the growing adoption of American lifestyles hybridized with local specificities, are on the rise among middle classes. This statement, however, does not contradict the growing Egyptian boycott of American goods. In fact, both trends can coexist, much like Egyptian local fast food (*ful, falafel, koshari*) has not and will not be affected by McDonald's because it is simply cheaper and catering to different publics. Rather, one choice does not negate the other. Parallel markets allowed the creation of an indigenous version of McDonald's, namely Mo'men. One contrast with Singapore's Asianization of McDonald's is that the Egyptianization of McFalafel failed because it could not compete in price with the local *falafel*.

II

Western social theory has produced a rich critique of the "culture industry" by the Frankfurt school, expanded later by Jean Baudrillard, Zygmunt Bauman and Mike Featherstone. We should be reminded that the 1968 student movement in Europe went to the streets to rebel against patriarchal, capitalist norms and the "terror of consumerism" that produced a well to do meaningless bourgeois society. On the other hand, urban sociologists dreamed of utopian city-malls, but then warned about ghost malls littering the landscape. My impression is that the Arab World is merely recycling consumer culture, without producing any self–reflexivity. Perhaps we are still in the phase of ecstasy, or rather an amnesia that enables us to live in a city-slum without ever noticing poverty. Consumerism immunizes us and detaches us from national authoritarian policies, which extend even to our dream malls. This brings me to Ashis Nandy's critique of the failure or "sterility" of modernity and progress in the South (with the exception in the domain of visual arts, literature and music) in stimulating creativity and original theorization. Nandy argues: "The concept of modernity has been sterile in the South because there is little understanding of the loss that is brought about the victory of modernity itself".[1] While according to Nandy, Western philosophical thinking exemplified in Theodor Adorno, Karl Marx, and Sigmund Freud, theorized this sense of loss, is absent among the social scientists of the South. I think that the absence of the "sense of loss" applies well to the consumer sphere and the devastating consequences of mimicry in the South. Perhaps consumerism as *Ersatz* to the weakened emotional and familial ties is lacking in the South and is yet to come. By *Ersatz*, I mean that consumerism has been substituting stable, long-term emotional relations and long-term secure careers and jobs. Consumerism as a consequence is creating a novel form of narcissism and narcissistic love relations through the body as a site of consumption. This has been a focal point of research in Western sociological theory, but could it generally apply to the South? What about tradition and traditional support family networks in the South, which are strongly operative if not reinvented for modern conditions, that accommodate well with consumerism?

This brings me to the next point: alienation and the metropolis. My concern is whether the loneliness can be similarly experienced in Cairo as it is in Berlin or London. "The loneliness of the city dweller" is a topos in literary works[2] much similar to how alienation evolved as a key concept in sociological theory. Walter Benjamin's flâneur is a melancholic loner and daydreamer whose final aim is to get lost in the labyrinth of the city.[3] Definitely, alienation can be experienced in any place in the world, but the high population density, the different body language related to close proximity, and the lively street communication associated with constant tight space management requires reflection. On the other hand, the sight of young

---

[1] Ashis Nandy, "Modernity and the Sense of Loss. Those in India who Want to Lead a Modern Life must Dig up their Roots: Old Traditions Irritate the new Elites" *Zeitschrift fuer Kultur Austausch*, 55, Jahrgang 1/05. pp. 44–42, p. 41.

[2] Alexander Welsh, *The City of Dickens*, pp. 11–12.

[3] Concerning this point see the striking text of Susan Sontag on Walter Benjamin, *Under the Sign of Saturn*, Farrar, Strauss, Giroux, New York, 1980, p. 112.

lonely male flâneurs in Cairene malls is frequent and they remind us that experiencing loneliness among dense masses is no different in Cairo from elsewhere.

III

Western intellectuals have expressed concern that cities have little to do with, and are not developing towards, what Richard Sennett has advocated in his work,[4] the return of the "humane city". Third World cities are today becoming infernal places, with growing pollution, poverty and overpopulation problems. Cairo has the record as one of the world's most densely populated cities. I am far from being an apologist for the frantic consumerist lifestyles of the new Third World bourgeoisie, but it seems that the resistance of the poor takes forms that are difficult to grasp in an atmosphere of harsh repression of human rights and the prevalence of political correctness among intellectuals on the one hand, and the decline of Marxism on the other. Parallel with the fascination of Carrefour, a friend told me that a new type of "simulating" shoppers has emerged. These, who are probably unable to afford to purchase anything there, experience an ephemeral joy by filling their trolley to the utmost, to leave it just before reaching the cashier. The "make believe" act seems to somehow replace window-shopping and evidently the real shopping, thus confirming what Jean Baudrilard had long ago predicted.

The mall has become a new space for social interaction, for shaping lifestyles and needs for consumption, a space for youth and the new professionals. Restaurants, shops and the service sector have absorbed large segments of youth. This certainly affects ways of "dressing" and looking modern in order to go to work. I recall a scene I often witnessed in shopping centres. Women removed their head scarves or "Islamic attire" when taking up their function as cashiers, waiters or saleswomen and put them back on when going home. This masquerade says a lot about how young women have to negotiate between different lifestyles. The same thing can be noticed among young girls who change their dress or their school

---

[4] Richard Sennett, *The Conscience of the Eye: The Design and Social Life of Cities*, New York, Knopf, 1990. See also Anthony Giddens, *Sociology*, Polity, 2001, 4th edition, pp. 585–86.

uniform according to place. This duality and constant changing of attire, in order to adapt to the two worlds, the inside/outside – the dense, highly socially controlled, poor, popular quarters versus the modern public spheres of work in malls – needs further study. It is thus possible to argue that what makes malls interesting in Cairo is not shopping, but rather that they are a locus and meeting place for groups of young girls. Malls are ideal places for mixing, for flirting between sexes and for strolling. They provide an outlet where the crowd finds warmth and friendliness. The mall is the place where the crowds are formed.

It is the place of entertainment, which replaces gardens, and public spaces, which are scarce in Cairo. One might even speak of their democratizing effects, as these spaces are accessible to all classes, despite the abrupt elimination of popular quarters and the economy of survival exemplified in the informal sector. Social scientists have pointed to the fact that, in recent years, Egyptian society has witnessed a growing Islamization in political and everyday spheres of life. Observers argued that "public religion" has gained visibility in Egypt as well as in the Middle East generally in the last decades of the twentieth century. This is not an erroneous argument. It is, nevertheless, a one sided point of view. My observations lead me to think that the Islamization of public space in the 1990's coincides with survival strategies taking the form of a "relaxation of norms" among youth, within an Islamic frame of reference.

One might interpret the phenomenon of *'urfi* (unregistered and thus illegal) marriage among youth as a circumvention that effectively resolves sexual tensions among youngsters. Similarly, the attire labelled "Islamic" can become a protective mechanism, to allow further mixing of the sexes, and allows young women to be left in peace. Islamic attire allows youth to smoke cigarettes or water pipes in public, and it allows flirtation in the intimate spaces of the coffee houses. Indeed, the younger generation, through meeting in coffee houses, seems to have gained some previously unknown liberties. While the 1970's witnessed a growing policing and segregation of public space, which coincided with the ascendance of Islamism, the 1990's witnessed a growing availability of such reshaped spaces and a new form of "mixing" of norms and tastes.

I would like to conclude here with a scene I experienced in the annex of the billiard room of the Hilton Ramses. I went there a few years ago with a female photographer to start my project on malls. In the large billiard room there were only two women, who were smoking and playing billiards. Both wore jeans, but one wore a headscarf. These two women intrigued my friend and because they seemed so self-assured with their game. Besides that they were very good players. When we approached them and explained my interest in malls, they did not mind being photographed. They were happy that the four of us understood one another; that we would highlight women's changing role in public in the article we were preparing. It turned out that one was a medical practitioner, while the one who wore the Islamic attire was an independent businesswoman and a dealer on the stock exchange. They came to the Hilton once a week for relaxation and seemed to have found an enjoyable partnership in playing together. Their independence and self-confidence says something about women today in Egypt. It seems to me that women are increasingly conquering public space without the need for a male presence to protect them. Certainly, Islamism does not do any favours to the feminist cause, but everyday reality tells us that women are continuing to invent survival strategies. It is the art of circumvention that tells us a great deal about how women continue to remain visible in the public sphere.

BIBLIOGRAPHY

Works in Arabic

Books and articles

'ABD AL-KERIM, Khalil. *Quraish minal al-qabila ilal-dawla al-markaziyya* (Quraish: From the Tribe to the Centralized State). Cairo: Sina lil-Nashr, 1997.

AL-'AIDI, Ahmed. *An Takun 'Abbas al-'Abd* (To Be 'Abbas al-'Abd). Cairo: Miret, 2003.

AL-HIDDINI, Amani. *Al-muhammashun wal-siyasa fi-misr* (The Marginalized and Politics in Egypt). Cairo: Centre for Political and Strategic Studies, Al-Ahram, 1999.

AL-MESSIRI, 'Abd al-Wahhab. *Fiqh al-tahayyuz* (The Problematic of Bias). Cairo: IIIT and the Syndicate of Engineer, 1996.

AL-WARDANI, Mahmud. *Musika al-Mool* (Mall Music). Cairo: Miret, 2005.

AMIN, Galal. *Matha hadatha lil-masriyyin?* (Whatever Happened to the Egyptians?), Cairo: Dar al-Hilal, 1998.

——. *'Asr al-jamahir al-ghafira* (The Era of Abundant Masses). Cairo: Dar al-Shuruq. Translated as *Whatever Else Happened to the Egyptians*, 2003.

DENYS, Eric. "Al-takhtit al-hadari wal-numuw fil-qahira" (Urban Planning and Cairo's Growth) in Mustafa Kamel al-Sayyed, Asef Bayat (eds.), *Al-qahira fi-lahzat tahawul (Cairo in a Moment of Transformation)*. Cairo: Centre for the Study of Developing Countries, Cairo University, 1998.

IMAM, Samia Sa'id. *Man yamluk misr* (Who Owns Egypt?), Cairo: Dar al-Mustaqbal al-'Arabi, 1986.

RIAD, Mohammed. "Al sakan al-'ashawa'i fi jumhuriyyat masr al-'arabiyya, anwa' al-'asha'iyyat wa tawzi'aha al-gughrafi wa-halat al-quahira al-kubra bishi' minal tafsil" (Slums in Egypt, Types of Slums, Geographical Distribution in the Case of Grand Cairo: Case Studies), in Fathi Mohammed Musilhi (ed.), *Al-'Umran al-'ashwa'i fi-misr (Unplanned Construction in Egypt)*, Cairo: Al-majlis al-a'la lil thaqafa, 2002.

THABET, Ahmed. "Nukhbat rigal al-a'mal fi-misr" (The Elite Businessmen in Egypt), in Ahmed Zayed, Arous Al-Zubair (eds.), *Al-nukhab al-ijtima'iyyah halat al-gaza'ir wa masr* (Elites in Algeria and Egypt), Cairo: Madbuli, 2005.

Newspapers and magazines

Akher Sa'ah
Al-Ahram
Al-Ahram al-Ta'alimi
Al-Bayt
Al-Hayat
Al-Mussawar
Al-Safir
Nisf al-Dunya
Rose al-Youssef

Works in Western Languages

Works in Western Languages

Books and articles

ABAZA, Mona. "Shopping Malls, Consumer Culture and the Reshaping of Public Space in Egypt", *Theory, Culture and Society*, 18 (5): 97–122, 2001.
——. "Perceptions of *'Urfi* Marriage in the Egyptian Press", *ISIM Newsletter*, 7/01: 20–21, 2001.
——. *Shifting Worlds: Debates on Islam and Knowledge, Egypt-Malaysia*, London: Kurzon-Routledge, 2002.
ABDEL MALEK, Anouar. *Ägypten: Militärgesellschaft. Das Armeeregime, die Linke und der Soziale Wandel unter Nasser* Frankfurt/M: Suhrkamp Verlag, 1971.
ABU-LUGHOD, Janet. "Tale of Two Cities: The Origins of Modern Cairo", *Comparative Studies in Society and History*, 7 (4): 429–457, 1965.
——. *Cairo: 1001 Years of the City Victorious*, Princeton: Princeton University Press, 1971.
——. "The Islamic City: Historic Myths, Islamic Essence, and Contemporary Relevance", in Richard T. LeGates, Frederic Stout (eds.), *The City Reader*, London: Routledge, 1996/2003.
ADAMS, Bert N.; R.A. Sydie. *Contemporary Sociological Theory*. Thousand Oaks: Pine Forge Press, 2002.
AGSTNER, Rudolf. "Dream and Reality: Austrian Architects in Egypt: 1869–1914" in Mercedes Volait (ed.), *Le Caire-Alexandrie, Architectures europeennes, 1850–1950*, Etudes Urbaines, 5, Cairo: CEDEJ-IFAO, 2001.
AL-ASWANI, Alaa. *Yacoubian Building*, The American University Press in Cairo, 2004.
ALBROW, Martin; KING, Elizabeth. *Globalization, Knowledge, and Society: Readings from International Sociology*. London: Sage Publications, 1990.
AMIN, Galal. *Whatever Happened to the Egyptians. Changes in Egyptian Society from 1950 to the Present*. Cairo: The American University in Cairo Press, 2000.
——. *Whatever Else Happened to the Egyptians? From the Revolution to the age of Globalization*. Cairo: The American University in Cairo Press, 2004.
AMBRUERE, Francis. *La vie secrète des Grands magasins*. Paris: Flammarion, 1932.
APPADURAI, Arjun (ed.), *The Social Life of Things: Commodities in Cultural Perspective*. Cambridge: Cambridge University Press, 1986.
APPADURAI, Arjun. "Introduction: Commodities and the Politics of Values", in Arjun Appadurai (ed.), *The Social Life of Things: Commodities in Cultural Perspective*. Cambridge: Cambridge University Press, 1986.
——. "Disjuncture and Difference in the Global Cultural Economy", *Theory, Culture and Society*, 7: 295–310, 1990.
ARMBRUST, Walter. *Mass Mediations: New Approaches to Popular Culture in the Middle East and Beyond*. Berkeley: University of California Press, 2000.
——. "The Riddle of Ramadan: Media, Consumer Culture and Christmas-ization of a Muslim Holiday", (http://nmit.georgetown.edu/papers/warmbrust.htm)
ASLAN, Ibrahim. *Nile Sparrows* (translation Mona El-Ghobashy). Cairo: The American University in Cairo Press, 2004.
AWAD, Mohamed Fouad; PALLINI, Cristina. "The Italianisation of Alexandria: An Analogy of Practice", Mercedes Volait (ed.), *Le Caire-Alexandrie, Architectures europeennes, 1850–1950*, Etudes Urbaines, 5, Cairo: CEDEJ-IFAO, 2001.
BACKES, Nancy. "Reading the Shopping Mall City", *Journal of Popular Culture*, 31 (3): 1–17, 1997.
BASYOUNY, Iman Farid. *"Just a Gaze" Female Clientele of Diet Clinics in Cairo: An Ethnomedical Study*, Cairo Papers in Social Science, 20 (4), 1997.

BAUDRILLARD, Jean. *The Consumer Society: Myths and Structures* (with an introduction by George Ritzer). London: Sage Publications, 1998/2002.

BAUMAN, Zygmunt. "From Pilgrim to Tourist or a Short History of Identity", in Stuart Hall, Paul du Gray (eds.), *Questions of Cultural Identity*, London: Sage Publications, 1996.

——. (2000). *Liquid Modernity*, Polity Press.

BAYAT, Asef. "Cairo's Poor: Dilemmas of Survival and Solidarity", *Middle East Report*, Winter, 2–8, 1997.

——. "The Street and the Politics of Dissent in the Arab World", *Middle East Report*, Spring, 2003.

BECH, Henning. "Citysex, Representing Lust in Public", in Mike Featherstone (ed.), *Love and Eroticism*. London: Sage Publications, 1999.

BEININ, Joel. *The Dispersion of Egyptian Jewry: Culture, Politics and the Formation of a Modern Diaspora*. Berkeley: University of California Press, 1998.

BENG HUAT, Chua; Anandah Rajah. "Hybridity, Ethnicity and Food in Singapore", Working Paper no.33, Department of Sociology, National University of Singapore, 1996.

BENG HUAT, Chua (ed). *Consumption in Asia: Lifestyles and Identities*, London: Routledge.

——. (2000). "Consuming Asians: Ideas and Issues", in Chua Beng Huat (ed.), *Consumption in Asia: Lifestyles and Identities*. London: Routledge, 2000.

——. "Singaporeans Ingesting McDonalds", in Chua Beng Huat (ed.), *Consumption in Asia: Lifestyles and Identities*, London: Routledge, 2000.

——. *Life is Not Complete Without Shopping, Consumption Culture in Singapore*. National University of Singapore, 2004.

BONTEMPS, Maurice. *Du vol, les grands magasins et le vol a l'étalage, etude medico-légal*, Thèse a la faculté de medicine et de pharamacie de Lyon, 1894.

BOUDISSEAU, Guillaume. *Espaces commerciaux, centralité et logiques d'acteurs à Beyrouth: le cas de Hamra et de Verdun*, Thèse présentée pour l'obtention du Doctorat de l'Université François Rabelais de Tours, 2001.

——. "Espace commercial. Les temples du shopping", *Le Commerce du Levant*, Avril, 60–63, 2002.

——. "Pas de Monopirx a Hamra", *Le Commerce du Levant*, Aout, 2003.

——. "Les nouveaux rois du shopping", *Le Commerce du Levant*, Octobre, 60–65, 2004.

——. "Le combat des chefs", *Le Commerce du Levant*, Octobre, 68–70, 2004.

BOURDIEU. Pierre. *Questions de Sociologie*, Paris: Editions de Minuit, 1980.

——. *Distinction, A Social Critique of the Judgment of Taste*, translated by Richard Nice, Harvard University Press, Cambridge, Massachussets, 1984.

BOWLBY, R. *Just Looking*, London: Methuen, 1985.

CAGLAR, Ayse S. "Hyphenated Identities and the Limits of Culture", in Pnina Werbner, Tariq Modood (eds.), *Debating Cultural Hybridity: Multi-Cultural Identities and the Politics of Anti-Racism*. London: Zed Books, 1997.

CALHOUN, Craig. "Introduction: Habermas and the Public Sphere", in Craig Calhoun (ed.), *Habermas and the Public Sphere*. Cambridge: MIT Press, 1992.

CELIK, Zeynap Z. *Urban Forms and Colonial Confrontations: Algiers under French Rule*, Berkeley: University of California Press, 1997.

CHENGZE, Simon Fan. "Economic Development and the Changing Patterns of Consumption in Urban China", in Chua Beng Huat (ed.), *Consumption in Asia: Lifestyles and Identities*. London: Routledge, 2000.

CIRANNA, Simonetta. "Italian Architects and Holy Space in Egypt" in Mercedes Volait (ed.), *Le Caire-Alexandrie, Architectures europeennes, 1850–1950*, Edutes Urbains, 5, Cairo: CEDEJ-IFAO, 2001.

COOPER, Artemis. *Cairo in the War, 1939–1945*. London: Hamilton, Penguin, 1989.

CORRIGAN, Peter. *The Sociology of Consumption: An Introduction*. London: Sage Publications, 1997.

DE GRECE, Michel. "Grand Oriental Hotels" in *Masr al-Mahrusa, Impressions of Egypt, Grand Hotels of Egypt*, Vol. XVIII: 8–10, 2002.

DENYS, Eric. "Urban Planning and Growth in Cairo", *Middle East Report*, Winter: 7–1, 1996.

EICKELMAN, Dale F.; Jon W. Anderson. "Redefining Muslim Publics", in Dale F. Eickelman, Jon W. Anderson (eds.), *New Media in the Muslim World: The Emerging Public Sphere*, Bloomington & Indianapolis: Indiana University Press, 1999.

EICKELMAN, Dale F.; Armando Salvatore. "The Public Sphere and Muslim Identities", *Arch. Europ. Socio.*, XLIII (1), pp. 92–115, 2002.

ELKADI, Galila. *L'Urbanisation Spontanée au Caire*. Centre d'Études et des Recherches Urbama, Tours, 1987.

EL-MESSIRI, Sawsan. *Ibn Al-Balad: A Concept of Egyptian Identity*, Leiden: E.J. Brill, 1978.

EWEN, Steward. *All Consuming Images: The Politics of Style in Contemporary Culture*, Basic Books, 1988.

FATHY, HASSAN. *Construire pour le peuple*, Paris: Sindbad, 1970.

FEATHERSTONE, Mike, Mike Hepworth, Bryan Turner. *The Body: Social Process and Cultural Theory*, London: Sage, 1991.

FEATHERSTONE, Mike. *Consumer Culture and Postmodernism*, London: Sage Publications, 1991.

——. "The Flâneur, the City and the Virtual Public Space", *Urban Studies*, 35 (5–6): 909–925, 1998.

——. (ed.) *Body Modification*, London: Sage Publications, 2000.

FERGANY, Nader. *The Growth of Poverty in Egypt*. Cairo: Al-Meshkah Research Centre, 1998.

FISHMAN, Robert. "Beyond Suburbia: The Rise of the Technoburb", in Richard T. LeGates, Frederic Stout (eds.), *The City Reader*. London and New York: Routledge, 1996/2003.

FITCHETT, Joseph. "Rendez-vous at the Shepheard's", in *Masr al-Mahrusa: Impressions of Egypt, Grand Hotels of Egypt*, Vol. XVIII: 103–121, 2002.

FREITAS, Ricardo Ferreira. *Centres commerciaux: îles urbaines de la post-modernité*, Paris: L'Harmattan, 1996.

FRIEDBERG, Anne. *Window Shopping: Cinema and the Postmodern*. Berkeley: University of California Press, 1993.

FRIEDMAN, Jonathan. *Cultural Identity and Global Process*. London: Sage Publications, 1994.

FRIERSON, Elizabeth B. "Gender, Consumption, and Patriotism: The Emergence of an Ottoman Public Sphere", in: *Islam and the Common Good*, Armando Salvatore and Dale Eickelman, (eds.), Brill, Leiden-Boston, 2004.

FROMM, Erich. *On Disobedience and Other Essays*, London: Routledge and Kegan Paul, 1984.

GHANNAM, Farha. *Remaking the Modern: Space Relocation and the Politics of Identity*. Berkeley: University of California Press, 2002.

GIDDENS, Anthony. *Sociology*, Polity, 2001, 4th edition, 2001.

GIROUARD, Mark. *Cities & People: A Social and Architectural History*. New Haven and London: Yale University Press, 1985.

GOLDING, Peter. "The Mass Media and the Public Sphere: The Crisis of Information in the Information Society", in Stephen Edgell, Sandra Walklate, Gareth Williams (eds.), *Debating the Future of the Public Sphere*. Brookfield: Avenbury, 1995.

GOLIA, Maria. *Cairo, City of Sand*. Cairo: The American University in Cairo Press, 2004.

HABERMAS, Juergen. *Der gespaltene Westen*. Suhrkamp, 2004.

HAMAMSY, Chafika Soliman. *Zamalek: The Changing Life of a Cairo Elite, 1850–1945*. Cairo: The American University in Cairo Press, 2005.

HANNA, Nelly. "Boulaq – An Endangered Historic Area of Cairo", in M. Meinecke (ed.), *Islamic Cairo: Architectural Conservation and Urban Development of the Historic Centre*. London: Art and Archeology Research Papers, 1980.

——. "An Urban History of Bulaq in the Mamluk and Ottoman Periods", *Supplement aux Annales Islamologiques*, cahiers no. 3, 1983.

——. *In Praise of Books: A Cultural History of Cairo's Middle Class, Sixteenth to the Eighteenth Century*. Cairo: The American University in Cairo Press, 2004.

IBRAHIM, Saad Eddin. (1. *Egypt, Islam and Democracy: Twelve Critical Essays*. Cairo: The American University in Cairo Press, 1996.

IBRAHIM, Sonallah. *Zaat* (translation Anthony Calderbank). Cairo: The American University in Cairo Press, 2001.

ILLOUZ, Eva. *Der Konsum der Romantik Liebe und die Kurturellen Widersprüche des Kapitalismus* (English Version, *Consuming the Romantic Utopia*). Berkeley: The University of California Press, 1997.

JOSEPH, Isaac. "Les Compétences de rassemblement, une ethnographie des lieux publics", *Enquetes*, 4: 107–122, 1996.

KANDIYOTI, Deniz; CAGLAR, Ayse Saktanber (eds.), *Fragments of Culture: The Everyday of Modern Turkey*. London & New York: I.B. Tauris, 2002.

KARNOUK, Liliane. *Modern Egyptian Art, 1910–2003*. AUC Press, Cairo-New York, 2005.

KHOSROKHAVAR, Ferhad; ROY, Olivier. *Iran: comment sortir d'une révolution religieuse*. Paris: Editions du Seuil, 1999.

KIRLI, Cengiz. "Coffeehouses: Public Opinion in the Nineteenth-Century Empire", in *Public Islam and the Common Good*, Armando Salvatore and Dale Eickelman (editors), Brill, Leiden-Boston, 2004.

KRAEMER, Gudrun. *The Jews in Modern Egypt, 1914–1952*. London: I.B. Tauris and Co. Ltd., 1989.

LANCASTER, Bill. *The Department Stores: A Social History*. London & New York: Leicester University Press, 1995.

LANDLER, Mark. "Has Malaysia's Leader Won His Risky Gamble?", *International Herald Tribune*, 4–5 September, 1999.

MACKAY, Hugh (ed.), *Consumption and Everyday Life*. London: Sage Publications, 1997.

MEHREZ, SHAHIRA. "Hassan Fathi Citoyen du Monde", unpublished paper.

——. *The Arab Interior, Between Orient, Orientalism and Globalization*, paper presented at a Conference on the Arab Interior, Vitra Design Museum, Berlin, October, 2003.

MILES, Steven. *Consumerism as a Way of Life*. London: Sage Publications, 1998.

MILLER, David et al. *Shopping, Place and Identity*. London and New York: Routledge, 1998.

MILLER, Michael B. *The Bon Marche: Bourgeois Culture and the Department Store, 1869–1920*. Princeton: Princeton University Press, 1981.

MITCHELL, Timothy. *Rule of Experts: Egypt, Techno-Politics, Modernity*. Berkeley: University of California Press, 2002.

——. "Dreamland: The Neoliberalism of Your Desire", *Middle East Report*, Spring, 28–33, 1999.

MORRIS, Meaghan. "Things to do with Shopping Centres", in Simon During (ed.), *The Cultural Studies Reader*, London and New York: Routledge, 1993.

NANDY, Ashis. "Modernity and the Sense of Loss. Those in India who Want to Lead a Modern Life must Dig up their Roots: Old Traditions Irritate the new Elites" *Zeitschrift fuer Kultur Austausch*, 55, Jahrgang 1/05. pp. 44–42.

NAVA, Mica. "Modernity's Disavowal: Women, the City and the Department Store", in Mica Nava, A. O'Shea (eds.), *Modern Times: Reflections on a Century of English Modernity*, London: Routledge, 1996.

——. (forthcoming). "Cosmopolitan Modernity: Everyday Imaginaries and the Allure of Difference", *Theory, Culture and Society*.

NELSON, Cynthia. "Religious Experience, Sacred Symbols, and Social Reality", *Humaniora Islamica*, 2: 253–266, 1974.

PARTSCH, Susanna. *Kunst-Epochen 20. Jahrhundert*: Reclam, 2002.

RAFAAT, Samir. W. *Cairo, the Glory Years: Who Built What, When, Why and for Whom*, Alexandria: Harpocrates, 2003.

RAYMOND, André. (ed.), *The Glory of Cairo: An Illustrated History*. Cairo: The American University in Cairo Press, 2002.

RAYMOND, André. *Cairo: City of History*. Cairo: The American University in Cairo Press, 2001.

REYNOLDS, Nancy Young. "Sharikat al-Bayt al-Masri: Domesticating Commerce in Egypt 1931–1956", *Arab Studies Journal*, VII (2) and VIII (1): 75–107, 1999/2000.

——. *Commodity Communities: Interweavings of Market Cultures, Consumption Practices, and Social Power in Egypt, 1907–1961*, Ph.D. Dissertation, Department of History, Stanford University, 2003.

RITZER, George. "Introduction", in Jean Baudrillard, *The Consumer Society: Myths and Structures*. London: Sage Publications, 1998.

——. *The McDonaldization Thesis*, London: Sage Publications, 1998.

ROBERTSON, Jennifer. *Takarazuka, Sexual Politics and Popular Culture in Modern Japan*. Berkeley: University of California Press, 1998.

ROBERTSON, Rolland.; Habib Haque Khondker. "Discourses of Globalization: Preliminary Considerations", *International Sociology*, 13 (1): 25–40, 1998.

ROBERTSON, Rolland. *Globalization: Social Theory and Global Culture*. London: Sage Publications, 1992.

RODENBECK, Max. *Cairo, The City Victorious*. Cairo: The American University in Cairo Press, 1999.

RUSSELL, Mona L. *Creating the New Egyptian Woman. Consumerism, Education, and National Identity 1863–1922*. Palgrave Macmillan, 2004.

SAID, Edward W. *Out of Place, A Memoir*. Alfred Knopf, 1999.

SALAMA, Ashraf. "The Architecture of Gamal Bakry", *Medina*, 21. April 2002, p. 28, 2002.

SALVATORE, Armando. "Public Islam and the Nation-State in Egypt", *ISIM Newsletter*, 8, p. 20, 2001.

SALVATORE, Armando. EICKELMAN, Dale F. (eds.), *Public Islam and the Common Good*, Brill, Leiden-Boston, 2004.

SASSATELLI, Roberta. "Interaction Order and Beyond: A Field of Analysis of Body Culture within Fitness Gyms", in Mike Featherstone (ed.), *Body Modification*, London: Sage Publications, 2000.

SCHARABI, Mohamed. *Kairo Stadt und Architektur im Zeitalter des Europäischen Kolonialismus*, Verlag Ernst Wasmuth Tübingen, 1989.

SCHIELDS, Robert. "Social Spacialization and the Built Environment: The West Edmonton Mall", in *Environment and Planning: Society and Space*, 7: 147–164, 1989.

SENNETT, Richard. *The Conscience of the Eye: The Design and Social Life of Cities*, New York: Knopf, 1990.

SCHILLINGS, Chris. *The Body and Social Theory*. London: Sage Publications, 1993/2003.

SIDKY, Ahmed. "L'Oeuvre de Mario Rossi au Ministère des Waqfs: Une reinterpretation italienne de l'architecture islamique", in *Masr al-Mahrusa: Impressions of Egypt, Grand Hotels of Egypt*, Vol. XVIII: 49–57, 2001.

SIMMEL, Georg. *On Individuality and Social Forms: Selected Writings*. Chicago: The University of Chicago Press, 1971.

SIMS, David. *Informal Residential Development in Greater Cairo: Summary Findings*, ms.

——. *Residential Informality in Greater Cairo: Typologies, Representative Areas, Quantification*,

Valuation and Casual Factors, unpublished report for Institute for Liberty and Democracy, Lima, Peru, 2000.

SONTAG, Susan. *Under The Sign of Saturn*. Farrar. Straus. Giroux, New York, 1980.

STROHMENGER, Steffen. *Gespräche über Liebe*. Eine ethnographische Collage in 12 Szenen, Wuppertal: Edition Trickster im Peter Hammer Verlag, 1996.

TALIB, Rokiah. "Malaysia: Power Shifts and the Matrix of Consumption", in Chua Beng Huat (ed.), *Consumption in Asia: Lifestyles and Identities*. London: Routledge, 2000.

TARLO, Emma. *Clothing Matters, Dress and Identity in India*. The University of Chicago Press, 1996.

TOLKIEN, Tracy. *Schick und Schrill, Klassiker der Designermode*. Knesebeck, München, 2001. English title: *Vintage-The Art of Dressing up*. Pavilion Books Limited, 2000.

TRABOULSI, Fawwaz. "Public Spheres and Urban Space: A Critical Comparative Approach", *paper presented at The Fifth Mediterranean Social and Political Research Meeting, Florence Montecatini Terme*, 24–28 March 2004, workshop X, 2004.

TURNER, Bryan. *The Body and Society*, Basil Blackwell, 1984.

VAN DER VEER, Peter. "Secrecy and Publicity in the South Asian Public Arena", in: Armando Salvatore and Dale F Eickelman, (eds.) *Public Islam and the Common Good*, Brill, Leiden-Boston, 2004.

VEBLEN, Thorstein. *The Theory of Leisure Class: An Economic Study of Institutions*. New York: The Modern Library, 1934.

VOLAIT, Mercedes. *L'Architecture moderne en Egypte et la revue Al-`imara, 1939–1959*, Cairo: CEDEJ, 1988.

WARNER, Michael. "Publics and Counterpublics", *Public Culture*, 14 (1): 1–90, 2002.

WATERS, Malcom. *Globalization*. London and New York: Routledge, 1995.

WATSON, James L. "Introduction: Transnationalism, Localization, and Fast Foods in East Asia", in James L. Watson (ed.), *Golden Arches East: McDonald's in East Asia*, Stanford, California: Stanford University Press, 1997.

——. (ed.), *Golden Arches East: McDonald's in East Asia*, Stanford, California: Stanford University Press, 1997.

WEBNER, Pnina. "Introduction: The Dialectics of Cultural Hybridity", in Pnina Webner, Tariq Modood (eds.), *Debating Cultural Hybridity: Multi-Cultural Identities and the Politics of Anti-Racism*. London: Zed Books, 1997.

WELSH, Alexander. *The City of Dickens*. Harvard University Press, Cambridge Massachssets and London, England, 1986.

WHITE, Jenny B. "Islamic Chic", in Caglar Keyder (ed.), *Istanbul between the Global and the Local*. Lonham: Rowman and Littlefield Publishers, 1999.

WILSON, Elizabeth. *The Sphinx in the City: Urban Life, the Control of Disorder, and the Women*. Berkeley: University of California Press, 1991.

——. "The Invisible Flâneur", *New Left Review*, 191: 90–116, 1992.

——. *The Contradictions of Culture*. London: Sage Publications, 2001.

WINEGAR, Jessica. "Governing Culture: Struggles for Sovereignty in the Globalization of Egyptian Art", paper presented at the Fifth Mediterranean Social and Political Research Meeting, workshop IV, 24–28 March, Monte Catini Terme, 2004.

WOLFF, Janet. "The Invisible *Flâneuse*: Women and the Literature of Modernity", *Theory, Culture and Society*, 2 (3): 37–46, 1985.

ZAKI, Moheb. *Egyptian Business Elites: Their Visions and Investment Behavior*, Konrad-Adenauer-Stiftung and Arab Centre for Development and Future Research, 1999.

ZUBAIDA, Sami. *Islam, the People and the State*, London and New York: Routledge, 1989.

——. "Religious Authority and Public Life", *ISIM Newsletter*, 11/2002, p. 19, 2002.

——. *L'art contemporain d'Égypte*, Ministère del a culture et de l'orientation nationale, Maison d'edition Jugoslavija, 1964.

——. *Experiment Bauhaus*, Das Bauhaus Archiv, Berlin, (West) zu Gast im Bauhaus Dessau, 1988.

——. *Egypt Almanac: The Encyclopedia of Modern Egypt*, Egypto-file, Ltd., LLC, Wilmington, 2003.

——. *The Ultimate Guide to Shopping in Cairo*, Shopping supplement, issue 2, AG Universal Line Publications Ltd., 2004.

Newspapers and magazines

Al-Ahram Weekly
Business Monthly
Business Today
Cairo Magazine
Cairo Times
Community Times
Der Spiegel
Egypt Today
Horus
International Herald Tribune
La Revue d'Egypte
Le Commerce du Levant

Web Sites

http://www.abc.com.lb
http://www.ameinfo.com
http://www.amcham.org.eg
http://www.boycottisraeligoods.org
http://www.businesstoday.com
http://www.cipe.org
http://www.countrystudies.us
http://www.crossborderreports.com
http://www.cyberegypt.com
http://www.ebusinessforum.com
http://www.egy.com
http://www.emaar.com
http://www.hrw.org
http://www.lefturn.org
http://www.icse.org
http://www.islamonline.net
http://www/mcdonalds.com
http://www.merip.org
http://www.motherearth.org
http://www.opendemocracy.net
http://www.orascom.com
http://www.otlob.com
http://www.redsea-realestate.com
http://www.sabbour-associates.com
http://www.spiegel.de
http://www.strategis.ic.gc.ca
http://www.touregypt.net
http://www.usembassy.egnet.net
http://www.thearlqatar.com
http://www.weekly.ahram.org.eg

Interviews and Personal Communications

'Adel 'Abdel Ghaffar: November 12, 2004, Giza.
'Afaf Abaza: November 23, 2004. Zamalek.
Ahmad al-Sukkary: March 14, 2005. Zamalek.
Ahmad Hamid: May 15, 2005. Zamalek. AUC.
Amru Kamal: December 2003. Arkadia Mall.
Amina al-Lozy: November 11 and October 15, 2004. Zamalek.
Ashraf Abu 'Aref: March 14, 2005. Yamama Centre, Zamalek.
Darwish Hashoush: January 18, 2005. Beirut.
David Sims: May 5, 2005. Zamalek.
Dolly Debs-Braidi: January 24, 2005. Keslik, Lebanon.
Gamal Bakry: October 3, 2004. Dokki.
Hussein Foda: March 3, 2005. Zamalek.
John Sfakianakis: March 20, 2005. Zamalek.
Joyce Foda: March 3, 2005. Zamalek.
Mehri Foda: March 3, 2005. Zamalek.
Menha al-Battrawi: November 1, 2004. Downtown.
Samir Gharib: 26 July, 2005. Zamalek.
Salwa Mesbahi: September 23, 2004. Zamalek.
Shahira Mehrez: May 15, 2005. Dokki.
Cairo shopping malls interviews are not included.

INDEX